ETHNICITY AND EDUCATION
IN ENGLAND AND EUROPE

Studies in Migration and Diaspora

Series Editor:
Anne J. Kershen, Queen Mary, University of London, UK

Studies in Migration and Diaspora is a series designed to showcase the interdisciplinary and multidisciplinary nature of research in this important field. Volumes in the series cover local, national and global issues and engage with both historical and contemporary events. The books will appeal to scholars, students and all those engaged in the study of migration and diaspora. Amongst the topics covered are minority ethnic relations, transnational movements and the cultural, social and political implications of moving from 'over there', to 'over here'.

Also in the series:

Migration, Citizenship and Intercultural Relations
Looking through the Lens of Social Inclusion
Edited by Fethi Mansouri and Michele Lobo
ISBN 978-1-4094-2880-0

Masculinity, Sexuality and Illegal Migration
Human Smuggling from Pakistan to Europe
Ali Nobil Ahmad
ISBN 978-1-4094-0975-5

Globalization, Migration and Social Transformation
Edited by Bryan Fanning and Ronaldo Munck
ISBN 978-1-4094-1127-7

Childhood and Migration in Europe
Portraits of Mobility, Identity and Belonging in Contemporary Ireland
Caitríona Ní Laoire, Fina Carpena-Méndez, Naomi Tyrrell and Allen White
ISBN 978-1-4094-0109-4

Experience and Representation
Contemporary Perspectives on Migration in Australia
Keith Jacobs
ISBN 978-0-7546-7610-2

Ethnicity and Education in England and Europe

Gangstas, Geeks and Gorjas

IAN LAW AND SARAH SWANN
University of Leeds, UK

ASHGATE

Published by
Ashgate Publishing Limited
Wey Court East
Union Road
Farnham
Surrey, GU9 7PT
England

Ashgate Publishing Company
Suite 420
101 Cherry Street
Burlington
VT 05401-4405
USA

www.ashgate.com

British Library Cataloguing in Publication Data
Law, Ian.
  Ethnicity and education in England and Europe : gangstas,
  geeks and gorjas. -- (Studies in migration and diaspora)
  1. Discrimination in education--England. 2. Minorities--
  Education--England. 3. Discrimination in education--
  Europe. 4. Minorities--Education--Europe. 5. Romanies--
  Education--Europe. 6. England--Ethnic relations.
  7. Europe--Ethnic relations.
  I. Title II. Series III. Swann, Sarah.
  371.8'29'0094-dc22

Library of Congress Cataloging-in-Publication Data
Law, Ian.
  Ethnicity and education in England and Europe : gangstas, geeks and gorjas / by Ian Law and Sarah Swann.
      p. cm. -- (Studies in migration and diaspora)
  Includes bibliographical references and index.
  ISBN 978-1-4094-1087-4 (hardback) -- ISBN 978-1-4094-1088-1 (ebook) 1. Ethnic relations-
-Great Britain. 2. Ethnic relations--Europe. 3. Education--Great Britain. 4. Education--Europe.
I.
Swann, Sarah. II. Title.
  GN496.L39 2011
  305.800941--dc23

2011023631

ISBN 9781409410874 (hbk)
ISBN 9781409410881 (ebk)

Printed and bound in Great Britain by
TJ International Ltd, Padstow, Cornwall.

Contents

List of Tables

Acknowledgements

The authors would like to thank all EDUMIGROM project colleagues including Evelyene Bartou, Monika Borovanová, Marcus Carson, Barbara Hobson, Jenny Kallstenius, Tina Kallehave, Ela Klementová, Kostlan, Zuzana Kusa, Sabine Mannitz, Radim Marada, Vera Messing, Bolette Moldenhawer, Michal Nekorjak, Mária Neményi, Marta Padovan-Özdemir, Joelle Perroton, Jessica Pouyau, Jurina Rusnakova, Claire Schiff, Kristina Sonmark, Gaby Strassburger, Júlia Szalai, Meryem Ucan, Róza Vajda, Eniko Vincze, Viola Zentai and János Zolney for contributions drawn on in Chapter 7. The authors would also like to thank all the many participants who contributed their time and effort in response to our surveys, interviews and conversations and in particular the young people in schools and community contexts. We must also thank our families for bearing with us, supporting us and encouraging us in this endeavour. Lastly we would like to thank the editorial and production teams at Ashgate, and also the peer reviewers who have all contributed to the development and quality of this publication.

The research leading to these results has been conducted under the auspices of the project EDUMIGROM: Ethnic Differences in Education and Diverging Prospects for Urban Youth in an Enlarged Europe, and has received funding from the European Community's Seventh Framework Programme (FP7/2007-2013), under grant agreement no. 217384.

Glossary

AST	Attendance Strategy Team
CME	Children Missing from Education
DCSF	Department of Children, Schools and Families
DfE	Department for Education
EDUMIGROM	European Commission 7th Framework Program project 'Ethnic differences in education and diverging prospects for urban youth in an enlarged Europe'
EMA	Education Maintenance Allowance
EMAG	Ethnic Minorities Achievement Grant
EOC	Equal Opportunities Commission
Gorjas	mainstream, settled communities as distinguished from Gypsy, Traveller and Roma young people and their communities
HCA	Housing and Community Agency
ISC	Independent Schools Council
ICT	Information and Communication Technology
LA	Local Authority
RRAA	Race Relations Amendment Act
SENCO	Special Needs Coordinator
TLRP	Travellers Law Reform Project

Ethnicity and Education
in England and Europe

For those unfamiliar with the designations used in the sub-title of this book, the three groups which form its spine are, young street orientated and educationally disaffected *gangstas* and young intellectually orientated *geeks*, both – in this context – of ethnic origin, together with *gorgas*, young Whites from mainstream settled communities. In addition, and most significantly, this study also embraces Gypsy, Traveller and Roma young people, for whom education is all too often a peripatetic and segregating episode. This is a volume which explores the impact of 'ethnic differences in education', on young people in the European Union. Though primarily focusing on education and ethnicity in England, the book, which evolved from a three year EU programme, provides a broader geographical perspective, and enables its readers to compare and contrast policy aims and outcomes, as well as pupil experience, in eight countries across Europe, which for the purposes of the programme were divided into clusters rather than compared and contrasted separately.

One of the prime, albeit negative, characteristics of multi-ethnic education is the segregation of the minority from the majority. Rarely, if at all, has this been the result of formal policy, as schools in the United Kingdom are bound to promote community cohesion and social inclusion. In fact it can be as the result of self segregation in urban or suburban locations, that some schools acquire a majority ethnic student body. For example, the authors describe a school where parental choice created an environment of educational separation in which there was a predominance of Pakistani students. The empirical research carried out in an unnamed northern city records ethnic and economic differences in that city and, accordingly, in academic achievement. In Northcity (the pseudonym given the location of the case study) ethnic diversity within the student body resulted in high levels of racial and ethnic segregation and, overall, lower than average pupil attainment. White flight and/or economic flight had created affluent middle class suburbs and pockets of social deprivation; residential divisions resulting in the formation of postcode gangs which were imported into the schools. Whilst this in itself is shown to have impacted on levels of achievement, the authors emphasise that ethnic minority children are often found to be living in, 'chaotic home environments'. Children from one parent homes, or Gypsy, Traveller or Roma families, many of whom lacked a stable or settled home life, were amongst the lowest school achievers. In support of this UK finding, the Europe wide research revealed that, with few exceptions, pupil achievement had a direct correlation to domestic stability.

The book highlights the contradictions of the acknowledgement of diversity which emphasises the schoolchild's otherness. In the authors' words 'young people yearned to escape being "othered"'; stereotyped and identified as different. This was particularly the case amongst Pakistani and African-Caribbean pupils who believed they suffered from their negative image; African-Caribbean boys perceived as drug dealers and Pakistani youths as taxi drivers. For these children the ladder to successful academic and professional achievement becomes an even tougher one to climb.

This is a book which challenges some of the preconceived ideas about ethnic minorities in the education system, suggesting that ethnicity should not be linked to low educational ambition – the exception being the children from Gypsy, Roma and Traveller backgrounds who tend to drop out of school at secondary level. As has been evidenced in Northcity and elsewhere in the UK, children of ethnic origin can and do achieve, if they have the ambition, support and tenacity; a fact highlighted by Michelle Obama on her visit to Oxford in the spring of 2011.

The book provides a number of recommendations which, if taken up, could improve the school and post-school lives of children from ethnic backgrounds. It highlights the need to address and reduce, if not eradicate, the negativity of emphasis on diversity, and replace this with an approach which is inclusive and which recognises the need for equality for all students. In this way it may be possible for ethnic gangstas and geeks as well as White gorgas to proceed from a level playing field and, for Gypsy, Traveller and Roma children to stand a chance of completing their schooling and go on to higher things.

Anne J Kershen
Queen Mary University of London

Chapter 1
Ethnic Relations Across Europe

Introduction

The power of ethnicity as a constitutive force within and across European societies is urgently felt in the twenty-first century. The strength of ethnic loyalties is evident in contemporary patterns of ethnic conflicts and hostilities which continue, despite international declarations and interventions, creative national policies and inter-ethnic mixing. The processes of racial and ethnic immiseration and inequality accompany many situations and social relations where ethnicity is not a central feature and where post-ethnic, mixed human relations are being actively constructed. How ethnicity works in education and how the relational logics of ethnicised education work across European societies is a central focus for this book. This book is also concerned with young people's lives and their world views whether street-orientated (gangsta) and educationally disaffected, intellectually-orientated (geek) with an obsessive thirst for certain aspects of knowledge and learning or inhabiting and performing elements of these two positions. It is also not only concerned with the lives of young people from minority ethnic groups but also with White identities, subcultures and the world views of the 'gorja', mainstream, settled communities as distinguished from Gypsy, Traveller and Roma young people and their communities.

This book arises from our involvement as the lead members of the UK team working on the European Commission 7th Framework Program project: EDUMIGROM[1] which ran from March 2008 to March 2011. This project: 'Ethnic differences in education and diverging prospects for urban youth in an enlarged Europe' was a comparative investigation in ethnically diverse communities with second-generation migrants and Roma. EDUMIGROM studied how ethnic differences in education contribute to the diverging prospects for youth and their peers in urban settings. It is a comparative endeavour involving nine countries from among old and new member states of the European Union, including Czech Republic, Denmark, France, Germany, Hungary, Romania, Slovakia, Sweden and the United Kingdom. It explored how far existing educational policies, practices and experiences in markedly different welfare regimes protect youth against marginalisation and eventual social exclusion. Despite great variations in economic development and welfare arrangements, recent developments seem to lead to similar consequences for certain groups of second-generation immigrants in the western half of the continent and Roma in Central and Eastern Europe.

---

1   EDUMIGROM is not an acronym, this is the EU 8-digit project name.

Formally citizens with full rights in the respective states, people affiliated with these groups tend to experience new and intensive forms of involuntary separation, social exclusion, and second-class citizenship. The project critically examined the role of education in these processes of 'minoritisation'. In ethnically diverse urban communities, schools often become targets for locally organised political struggles shaped by a broader political and civic culture of ethnic mobilisation. EDUMIGROM investigated how schools operate in their roles of socialisation and knowledge distribution, and how they influence young people's identity formation. The project also explored how schools contribute to reducing, maintaining, or deepening inequalities in young people's access to the labour market, further education and training, and also to different domains of social, cultural, and political participation. The results of macro-level investigations, a comparative survey and multi-faceted field research in local settings have provided rich datasets for intra- and cross-country comparisons and evidence-based policy making (http://www.edumigrom.eu/).

This chapter examines selected aspects of this terrain and puts ethnic relations in the UK into this European context. This chapter provides a comparative overview of the working of inter-ethnic relations and the state of groups across nine EU countries (Germany, France, Sweden, Denmark, Hungary, the Czech Republic, Slovakia, Romania and the UK. Firstly, the social significance of ethnicity is examined. Secondly, two key patterns of ethnic relations are examined, migrant workers and their descendants forming strong ethnic communities, for example Turks in Germany or Pakistanis in the UK, and the Roma. Common patterns of racism and discrimination are identified together with the formation of ethnic boundaries. Next, this chapter will also address the construction of official statistics on ethnicity, forms of self-identification and problems in the comparative analysis of ethnicity data and ethnic relations.

The main body of literature which examines ethnic identity discusses either macro level processes, policy formulations and effects, or micro-social settings and the integration of these three levels of analysis is a central objective for this book. The proposed three-level approach allows the mapping of variations in the construction of social status as it is forged through identity formation and empowerment in local communities, on the one hand, and through macro-level developments and policies in education and employment, on the other. With its focus on the combined effects of macro- and micro-level factors, along with individual experiences in shaping identity, this book aims to contribute to the advance of an interdisciplinary theory of identity formation.

The persistence, durability and, in some cases, increasing strength of ethnic identities, divisions and conflicts across these national contexts is evident. This contextualises the growing importance of ethnicity in forging young people's career paths and life chances, despite political, legal and policy interventions to tackle discrimination and target support.

There are significant variations and differences in migration processes, economic development, welfare provision and forms of citizenship here, but these have led to some strong similarities in the creation of patterns of ethnic exclusion and minoritisation across second-generation immigrants in the western half of the continent and Roma in Central and Eastern Europe. The overt and covert mechanisms through which socio-economic, political, cultural, and gender relations that make ethnicity a substantive component of inequalities in social status and power are examined here.

This cross-country comparative chapter provides a meta-analysis of the themes and issues examined by national research teams in the EDUMIGROM project.[2] In providing a comparative evaluation it is also important to acknowledge both the significance of specific contextual settings and the many dimensions of difference and diversity in these contexts. Many of the selected countries have long-established immigrant communities; in addition some are confronted with a more recent increase in migration. There are differences in the ethnic composition of these countries, such as overall size and types of ethnic groups, which makes a direct comparison of the countries rather difficult. The comparability of data is even more complicated due to different categorisations of groups used in the process of data collection, differences regarding the availability of differentiated data, and diverse educational systems. In addition, differences in processes of ethnic mobilisation and ethnic conflict are likely to be evident.

Why ethnicity matters

Ethnicity refers to the differentiation of groups of people, who have shared cultural meanings, memories and descent, produced through social interaction. In classical Greek the terms *ethnos/ethnikos* were used in a number of ways to refer to a collectivity that shares similar cultural or biological characteristics, for example a tribe of people or a band of friends, and who were not Greek, outside the nation, foreign, different and also inferior, barbarian and less-civilised. This distinction between ethnically marked 'others' and non-ethnically marked 'us' persists in modern popular usage with references to ethnic fashion, food, music, literature and forms of verbal and non-verbal communication. Sociological accounts of ethnicity are highly varied but tend to break the classical linkage

---

2   These reports cover ethnic relations in Romania, Slovakia, Hungary, the Czech Republic, France, Germany, the UK, together with a comparative report on Denmark and Sweden, which constitute the participating countries of the EDUMIGROM research project. The reports are, as follows: Schiff et al.: Country Report on Ethnic Relations: France; Kusá et al.: Country Report on Ethnic Relations: Slovakia; Magyari et al.: Country Report on Ethnic Relations: Romania; Law et al.: Country Report on Ethnic Relations: United Kingdom; Katzorová et al.: Country Report on Ethnic Relations: Czech Republic; Miera: Country Report on Ethnic Relations: Germany; Kallehave and Moldenhawer: Country Report on Ethnic Relations: Denmark and Sweden; Molnár and Dupcsik: Country Report on Ethnic Relations: Hungary.

between ethnicity and 'other', in asserting that we are all ethnically located in that our subjectivity and identity are contextualised by history, language, descent and culture. Ethnicity usually refers to the differentiation of social groups on the basis of five distinct criteria. Firstly, a notion of a 'homeland' or place of common origin is a key element, which is linked to the idea of a diaspora, where an ethnic group has migrated from that place to form communities elsewhere that identify with their place of origin. Secondly, a common language, either distinctive in itself or a distinctive dialect of a language shared with others, may be central to the construction of shared memories and affective belonging. Thirdly, identification with a distinct religion, e.g. Sikhism, or a religion shared with others can be a central feature of many ethnic groups. Fourthly, a common culture with distinctive social institutions and behaviour, diet and dress and, fifthly, a common tradition, or shared history of one's own 'people' or nation are other criteria used in specifying ethnic groups. This last marker, a shared history is particularly important for ethnic groups like the Roma. Not all markers are used to differentiate all ethnic groups, but identification of the five, or less, criteria provide a sound basis for mapping the complexities of ethnic differentiation.

How and why does ethnicity matter? In fleshing out some of the ways in which ethnicity matters we need to look closely at specific social contexts. The strength of ethnic loyalties is evident in contemporary patterns of ethnic conflict which continue, despite international declarations and interventions, creative national policies and inter-ethnic mixing. It is 'a world-wide phenomenon that has become the leading source of lethal violence in international affairs' (Esman 2004: 26). In organised structure of domination, such as exclusionary domination in apartheid South Africa or inclusionary domination such as the French Republican model of assimilation, ethnic relations across the globe encompass highly varied, complex forms of social relations. Apart from these more formal contexts, ethnicity may also be of high importance in informal social contexts (Jenkins 1997) such as:

- *Primary socialisation*: in the social construction of children's identities encountering and learning about oneself, who we are, and others may involve the use of ethnic labels and categories alongside other primary identities of gender, selfhood and human-ness.
- *Sexual relationships and marriage*: inter-ethnic sexual relationships have often been a key site for violence and conflict, for example in the British race riots of 1919 and 1948, and also for aspects of patriarchal power and control which may often be concerned to enforce ethnic exclusivity or group possession of women, for example where a female Irish Traveller may be 'outcast' if she marries outside the group.
- *Routine public interaction*: informal ethnic categorisation may often help to organise and interpret social interaction. Verbal and non-verbal cues including dress, language, humour and verbal abuse may often be key to the expression and mobilisation of ethnic identities and group boundaries, who is part of my group and who is not. Everyday cultural ignorance,

miscommunication and misrecognition of difference, where individuals coming from two contrasting ethnic communities may bring with them different value assumptions, expectations, verbal and nonverbal habits that influence social interaction and communication, may result in offensive behaviour, affronts to dignity and lack of respect which can all lead to ethnic conflict and violence.

So, the extent to which ethnicity matters may be highly variable dependent on society, time and context, but it is arguably 'a basic universal facet of the human cultural repertoire' (Jenkins 1997: 77). The leading contribution of Modood's work on ethnicity is widely acknowledged and his theoretical position is located as a bridge between political theorists of multicultural citizenship, including Parekh (2005) and Kymlicka (2007) and the long established tradition of sociological investigation of post-imperial migrant settlements in Western Europe. He emphasises five key dimensions of ethnic difference. These include:

Table 1.1   Dimensions of ethnic difference

1. cultural distinctiveness (norms and practices such as arranged marriage),
2. identity (affective meanings that may motivate or demotivate),
3. strategy (differential responses to a set of circumstances that may contribute to group consciousness),
4. creativity (group innovations e.g. clothing styles) and,
5. disproportionality (differential structural characteristics e.g. unemployment).

Source: Based on data in Modood, 2005: 189.

The purpose here is to capture both the subjective and objective features of a group defined by descent, and there is a central concern here to explore why certain social contexts over-determine or reduce the significance of ethnicity and the ways in which the different dimensions of ethnic difference may be operating in local circumstances. These issues are examined below in relation to the ethnic groups selected for analysis in this study.

Selected groups and inter-ethnic relations

The nature and complexity of relations between the movement of people (migration), the formation of boundaries between groups of people who have shared cultural meanings, memories and descent (ethnicity) and the formation and negative treatment of racial groups (racism) is a key focus for this study. Two key forms of ethnicity are examined in this study: *migrant workers* and their descendants forming strong ethnic communities, for example Turks in Germany or Pakistanis in the UK, and the *Roma*. This study is broadly concerned with comparing the situation of indigenous Roma in four Central and Eastern European countries with the situation of second generation migrants in five Western European countries. But, as the choice of selected minority groups shows, it is also concerned to identify how ethnicity and education operate across a range of different social and political contexts. Firstly, the situation of the Roma is examined in both Eastern and Western Europe, as the UK study also sets out to explore Gypsy and Traveller perceptions and experiences. Secondly, post-colonial migration flows to Europe are examined with a focus on a varied range of groups including North Africans, Black Caribbeans and Pakistani groups, which have differing patterns of educational achievement. Thirdly, other migrant groups including two guest worker migration flows from Southern Europe (Portuguese) and Turkey, and a refugee group, the Somalis, provide further detailed exemplars for the analysis of ethnicity.

Table 1.2   Selected groups

Country	Selected Ethnic Minority Groups
Hungary	Roma
Slovakia	Roma
Romania	Roma
Czech Republic	Roma
UK	Black Caribbeans, Pakistanis, Gypsy/Roma/Travellers
France	North Africans (Algerians, Moroccans, Tunisians), Turks
Germany	Turkish, Portuguese
Denmark	Pakistani, Somali

The migration history of each of these groups, and the resources and networks they have established, provide a set of key contextual factors that are likely to have a significant influence on patterns of educational achievement, together with the structural context of provision and discrimination. In examining this range of minority ethnic groups, it is to be expected that national, ethnic and intra-ethnic differentials in social, political and economic location and patterns of achievement will be significant and the complexity of positions and trends is important to capture, particularly for the purposes of policy intervention. Super-diversity is a concept that foregrounds a level and kind of ethnic complexity surpassing anything that has been previously experienced (this has been applied to the UK by Vertovec 2006). This is distinguished by a contrast with previous periods of migration and identification of the dynamic interplay of variables among an increased number of new, small and scattered, multiple-origin, transnationally connected, socio-economically differentiated and legally stratified immigrants.

This concept is employed here. It is also important to identify structural dynamics at the transnational level, the articulation of global market forces within local networks and transnational forms of political identification and action, as seen for example in the construction of European Roma identity, agencies and agendas. Although the mobilisation of ethnicity is operating differently across these groups examined here there may also be commonalities in forms of negative treatment and majority hostility.

Negative treatment: the commonality of discrimination and hostility

There has been an accumulating mass of research evidence from the 1960s onwards which has sought to both establish an evidence base and win social and political recognition for the reality of mundane everyday racial discrimination in Europe and elsewhere across the globe. The response of many governments and their politicians and policy makers has been ambivalent ranging from denial of the significance of discrimination to pro-active recognition and intervention. Reaching 'square one' on this issue, i.e. recognition, has been a long and arduous task, let alone building a platform of successful interventions to tackle these fundamental problems. Here, the compatibility between, on the one hand, racial and ethnic exclusionary practices, and on the other, institutional behaviours, environments and objectives may be one key link in explaining their durability and persistence, rather seeing these as the exceptional, unwitting or warped attitudes of isolated individuals. General trends in racism and discrimination in a range of EU member states were examined in fieldwork with 11,000 respondents from minority ethnic and migrant communities between 2001 and 2005 (FRA 2006a). This shows that a significant number of migrants in all 12 countries examined[3] have subjectively experienced discriminatory practices in their everyday life, with many being particularly vulnerable to such exclusionary behaviour in the spheres of employment, housing, education and in interactions with the police. This high level of everyday, often casual, racial discrimination and the resulting perception across many groups and communities of systemic hostility may have a range of significant effects including alienation.

The report also highlights a significant gap between the amount of experienced discrimination and the rate of reporting such discrimination to public authorities. This observation points to the theme of the availability and profile of institutions registering acts of discrimination. It may be that many victims either have no opportunity to report instances of discrimination, or are not aware of existing possibilities. About one third reported experiences of discrimination in employment including harassment at work, refused access to jobs and differential treatment in promotions. About a quarter reported harassment on the street, on public transport

---

3   The countries included in this study were Belgium, Germany, Greece, Spain, France, Ireland, Italy, Luxembourg, Netherlands, Austria, Portugal and UK and migrants groups selected for study came from a range of backgrounds, being those especially affected by racism and discrimination, including Black Africans, Turks and those from Arab countries.

and by neighbours with 15 per cent of migrants saying that they had been the victim of violence or other types of criminal offences. One in five reported being denied access to either restaurants or discotheques and discriminatory treatment in restaurants or shops because of their 'foreign background', even including being denied entry to a shop. In the context of private commercial transactions just under 30 per cent reported that they had experienced discrimination in settings of commercial transactions being denied access to housing, credit or loans. In institutional contexts, every sector investigated in this study uncovered a significant level of experiences of racial discrimination across these European countries. About one in four had been subject to discriminatory treatment by the police in the last year and slightly less in educational establishments. One in five experienced racial discrimination in interactions with providers of welfare benefits and with employment agencies with slightly lower rates in healthcare and social service institutions.

Across these differing national contexts targets and levels of discrimination vary widely. In Belgium for example Moroccan, Turkish, Congolese and Chinese people were key targets of discrimination with employment at 37 per cent being the sphere with the highest level of perceived discrimination. In Germany, Black people were key targets with 57 per cent reporting that they felt they had been denied a job for racist reasons, and in institutional contexts such as education the average rate of perceived discrimination was twice as high as for other groups such as Turkish people. In France over half of people from the Maghreb (North Africa) reported racial discrimination in access to jobs with slightly higher levels of discrimination being reported by people from Central African backgrounds. Lastly and most worryingly 86 per cent of those who had experienced discrimination did not report these incidents which indicate a gulf of trust between minorities, migrants and public and private institutions in

Table 1.3   Racial and ethnic hostility by selected country

Country	% hostile to the formation of a multicultural society	% opposed to civil rights for legal migrants	Aggregate hostility ranking
Germany	34	48	1
Denmark	22	41	2
Hungary	18	50	3
Slovakia	28	38	3
UK	20	48	3
France	22	40	3
Czech Republic	39	21	7
Sweden	12	34	8
Romania	12	15	9

Source: FRA 2005.

Europe. For this study, the finding that about a quarter of migrants reported perceived racial discrimination in education indicates the necessity of examining this sphere and assessing ethnic differentials and their causes.

A further study of the attitudes of majorities to minority ethnic groups (FRA 2005) provides a set of data on racial and ethnic hostility for our selected countries; UK, France, Germany, Denmark, Sweden, Czech Republic, Slovakia, Hungary and Romania (see Table 1.3).

This data indicates that firstly, there is a substantial level of popular hostility towards minority ethnic groups, towards the formation of a multicultural society and towards the granting of migrant rights. Secondly, there is wide variation between the countries under scrutiny here with no consistent pattern differentiating Western Europe from Central and Eastern Europe, which are indicated by for example the wide variation between the Czech Republic's level of hostility to a multicultural society (39 per cent) and Romania (12 per cent). There is however, a tendency for opposition to migrant rights to be higher in Western Europe, with the exception of Hungary where the level of opposition is at its highest (50 per cent). The aggregate ranking combines both of these sets of data and indicates three groupings of countries; very high levels of hostility in Germany and Denmark, similar and slightly lower levels of hostility in Hungary, Slovakia, UK and France, and lastly moderate levels of hostility overall in the Czech Republic, Sweden and Romania. The key drivers of majorities' attitudes towards minority ethnic groups were identified here and they include *immigration* (the actual and perceived numbers of asylum seekers, refugees, legal and illegal migrants together with immigration control and border policing), *Europeanisation (*the role of new Member States and their citizens in the EU, and future accession of other countries to the EU), *global conflicts* (the impact of on-going and recent global conflicts on relationships between populations within the EU – such as the attacks of 11 September 2001, the Israel/Palestine conflict, Iraq and Afghanistan), and lastly n*ew policies of diversity and multiculturalism* (the increasing recognition and promotion of diversity in different aspects of social/public life; public information about immigration, citizenship and cultural diversity). Majority concerns and anxieties over immigration, threats remain a long-standing terrain for the construction of racist and exclusionary discourse. The resurgence of defensive forms of nationalism as a reaction to processes of globalisation, and the 'de-centring of the West' which has been linked to shifting economic and power relations, are processes which have led to the undermining and fracturing of national identities in late-twentieth-century Europe. In addition, the renewed debates over nationalism in the face of Europeanisation are seen as highlighting the criteria for citizenship, belonging and identity and providing political and cultural space for the re-articulation of racist discourse. Also, international hostilities including 9/11, 7/7 and the War on Terror, the Israeli-Palestinian conflict, and other conflicts which may be driving the movement of asylum-seekers and refugees may all be relevant here in increasing local tensions and perceptions of insecurity, threat and risk. Lastly, hostility to inclusionary policies of various types has developed, often portrayed as majority resentment over unfair preferential treatment of minority ethnic groups.

There are a complex, wide-ranging set of causes and motivations for racial and ethnic hostility and related violence. Identifying potential factors which make this more likely, more acceptable and more durable involves consideration of a complex set of interlocking environments.

- Virtual environment, internet sites and networks which may be influential in encouraging hostility and violence.
- International conflicts and events including ethnic and racial conflicts, acts of terrorism, which heighten local perceptions of insecurity and fear and which are used to rationalise racist violence.
- National political and media messages on migration, ethnicity and racism which shape racial hostility.
- Economic factors including patterns of unemployment and low pay, economic decline, exclusion from new economic opportunities.
- Educational factors that make hostility more likely such as patterns of underachievement, exclusion, racial and ethnic segregation, lack of explicit focus in schools, failure to challenge racism through school curriculum and ethos.
- Family factors where hostility is socialised and legitimated across generations and genders, with old/young, female/male attitudes and talk promoting hostility in different ways.
- Local social/community factors, such as the balance between conflict 'preventors' and 'promoters', and the level and nature of social interaction across ethnic/racial lines.
- Adult/youth factors, active local cultures/sub-cultures, values and norms of peer groups which may encourage hostility.
- Activities of ideologically driven groups, e.g. far right groups, who encourage and promote hostility.

The macro, meso and micro contexts which collectively frame majority responses to migrants are highly dynamic with for example, changing migration flows, global conflicts, media images and national debates, yet the levels of racial and ethnic hostility reported by the FRA (2005, 2006a) appear to have remained relatively stable over the last decade. Changing times and environments play out across a fixed hard core of entrenched patterns of racial and ethnic discrimination and hostility.

The formation of ethnic boundaries: the Roma and anti-gypsyism

The long history of discriminatory treatment of Roma and Travellers, by both states and in civil society, has placed these groups as the most vulnerable to racism in Europe. Marginalisation, discrimination and persecution have always been defining characteristics of the social life of the Roma since their entry into Europe in the fourteenth century. Three competing forms of understanding and conceptualising Romani identity have been set out in recent debate (Vermeersch 2006), and as the Hungarian report confirms there are no universally agreed objective criteria to determine Roma ethnicity. The Roma have been, firstly, identified as a historical diaspora, emphasising common origin and descent of a group of people from a military caste in India with a common Romani language now scattered across Europe. This 'deliberate fabrication' of classic 'gypsyologists', Nazi scientists and contemporary academics has been challenged for its homogenising exoticism (Okely 1983, Vermeersch 2006: 14). Secondly, others have argued the Roma can be recognised by their affection for travelling/itinerant lifestyles, being marginal in national contexts and having a specific set of cultural practices and musical traditions. Yet, movement and migration characterises humanity and also most Roma in Central Europe do live in settled communities. Thirdly, others have argued that the Roma are genetically related and have biological kinship, although this raises the spectre of a return to forms of scientific racism through the use of racial and ethnic categories in the construction of genetic and genomic databases and related forms of mapping. The lack of agreed criteria for defining Roma ethnicity causes major problems for data collection and is discussed below.

An 'identity crisis' at the level of the Roma population in Romania has been identified as it is characterised by many internal divisions and fragmentations including differences between those who are characterised by cultural heterogeneity and by a rigid internal hierarchical stratification, which obstructs communication with the outside world, and those who comprise the fragile political class and especially the vocal civic Roma society. Trehan and Kóczé (2009) argue powerfully for the need to construct grassroots alternatives to the dominant, neo-liberal paradigms within which Roma peoples are materially and symbolically captured – paradigms informed both by 'older', dichotomised ('Occidental'/'Oriental') understandings of cultural difference and by 'newer' EU pressures brought to bear on eastern Europeans to prove their western credentials, which have only led at times to their further separation, or to the consolidation of a racialised social order in which they and other travelling peoples are ironically fixed in (last) place (Huggan and Law 2009). The Hungarian report identifies a growing divide between intellectuals and entrepreneurs and the mass of the Roma population living in increasing poverty.

The contemporary vilification, discrimination and hostility faced by the Roma in Europe and their selection for total annihilation along with Jews in the Nazi Holocaust arise from their positioning as a racial threat to national stability. The Romani people arrived in Europe in the 1400s, having moved from India in a succession of migrations due to Islamic invasion of Asia during the Ghaznavid Empire. The historical roots of anti-gypsyism can be traced from this period and some key causes for this specific form of racism have been identified by Hancock (1997). These include early associations between the Roma and an Islamic threat with terms such as heathen, Saracen, Tatars and Gypsies being used and the equation of Roma skin colour with darkness, sin, dirt and evil, with accusations that they were spies, carriers of the plague and traitors to Christendom. Exclusivist Roma culture with restrictions on contact with non-Roma, combined with their positioning as outside the state, with no protective territorial, military or economic strength, has facilitated their treatment as vulnerable scapegoats. This treatment included mass murder, enslavement and removal of children from families, for example in Germany from 1400 to 1800.

By the early 1800s Roma were referred to as 'the excrement of humanity' and the 'refuse of the human race' (Hancock 1997: 7). In Romania, Marshall Ion Antonescu's pro-Nazi government was vehemently anti-minority, and especially anti-Roma. Mass deportation of Roma began, particularly of nomadic Roma who were primarily thought to be criminals. Some 25,000 Roma were thus sent to land captured from the Soviet Union (Transdniestria), in 1942. The Romanian People's Court set up a War Crimes Commission in the aftermath of the war. According to the Commission, 36,000 Roma died in Romania during the war, the highest number from any European country (although as a percentage of the Roma population it was far lower than in countries such as Poland and Germany). After the Second World War socialist governments in Central and Eastern Europe (CEE) engaged in a concerted and culturally repressive effort to assimilate and settle the Roma populations. The target was to gradually eliminate national differences, but actually this meant the elimination of minority ethnic groups (i.e. their forced assimilation) (Pons 1999: 28). In all CEE countries, Roma culture was considered to be one of poverty and underdevelopment and by eliminating any references to Roma, the state denied the specificity of the Roma community. Although socialist policies improved conditions by increasing access to education and employment, they failed to provide equality of opportunity providing jobs that were mostly unskilled, low-paying and physically demanding and education marginalising them in the labour market, further weakening their access to decent housing, health and education and subjecting them to open racism and discrimination. In the 1990s anti-Gypsyism re-surfaced in European countries that were facing the prospect of increased numbers of Roma asylum seekers. At the same time, Central and Eastern European countries failed to tackle the reasons behind large numbers of Roma seeking to leave.

Segregation and discrimination against the Roma is evident in both housing and education. Across the EU migrants and settled minorities do generally appear to suffer higher levels of homelessness, poorer quality housing conditions, poorer residential neighbourhoods (such as shanty towns), and comparatively greater vulnerability and insecurity in their housing status. Very serious housing problems include lack of access to basic facilities such as drinking water and toilets, significantly higher levels of overcrowding than for other households, and exploitation through higher comparative rents and purchase prices. Persistent difficulties are faced by Roma, Travellers, Gypsies and Sinti, and refugees and asylum seekers, across the EU in securing adequate basic housing. There is also evidence of some improvement in patterns of housing conditions over time, but relative housing inequalities are highly durable. Poor mental and physical health, lower levels of educational attainment and lower income levels, together with many other dimensions of social exclusion, also have identifiable links with poor housing conditions. In Romania, 52.2 per cent of the Roma were identified as living in severe poverty in 2001, infant mortality is four times higher than the total population and unemployment rates (28 per cent in 2002) are almost three times the national level. In Hungary, 80 per cent of the Roma were identified as living in poverty, being less integrated than any other minority group. In Slovakia, the Roma have been severely affected by the continuing economic depression and their living and housing conditions deteriorated not only due to joblessness but also due to the halting of social programmes which ran under the communist regime, which together with insufficient political representation, political advocacy of Roma interests and comprehensive welfare programmes has led to general deterioration in their living conditions and life opportunities. These trends are evident across all CEE countries.

The Roma population in Europe is disproportionately young, due to both a relatively high birth rate and a short life expectancy. The parents of Roma children who are starting school today already belong to the generation that have never been permanently employed in their lifetime, and this circumstance heavily influences these children's opportunities of further education. Some Roma children receive no formal education at all, particularly in Romania for the nomadic groups in remote parts of the country, due to ongoing racial discrimination and processes of exclusion, and those that do attend may suffer racist humiliation and physical abuse by their teachers and peers. Also very few Roma will ever learn, in school, about Roma culture, history or language, or about the rich contributions Roma have made to the societies in which they live (ERRC 2008, OSI 2007). Enrolment and attendance in primary education is low in most European countries and absenteeism is a persistent, common and serious problem affecting all Roma and Traveller pupils. Transition to secondary education is low and dropout rates increase with age, as a result of both moves into employment and low levels of educational attainment. Indirect discrimination in enrolment resulting from differential application of bureaucratic regulations requiring proof of residence status, or other documentation not readily available, and direct discrimination by open refusal of school authorities to enrol Roma and Traveller children have been well established (FRA 2006b). Punishing Roma and Traveller pupils by placing them in classes lower than their age group, largely as a result of erratic attendance, academic failure or temporary abandonment of school has also been found, which prevents peer group integration, has a demoralising effect and can result in higher dropout rates. Formal and informal practices of segregating Roma and Traveller pupils persist, despite strategies and policies that have been developed to combat them. Although systematic segregation no longer exists as educational policy, segregation is practised by schools and educational authorities in a number of different, mostly indirect, ways sometimes as the unintended effect of policies and practices and sometimes as a result of residential segregation.

Wider patterns of anti-Roma hostility in relation to education are also evident. In Bulgaria, 86 per cent of respondents in a 2005 Gallup Poll, said they would not want their children attending school where more than half the children were Roma. This partly explains government failures to implement school desegregation programmes. In Hungary, general anti-Roma hostility was reported by about 37 per cent in 2003, with increasing levels of hostility up to the present and it therefore affects a large section of Hungarian society (OSI 2007). In Romania, research conducted by the National Council for Combating Discrimination in 2004 showed a significant level of discrimination in relation to employment, authorities and schools. In Serbia, discrimination has been identified as one of the key obstacles to equal access to education for Roma. In Macedonia, a UNICEF report on the Situation Analysis of Roma Women and Children states that 80 per cent of people polled apply negative stereotypes to the 'Gypsies' (OSI 2007). In the Czech Republic many common people still equate Roma distinctiveness with biologically inherited shortness.

The Roma and other selected minority ethnic groups

Outside Central and Eastern Europe, the Gypsy and Traveller population is also being studied as part of the UK project and here this group appears to be both in the most vulnerable position of economic, political and social marginality of any minority ethnic group and subject to continuing hostility and discrimination, although data for this group is much more limited (Cemlyn and Clark 2005). Analysis of the position of the other selected groups in the UK shows that the African-Caribbean population tends to be economically disadvantaged and socially assimilated, in terms of cohabitation and marriage patterns, and with some significant degree of political incorporation; and the Pakistani population tends to be in a position of greater economic marginality and poverty, with more social distinctiveness, due partly to social closure, and less political incorporation (Peach 2005, Modood 2005) (see Chapter 2 for a full account). Both of these groups had the right to settle in the UK, to acquire citizenship and participate in electoral politics due to previous British colonial relations and obligations (Robinson and Valeny 2005).

So within the UK, comparative analysis of ethnicity indicates that the Gypsy and Traveller groups, who are a part of the Roma diaspora, despite centuries of residence are doing worse, particularly for example in educational attainment than more recent migrant groups. A similar picture emerges in both comparing the Roma in Central and Eastern Europe with post-colonial migrant groups examined here including North Africans (Algerians, Moroccans, Tunisians) in France, and guest workers such as Turks in Germany and France. The population of North African origin and the Maghrebian second generation (the Beurs) in France have high levels of social marginalisation and racial hostility. Whereas the Turkish group of migrants tend to have lower levels of cultural integration and inter-ethnic relations of marriage and friendship than North Africans, and also high failure rates at school. In France, about 50 per cent of Turks and 45 per cent of North Africans (less for women) have no school qualifications. Turks and Portuguese migrants to Germany came as guest workers from the mid 1950s onwards subsequently settling, establishing a permanent presence with increasing levels of intermarriage. Ethnic differentials in education remain striking with 23 per cent of Turkish students failing to achieve school qualifications compared to 1.5 per cent of non-immigrants, with Portuguese migrants doing better than Turks but remaining well below the position of non-immigrants. In Denmark, Somali migrants are primarily a refugee group and have the lowest levels of educational and labour market outcomes, with Pakistani migrants, a guest worker group, occupying a better position, but still showing a considerable level of ethnic inequality in comparison to the majority population. Although broad comparative patterns of ethnicity can be identified, there is still considerable difficulty in carrying out systematic comparison of the relative position of these groups.

Categorising ethnicity

The problem of identifying the Roma population has led to the use of variously termed methods (hetero/ascription/outsider/external-identification) in addition to census self-assessment. In Romania data on ethnicity is obtained through the national census using self-definition. The real number of this minority remains more or less hidden to the authorities, partly due to the traditional tendency to be an 'untouchable ethnicity'. Ahmed et al. (2001) notes in a study using hetero-identification that about 10 per cent of the respondents who self-identified as non-Roma were designated as Roma by interviewers. Here, the external characteristics of an individual affected the probability of being hetero-identified as Roma: residence in a (perceived) majority Roma/Gypsy settlement, low level of education (elementary or less), number of people in the household and low income. Residence in Roma neighbourhoods increased this probability by twelve times, the lack of education around three times, and poverty and agglomeration each around one and half times. The tool of 'Roma Social Mapping' has been developed (Sandu 2005) to improve data collection. This uses both Roma and non-Roma local informers to identify compact local communities and estimates of population size are then made, without attributing ethnic identities to individual respondents.

In Hungary, similar problems of data collection on ethnicity arise, this position is described as 'statistical chaos' (Kocsis and Kovács 1999: 13). caused by the legal prohibition of the registration of ethnicity as well as the methodological difficulties of defining 'who is a Gypsy' which creates serious difficulties for research. The lack of objective criteria to determine Roma ethnicity has led to a reliance on census self-identification data, and identification by outsiders with the both methods being the subject of intense debate and are highly contested. Current approaches seek to combine these methods whilst maintaining that everyone has a right to decide their own identity. In Slovakia, a similar problem of census under-enumeration exists. During the 1990s, several administrative bodies surveyed (externally attributed) ethnicity and collected data on kindergarten attendance, births, infection diseases and criminal cases, but such practice has now ceased. Sociographic mapping of Roma settlements was carried out in 2003-2004 and has brought about the most precise information about the residence and habitation conditions of the Roma population. This was based on local expert interviewing (such as mayors and other municipal representatives, teachers, priests and like) and done in 1,087 towns and villages (38.4 per cent of all in Slovakia) and has been processed into a typology of Roma communities according to their level of disadvantage which has been used in various official classifications and policies. Currently discussion about implementing legislation to facilitate collection of ethnic data is underway. In the Czech Republic statistical data on the Roma are generally not reliable and the problem of Roma non-declaration of ethnicity also persists. Here, nationality is a key identifier which permits the production of more reliable data on the Vietnamese minority as they appear to have no major concerns with self-declaring as Vietnamese nationals. The unreliability of data on the Roma has led to the use of proxy categories such as socially weak, disadvantaged or excluded, but there is a poor fit here as at least half the Roma population do not live in localities containing concentrations of socially excluded people.

In the UK no national census data on European Roma has yet been collected, although discussion is taking place about possible inclusion in the 2011 census. Since 2003 data has been collected in schools and Gypsy/Roma and Travellers of Irish heritage are two distinct ethnicity group categories within the School Census. The Gypsy/Roma category includes pupils who identify themselves as Gypsies, and/or Romanies, and/or Travellers, and/or Traditional Travellers, and/or Romanichals, and/or Romanichal Gypsies, and/or Welsh Gypsies/Kale, and/or Scottish Travellers/Gypsies, and/or Roma. It includes all children of a Gypsy/Roma ethnic background, irrespective of whether they are nomadic, semi nomadic or living in static accommodation. The Travellers of Irish Heritage category are either ascribed and/or self-ascribed and include: Minceir, Travellers, Travelling People, and Travellers of Irish heritage. Travellers of Irish heritage speak their own language known as Gammon, sometimes referred to as 'Cant' and which is a language with many Romani loan-words, but not thought to be a dialect of Romani itself.

The school census guidance explains that for children aged up to 11, those with parental authority should make the decision on the ethnic background of the child. Children aged 11-15 should make this decision with the support of their parents. Young people aged 16 and over can make the decision for themselves. However, an individual's perception of their own ethnic identity is considered sensitive personal data and ultimately it is the 'data subject', i.e., the pupils who determine their own identity by ethnic group. For children aged 11 and above, it is the child's decision that matters and should take precedence over that of their parents. In the event of a significant disagreement arising either between parents or between parents and their child over ethnic identity, the matter should be referred to the relevant government department. When a parent fails to return the ethnic group collection form, the school can use its best judgement to determine the ethnic group of the pupil. This process is also known as 'third party' ascription. If ascription is to be carried out then the information should be requested from the parent by post along with a letter that explains that the school will ascribe an ethnic group to their child if there is no response and parents do not formally refuse to provide this information. If a formal refusal is made, schools must not ascribe an ethnic group. Parents should be informed of the school's decision and given the opportunity to see, amend or remove the ethnic group record. The ethnic group record will be marked as 'ascribed by the school.' If the school has a confident belief that the children in question are likely to be, or have a Traveller heritage, then they should be encouraged to declare it within the context of the ethnic group completion form, but only after establishing, through diplomatic questioning, whether they agree to subscribe to the ethnic status of either Gypsy/Roma or Traveller of Irish Heritage. The historic social status of Gypsy/Roma and Travellers of Irish Heritage has been negative and there may well be some parents who feel that they are protecting their children by not declaring their ethnic background. In these circumstances, every encouragement and reassurance should be given to these families by carefully explaining the value to be gained for the child from the exercise. So, clear guidance is in place for dealing with the difficulties that may arise in ethnic monitoring and the rights of the 'data subject' are prioritised.

Danish, Swedish, German and French data is very limited with no collection of information on self-declared ethnicity. These countries rely primarily on identification of country of birth, lines of descent and citizenship status. For example in Denmark the 'immigrant' category refers to people who were not born in Denmark and whose parents were not born, or are not Danish citizens. So, the Pakistani and Somali groups and their descendants are defined by both nationality and whether they are Danish or foreign citizens. The Roma cannot be identified in Denmark in national data. In Sweden the only way to identify ethnic origin is through information of place of birth or citizenship. Here, the Roma are an officially recognised minority group of 40-50,000 people.

In Germany, similar problems arising from reliance on citizenship and country of birth data has led to a wider debate which has led to the creation of a new category, 'persons of migrant background', which was included in the 2005 micro census which roughly doubled the count of migrants and included identification of second-generation migrants. In France, legal regulations prohibit the collection of data on ethnic or racial origins but there is recent debate that may lead to relaxation of these laws. So, data in this country also draws on citizenship and country of birth to identify immigrants and their descendants. Also, in Germany and France it is not possible to identify the Roma population. In the UK measurement and classification of ethnicity in national statistics began in 1976, prior to this proxy measures such as country of birth and nationality were used. The national decennial census, the Labour Force Survey and the four national surveys of minority ethnic groups conducted by the Policy Studies Institute provide benchmark data sources, together with local education authority data, the school pupil census and excellent national data sets on entrants to higher education providing more detailed information on education. The lack of consistent cross-national data on ethnicity remains a key problem for social research in this field.

Conclusion

How should we understand the meaning of racism and ethnicity in a post civil-rights, post-apartheid, post-colonial, post-national, post-racial, post-communist world? Up to 1990 in Romania, but also in the entire communist world, scholars and political actors considered that the importance of ethnicity must decline along with the development of modernisation and homogenisation. But, as this chapter confirms, racism and ethnicity are not in decline, and many sociologists have been wrong in predicting their demise, including Max Weber,

> Weber may be criticised along with almost every other social thinker from the time of the French Revolution to the outbreak of World War 1 for failing to give sufficient weight to racial, ethnic and national conflicts. (Stone 2003: 29).

The strength of racial and ethnic loyalties and their practical adequacy for many people in making sense of their position in the world, in pre-modern, modern and contemporary times indicates the likelihood that such conflict will continue, despite international declarations and interventions, creative national policies and inter-ethnic mixing. The level of ethnic and cultural diversity in a society does not have any significant effect on the likelihood of racial and ethnic conflict and associated violence and genocide (Lattimer 2008). This proposition about ethnic diversity draws on quantitative longitudinal analysis of a range of causal hypotheses (Harff 2003) and provides an empirical challenge, particularly to national political discourse which seeks to either control or reduce migration, or reject the creation of multiethnic and multicultural societies in the name of reducing racial and ethnic conflict. Whereas factors such as the habituation to illegal violence among the armed forces or police, prevailing impunity for human rights violations, official tolerance or encouragement of hate speech against particular groups and, in extreme cases, prior experience of mass killing are all much more likely to increase the likelihood of violence and atrocities being committed. The multiplicity of groups under threat and the complexity of these contexts indicates the importance of both recognising the global significance of the forces of ethnicity, racism and migration and developing a wider understanding of these issues across a range of regional situations.

Across the EU, and particularly those member states under investigation here, there are commonalities of experience. All of these groups have been subject to racism, xenophobia, hostility, violence and practices of restriction and exclusion during the process of migration and settlement. They have also been subject to varying levels of political and cultural recognition, acceptance of racial and ethnic difference, inter-ethnic marriage and cohabitation and incorporation into political, economic, cultural and social spheres of activity. Many of the states under scrutiny here have strong national discourses which emphasise tolerance of minorities, but empirical evidence shows that interethnic relations are sharply competitive and conflictual, particularly in Romania for example in comparison with other Central-European countries (Culic, Horvath, Lazar and Magyari 1998). The rising 'ethnicisation of politics' in Central and Eastern European countries and the return to 'aggressive majoritarianism' (Gillborn 2008) in Western Europe are indicative of these trends.

The ongoing importance of ethnicity in a range of formal and informal contexts has been established in this chapter. Why certain social contexts over-determine, or make ethnicity of high importance, and why others under-determine or reduce the significance of ethnicity, together with examination of the ethnic difference in varying regional, national and local circumstances are central questions here. The nature and complexity of relations between the movement of people (migration), the formation of boundaries between groups of people who have shared cultural meanings, memories and descent (ethnicity) and the formation and negative treatment of racial groups (racism) has been examined. Migration, racism and ethnicity remain strong social forces and there is evidence of sharpening tensions and conflict in inter-ethnic relations. Two key forms of ethnicity are examined in this study: *migrant workers* and their descendants forming strong ethnic communities, for example Turks in Germany or Pakistanis in the UK, and the *Roma*. These groups collectively experience discriminatory practices in their everyday life, with many being particularly vulnerable to such exclusionary behaviour in the spheres of employment, housing, education and in interactions with the police. The selected minority ethnic groups chosen for study here indicate a varied hierarchy of ethnic differentials with the Roma in the most vulnerable and marginal position.

The macro, meso and micro contexts which collectively frame majority responses to these minority groups are highly dynamic with for example, changing migration flows, global conflicts, media images and national debates. Despite this changing context, levels of discrimination and hostility have been high and relatively stable and the resulting perception across many groups and communities of systemic negative treatment has a range of significant effects including alienation and political mobilisation. Increasing recognition of minority rights has accompanied increasing minority ethnic mobilisation. Although forms and levels vary across these countries it is clear that minority claims-making and, often inadequate and partial, national political and policy responses together with significant levels of majority hostility are common features. Multiculturalism as a normative principle has not gained ground in Central and Eastern Europe, and is under attack in the West. The value of diversity is in question and there is a majority backlash to values of tolerance. At the same time the rhetoric of equality is evident in integration and non-discrimination interventions, yet they have failed to deliver significant reductions in inequalities and sustained political recognition of minority rights. Education has been a key battleground in which these mainstream and minority claims and positions have been articulated and utilised in political struggles and policy debates. Beneath the politics of race and ethnicity, our selected minority ethnic groups have drawn creatively on their cultural distinctiveness and identity to formulate differential responses to these circumstances.

The next chapter provides an in-depth account of ethnic relations in the UK and introduces educational debates which are then examined more closely in Chapter 3. Following the presentation of new research on education and ethnicity in a Northern city of the UK in Chapters 4, 5 and 6 we return to the European level of cross-country comparative analysis in order to assess the significance of these findings alongside new evidence from the other country teams involved in the EDUMIGROM project.

Chapter 2
Ethnic Relations in the UK

Introduction

Ethnic relations in the UK are highly dynamic and this chapter charts contemporary changes. This chapter provides a wide-ranging account of a range of aspects of ethnic relations in the UK. Firstly the historical development of ethnic diversity is considered. Secondly, a new contemporary comparative analysis of African-Caribbeans, Pakistani and Gypsy and Traveller people is presented. Thirdly, consideration is given to the measurement of ethnicity. Next, inter-ethnic relations in the light of public discourses and current conflicts are evaluated. The post-war policy context in relation to racism and ethnic diversity is also mapped out with particular consideration of the impact of these policy approaches for education. Finally, future prospects for ethnic inequalities in the context of the contemporary economic crisis are considered in relation to patterns of poverty and exclusion. This chapter therefore provides a 'leading edge' account of ethnic relations in the UK and lays the basis for the detailed examination of ethnicity and education in the next chapter.

Historical development of ethnic diversity in the UK

The UK has always been ethnically diverse with a population developing from complex historical migration patterns and periods of conflict, conquest, state formation, empire and de-colonisation. Specific movements relevant here include sporadic in-migration of Gypsies and the importation of African slaves and servants from the sixteenth century onwards, mass migrations of Irish and Jewish people in the nineteenth century and post-war economic migration to Britain from the Caribbean, the South Asian subcontinent, China and Africa (Okely 1983, Shyllon 1977, Holmes 1988). In the postwar period there is both increasing mixing of ethnic groups and 'super-diversity'[1] (Vertovec 2006, see below) which have created an ethnically complex society. The UK is also undergoing substantial social

---

1   Super-diversity is a concept that foregrounds a level and kind of ethnic complexity surpassing anything the country has previously experienced, and this has been applied to the UK by Vertovec (2006). This is distinguished by a contrast with previous periods of migration and identification of dynamic interplay of variables among an increased number of new, small and scattered, multiple-origin, transnationally connected, socio-economically differentiated and legally stratified immigrants.

and cultural change due to globalisation, Europeanisation, devolution, the end of Empire, social pluralism and the acceleration of migration (Parekh 2000, Loury, Modood and Teles 2005). As Ulrich Beck reminds us, the increasing development of inter-cultural and inter-ethnic social relations across modern societies has been identified by a range of intellectuals and scholars including Kant, Goethe, Marx and Simmel, who all saw the modern period as the product of a transition from 'early conditions of relatively closed societies to "universal eras" [universellen Epochen] (Goethe)' (Beck 2006: 9) of societies marked by economic and social interdependence, together with increasingly complex patterns of movement and cultural interaction. The resulting swirl of social change has brought into being two opposing positions. On the one hand, cosmopolitanism brings with it an emphasis on openness to others, recognition and acceptance of difference and the universalist view that all are equal and everyone is different. Whereas anti-cosmopolitanism, which can be found across all political camps, organisations and countries, emphasises hostility to cultural, linguistic and cultural differences, and promotes exclusion of and contempt for racial, ethnic or cultural groups who are perceived as threatening in some way. These opposing forces are both central features of the European tradition and of twenty-first century Europe and provide the context for micro inter-ethnic interactions in educational and community contexts for this study of the UK. The 'selected minority ethnic groups' chosen for this study are the Gypsy/Roma/Traveller population, African-Caribbeans and Pakistanis. All of these migrant groups have been subject to racism, xenophobia, hostility, violence and practices of restriction and exclusion during the process of migration and settlement in the UK (Holmes 1991, Panayi 1996). They have also been subject to varying levels of political and cultural recognition, acceptance of racial and ethnic difference, inter-ethnic marriage and cohabitation and incorporation into political, economic, cultural and social spheres of activity.

The post-war period saw a sustained level of inward migration from commonwealth or former commonwealth countries to supply labour. Migration from the Caribbean was followed by that from India and Pakistan and subsequently Bangladesh. Although much primary migration was male, with family re-unification (that is, applying for dependants from abroad to join them here), being a subsequent step, this was not the case for Caribbean immigration where there were large numbers of women among primary migrants who came, for example, to take up work in the health service. These groups were from former British colonies, with people subject to initial rights of entry that were gradually restricted during the 1960s and early 1970s until only families of settled migrants could enter.

The 1948 Nationality Act gave rights of entry and citizenship to all citizens of British colonies and the Commonwealth and embodied the domestic need to ensure labour migration to re-build postwar Britain and the international objective of seeking to maintain a united British Commonwealth. So, citizenship and all the civil, political and social rights associated with it were held by most under post-colonial arrangements (Hansen and Weil 2001). From 1948 to 1962 the British state was involved in a long process of political and ideological racialisation, which focussed on dismantling and differentiating these rights in immigration policy (Saggar 1992). This culminated in the 1962 Commonwealth Immigrants Act which differentiated between British and Commonwealth citizens, with the specific intention of restricting non-White migrants. This was followed by an increasing succession of strong legislation with repeated attempts to stop Black and Asian migration to the UK. Immigration from the Caribbean was about 2,000 annually in the late 1940s and early 1950s, this doubled between 1959 and 1960 and this primary migration increased further in an attempt to beat the impact of new controls. 70 per cent of male Caribbean migrants arrived in the UK pre-1962. Indian and Pakistani migration was more evenly spread across the period of the mid-1950s to the mid-1980s (Saggar 1992: 51). After partition in 1947, Pakistan was divided into East and West, from the 1950s a civil war developed and in 1971 the independent nation state of Bangladesh was created from what had been East Pakistan. Thus the early arrivals from Bangladesh were actually Pakistani, whereas later arrivals from that region were Bangladeshis from the new state of Bangladesh. In this book reference to Pakistanis and Bangladeshis refers to current nationalities.

Large and eventually well-organised communities were formed, particularly through the establishment of community associations and places of worship (Vertovec 2006). Expulsion also resulted in settlement by numbers of Vietnamese and East African Asian families around 1970. Since 1970, most primary immigration for employment has been at a standstill, with family re-unification and fertility being the routes through which minority groups have expanded. Refugees have also contributed to a diverse minority group population, a recent phenomenon being the arrival of asylum seekers from within Europe as well as from further afield.

The differentiation in economic position, migration history, political participation and perceptions of social citizenship are significant across minority ethnic groups in the UK and they are becoming increasingly evident. Recent debate has highlighted the problem of hyper- or super-diversity where professionals and managers face substantial dilemmas in responding to the needs of culturally complex societies (Vertovec 2006, Mir 2007). Vertovec argues that the new context of super-diversity in the UK arising from the 1990s onwards requires consideration of the following factors in both research and policy:

- country of origin (comprising a variety of possible subset traits such as ethnicity, language[s], religious tradition, regional and local identities, cultural values and practices),
- migration channel (often related to highly gendered flows and specific social networks),
- legal status (determining entitlement to rights),
- migrants' human capital (particularly educational background),
- access to employment (which may or may not be in immigrants' hands),

- locality (related especially to material conditions, but also the nature and extent of other immigrant and ethnic minority presence),
- transnationalism (emphasising how migrants' lives are lived with significant reference to places and peoples elsewhere),
- uneven responses by local authorities, services providers and local residents (which often tend to function by way of assumptions based on previous experiences with migrants and ethnic minorities).

The implication of addressing 'super-diversity' in schools is that it may be impossible to give teachers appropriate knowledge about the language and culture of an increasing breadth of newcomer children. Whereas the development of generic skills in teacher training for the broad appreciation of cultural difference may be more appropriate.

There is a complex system of citizenship rights, forms of membership and restrictions and exclusions which cross-cut differing categories and groups of migrants to the UK. This produces an ad hoc and variable pattern of denial of service and responses to individual needs so that people in the same migrant category may receive different services and entitlements. This produces a situation where 'neither service providers, advice-givers nor migrants themselves are clear as to what services they might be entitled' (Morris 2002, 2004, Arai 2006, Vertovec 2006). This is particularly relevant in the provision of welfare and associated benefits which are discussed below. The recent national evaluation of Sure Start (Craig et al. 2007), a cross-departmental initiative which aimed to enhance the life chances of children less than four years old growing up in disadvantaged neighbourhoods, identified the basic failure to address ethnicity which, in the implementation of this programme, was 'fragmented, partial or lacking altogether'. This indicates a wider national failure of welfare providers to develop consistent and coherent national policy and practice in relation to the varying needs of migrant groups.

Selected ethnic groups in the UK: a comparative overview

This section introduces a comparative overview of three selected groups and shows that, the African-Caribbean population tends to be economically disadvantaged and socially assimilated, in terms of cohabitation and marriage patterns, and with some significant degree of political incorporation; the Pakistani population tends to be in a position of greater economic marginality and poverty, with more social distinctiveness, due partly to social closure, and less political incorporation (Peach 2005, Modood 2005). Both of these groups had the right to settle in the UK, to acquire citizenship and participate in electoral politics due to previous British colonial relations and obligations (Robinson and Valeny 2005). The Gypsy and Traveller population appears to be in the most vulnerable position of economic, political and social marginality of any these groups, although data for this group is much more limited (Cemlyn and Clark 2005). Although this group have formal voting rights, they are likely to have much lower levels of electoral registration and they have no elected representatives in either local or national government.

Gypsy, Roma and Traveller people

Gypsies are believed to have moved into the UK from Europe from the sixteenth century onwards, with a significant community being established around London by the eighteenth century. The origins and differentiation of groups within this category are complex and may include the formation of groups with both indigenous and non-UK roots. Migration to the UK has been mainly driven by expulsion and repression in mainland Europe together with rejection of sedentary lifestyles and feudal bonds. They have often being subject to oppressive vagrancy legislation. There has been a history of conflict between this group and the state particularly in relation to the enforcement of housing, urban planning and land control laws which has affected family travel and mobility (Morris and Clements 1999).

Welfare outcomes are particularly poor for this group (Cemlyn and Clark 2005), for example they have higher levels of infant mortality and lower life expectancy due to difficulties in accessing health services than most other groups (Morris and Clements 2001), life expectancy for men and women is 10 years lower than the national average and Gypsy and Irish Traveller mothers are 20 times more likely than mothers in the rest of the population to have experienced the death of a child (Van Cleemput et al. 2004). In education, as well as some of the lowest levels of educational attainment (DCFS 2008), some schools are refusing to admit children from this group, imposing discriminatory conditions on admission or delaying registration (Clark 2004), whereas some central and local government initiatives have sought to challenge these processes and prioritise inclusion work. Also a recent study found that of those that do get access to education, at least half of gypsy and traveller children in England and Wales drop out of school between Key Stages 1 and 4 and the same study also showed very high rates of exclusions (DfES 2005). Furthermore, there is increasing evidence of almost total failure of access to higher education for this group (Clark 2004).

This group has much diversity within it and is estimated to include 200,000-250,000 people (Morris 2003, Clark 2004, Clark and Greenfields 2006). In Britain there are UK Irish Travellers, Scots Travellers (Nachins), Welsh Gypsies (Kale) and English Gypsies (Romanichals) among others. There are also Travelling Showpeople (Fairground Travellers), Boat Dwellers (Bargees) and Circus Travellers. Ethnic identifiers, including language, identity, names and traditions vary across these sub-groups, and many can opt to conceal their ethnicity as phenotypical characteristics are more difficult to use to mark out this group. They are therefore on the margins of racial visibility, but they are clearly social and ethnically identifiable, particularly in terms of a long shared history, of which the group is conscious as distinguishing it from other groups, and the memory of which it keeps alive; and a cultural tradition of its own, including family and social customs and manners. In the decennial census of population these groups, where enumerated, are included in the 'White' category.

In 1985 the Swann report identified Gypsy, Roma and Traveller pupils as being strongly affected by many factors influencing the education of children from other minority ethnic groups including racism, stereotyping and the need for more positive links between Gypsy, Roma and Traveller parents and their children's schools. The Department for Children Schools and Families (DCSF) confirmed recently its commitment to raising the attendance and achievement of Gypsy, Roma and Traveller pupils. In 2003, the Department (DfES which became the DCSF in 2007) published *Aiming High: Raising the Achievement of Minority Ethnic Pupils*, and *Aiming High: Raising the Achievement of Gypsy Traveller Pupils: A Guide to Good Practice.*

Gypsy/Roma and Travellers of Irish Heritage are identified as racial groups and covered by the Race Relations Acts as legitimate minority ethnic communities. Gypsy/Roma people have been recognised as a racial group since 1988 (CRE v Dutton). Travellers of Irish heritage received legal recognition in law as a racial group in 2000 (O'Leary v Allied Domecq). Gypsy, Roma and Traveller communities frequently experience social exclusion and discrimination which can be intentionally or is unintentionally racist in character on account of the lack of knowledge by the perpetrator(s) of their legal minority ethnic status. Legal recognition of this group is necessary in order to secure protection from racial discrimination. Members of a group that is not recognised cannot legally pursue complaints of racial discrimination. Therefore, prior to this formal recognition racial discrimination against Gypsies and travellers was lawful and could not be challenged in the courts or in industrial tribunals. Since 2003 Gypsy/Roma and Travellers of Irish heritage are two distinct ethnicity group categories within the School Census. These two groups are defined as follows:

> *Gypsy/Roma*   This category includes pupils who identify themselves as Gypsies and or Romanies, and or Travellers, and or Traditional Travellers, and or Romanichals, and or Romanichal Gypsies and or Welsh Gypsies/ Kaale, and or Scottish Travellers/Gypsies, and or Roma. It includes all children of a Gypsy/Roma ethnic background, irrespective of whether they are nomadic, semi nomadic or living in static accommodation.

> *Traveller of Irish Heritage*   A range of terminology is also used in relation to Travellers with an Irish heritage. These are either ascribed and or self-ascribed and include: Minceir, Travellers, Travelling People, and Travellers of Irish heritage. Travellers of Irish heritage speak their own language known as Gammon, sometimes referred to as 'Cant' and which is a language with many Romani loan-words, but not thought to be a dialect of Romani itself.

The School Census categorisation does not include Fairground (Showman's) children; the children travelling with circuses; or the children of New Travellers or those dwelling on the waterways unless, of course, their ethnicity status is either of that which is mentioned above. Although most of these people have full citizenship rights, this category of Gypsy/Roma will also include people whose immigration status will be either, asylum seeker or refugee, and or migrant worker who have moved to the UK more recently from other EU states. The most recently arrived Roma in the UK have been subject to highly visible media hostility and vilification (Craske 2000).

Data on household formation, economic activity, occupations and incomes is very limited, a useful summary of evidence has been provided by Cemlyn and Clark (2005). They identify Gypsy and Traveller culture as strongly family-orientated and child-centred and these family and extended family networks are seen as primarily provide support in difficult times. Gypsy and Traveller economies have been largely identified as family based self-employed activities, which are flexible, adaptable and opportunistic in relation to gaps and opportunities in mainstream economic markets. This includes declining traditional work in areas such as, farm work and scrapping, and other newer economic activity in market trading and construction. Regulations and restrictions on self-employment on official sites have limited opportunities and many find that simply being a Gypsy or Traveller, and lacking basic literacy skills, will prevent them accessing mainstream wage labour jobs or training (Cemlyn and Clark 2005). There are an increasing number of local needs studies that have examined housing, health and educational needs, for example in West Yorkshire, but there is an urgent need to collect and collate data at national level.

African-Caribbean people

There is extensive historical evidence of the establishment of Black communities in selected British cities from the seventeenth century onwards, often remaining a key focal point for people of African descent in the UK for centuries (Walvin 1973, Law 1981). There is also extensive historical evidence of both the depth and pervasiveness of anti-Black racism and associated violence, discrimination and hostility, as well as more positive forms of social interaction, including inter-racial marriage and cohabitation with White people which has increasingly formed a large mixed population. Early Black communities established in the nineteenth century, for example Liverpool and Cardiff, were built on these social relations of inter-ethnic marriage and cohabitation, and this trend continues (Berthoud 2005), which is in marked contrast to other national contexts e.g. the USA.

African-Caribbeans are people of African descent who were born in the Caribbean or who come from families which include people born in one of the Caribbean islands. In the post-war period this group mainly arrived in the UK during the 1950s and 1960s from Jamaica and other islands including Barbados, Grenada and Trinidad and Tobago, in response to demand for labour in the UK due to post-war reconstruction and economic growth (Peach 1996, Robinson and Valeny 2005). This group generally came as families and by 2001 constituted about 1 per cent of the UK population, about half a million people (566,000). The Black Caribbean group are now mainly British born (57 per cent born in UK) and of Christian religious background (74 per cent). In comparison to the White British population they tend to have a younger age profile, a broadly similar socio-economic profile with, unusually, men tending to fare less well in both education and employment than women (ONS 2006). For example, the proportion of African-Caribbean men in routine and manual occupations (37 per cent) exceeded the proportion in professional and managerial occupations (24 per cent) compared to the contrasting respective figures of 24 per cent and 30 per cent for African-Caribbean women. The income poverty rate for African-Caribbeans is 30 per cent compared to 20 per cent for Whites, for Bangladeshis it is much higher at 65 per cent (Palmer and Kenway 2007). In terms of housing needs, African-Caribbeans are over-represented amongst the homeless (11 per cent of those households accepted by English local authorities as homeless and in urgent priority need were from this group).

In 2001, in recognition of the increasingly mixed heritage of certain groups of people, four new mixed categories were included in the national Census, one of these was Mixed White and African-Caribbean. This group was the largest of the mixed categories, comprising about 237,000 people who were largely born in the UK (94 per cent), it also was the youngest of these mixed groups with 58 per cent being under 16 and the one with the lowest socio-economic profile and high levels of unemployment and poor educational outcomes. Also 25 per cent of economically active younger people from this group were unemployed, with an average of 16 per cent overall for this group, and 25 per cent had no educational qualifications at all (Bradford 2006). African-Caribbean and Mixed White/Black Caribbean young men are increasingly subject as a group to internal socio-economic polarisation, as they are increasingly found both amongst the ranks of those with higher incomes and amongst the long-term unemployed (Berthoud 1999). Black young adults are also three times more likely to be in prison than White young adults, and this indicates a continuing crisis regarding the position of this group in relation to the criminal justice system (EHRC 2010).

Pakistani people

This group has been the most recent to settle in the UK of the three minorities under consideration here, with migration beginning in the 1950s. Men from Pakistan came as economic migrants with increasing numbers in the 1960s and 1970s with further rapid expansion through family reunification through into the 1980s. Three key problems were highlighted for this group; recent arrival from a rural peasant society lacking skills to access well-paid employment and often moving into low-skilled manufacturing occupations such as textiles, poor command of English and racial discrimination in housing and employment. Other key causes of educational under-achievement identified were low teacher expectations, racial hostility in school and community contexts, deprivation of home background, poor educational provision in Pakistan and missed schooling after arrival in the UK. Also cultural differences were seen as posing severe difficulties for schools in respect of halal food, sex education, religious education, uniforms and the observance of purdah. Social services were described as 'hostile and invasive' by Pakistani organisations and poor housing and material conditions led to a high incidence of ill-health.

Over the last two decades there has been both substantial change in some aspects of life, for example a rapid improvement in educational achievement at school, whereas in terms of housing, poverty and incomes there have been highly durable persisting inequalities for this group. In 2001 this group constituted 1.6 per cent of the UK population at about 747,000 people with almost half being born in the UK. Significant characteristics of this group are that over 92 per cent are Muslims, this group also has a much younger age structure with a particularly high proportion of children under 16 (the median age for Pakistanis being 24), and generally larger families with an average household size of 4.2 people (compared, for example, to 2.3 people for African-Caribbean and White British households) (Platt 2010). Due to high birth rates and net international immigration the Pakistani group grew faster than most other minority groups, by 56.6 per cent between 1991 and 2001. Between 1994 and 2000 after adjusting for education and age Pakistanis experienced significant increases in unemployment rates, with unemployment effects being as great for the second generation as the first, illustrating their position of economic vulnerability and the hypercyclical cause of this trend; being more severely affected by economic cycle changes than the majority (NEP 2010). 44 per cent of Pakistani women are still economically inactive although more women from this group are moving into higher education and the labour market (NEP 2010). High levels of fertility are declining with the rate of teenage motherhood falling along with declining family size and there are indications of a convergence with White fertility rates (Berthoud 2005). Pakistani families are moving through a period of change, re-negotiating core values and converging on the wider patterns across the UK, whereas African-Caribbean family structures are moving very differently, away from standard White norms. This Black group have an increasing number of unpartnered parents, over 50 per cent of families, a very low rate of marriage and a high proportion of White partners, over 25 per cent of families (Berthoud 2005: 236). Berthoud argues that West Indian cultural traditions, with mothers and children living separately from the father, the relative acceptability of non-marital and non-residential partnerships, a preference for less committing family forms, 'modern individualism' and the importance placed on personal choice rather than conventional obligation and greater social acceptance of mixed partnerships all play a part in explaining these trends. These contrasting patterns of family formation do show however that all groups are moving in the same direction from 'old-fashioned values' to 'modern individualism' with African-Caribbeans ahead of the position of White families and Pakistanis behind them.

Measuring ethnicity

In the UK measurement and classification of ethnicity in national statistics began in 1976, prior to this proxy measures such as country of birth and nationality were used. Since 1976 terminology and categorisation of groups have been subject to revision and change. The GRT population has only been identified by the School Census which began in 2003, but it is likely that this group will be identified in the national Census, for the first time, in 2011. The African-Caribbean group was referred to as West Indian prior to 1991, as Black was considered to be derogatory. The Pakistani category has remained constant over time in national statistics (ONS 2006). The national decennial Census, the Labour Force Survey and the four national surveys of ethnic minorities conducted by the Policy Studies Institute provide benchmark data sources, together with local education authority data, the school pupil census and excellent national data sets on entrants to higher education providing more detailed information on education.

For the school census, DCSF Guidance explains that for children aged up to 11, those with parental authority should make the decision on the ethnic background of the child. Children aged 11-15 should make this decision with the support of their parents. Young people aged 16 and over can make the decision for themselves. However, an individual's perception of their own ethnic identity is considered sensitive personal data and ultimately it is the 'data subject', i.e., the pupil who determines their own identity by ethnic group. For children aged 11 and above, it is the child's decision that matters and should take precedence over that of their parents. In the event of a significant disagreement arising either between parents or between parents and their child over ethnic identity, the matter should be referred to the DCSF. When a parent fails to return the ethnic group collection form, the school can use its best judgement to determine the ethnic group of the pupil. This process is also known as 'third party' ascription. If ascription is to be carried out then, the information should be requested from the parent by post along with a letter that explains that the school will ascribe an ethnic group to their child if there is no response and parents do not formally refuse to provide this information. Also if a formal refusal is made, schools must not ascribe an ethnic group. Parents should be informed of the school's decision and given the opportunity to see, amend or remove the ethnic group record, and the ethnic group record will be marked as 'ascribed by the school.'

If the school has a confident belief that the children in question are likely to be, or have a Traveller heritage, then they should be encouraged to declare it within the context of the ethnic group completion form, but only after establishing, through diplomatic questioning, whether they agree to subscribe to the ethnic status of either Gypsy Roma or Traveller of Irish Heritage. The historic social status of Gypsy Roma and Travellers of Irish Heritage has been negative and there may well be some parents who feel that they are protecting their children by not declaring their ethnic background. In these circumstances, every encouragement and reassurance should be given to these families by carefully explaining the value to be gained for the child from the exercise. So, clear guidance is in place for dealing with the difficulties that may arise in ethnic monitoring and the rights of the 'data subject' are prioritised.

Table 2.1   Ethnic composition of the UK population, 1991-2001, in 000s

Group	1991 population	2001 population	% change
All ethnic groups	54,887	57,104	4.0
White	51,873	52,481	1.2
Mixed*	-	674	-
Asian	1,677	2,329	38.9
Indian	840	1,052	25.2
Pakistani	477	747	56.6
Bangladeshi	163	283	73.6
Other Asian	197	247	25.4
Black	890	1,148	29.0
Black Caribbean	500	566	13.2
Black African	212	485	128.8
Other Black	178	97	-45.5
Chinese	157	243	54.8
Other ethnic groups	290	229	-21.0
All non-White	3,014	4,623	53.4
Gypsy/Traveller	-	200-250 (estimate)	-

Note: * Mixed ethnic group categories were not included in 1991 census.

Source: 1991 census, 2001 census, Office for National Statistics; 2001 census, General Register Office for Scotland.

In December 2008 the Office of National Statistics, after a long process of consultation, agreed a new categorisation of ethnic group in the 2011 national census. This has important implications for many public sector agencies and researchers and is examined here. The purpose of the ethnic origin question is primarily to allocate resources, for example to local government, and facilitate the monitoring of racial and ethnic discrimination. Despite the detail of existing categorisation of ethnic group it is interesting to note that in the consultation process over 40 per cent of data users felt that this failed to meet their information requirements and this indicates the importance of making revisions.

New categories which have been included in the 2011 Census are 'Gypsy or Irish Traveller' and 'Arab' and they were introduced due to the recognised user need in relation to informing appropriate delivery of public services and the current lack of data. The Office of the Deputy Prime Minister (now known as Communities and Local Government) stated that the collection of such information would 'enable those authorities responsible for providing accommodation, education and health services to ensure that the needs of the Gypsy and Irish Traveller community are accurately assessed and resources properly targeted' (ONS 2008: 19).

The debate over the Arab category elicited some confusion. Some viewed the term as too specific others suggested the category was too broad. For example one local authority argued, '"Arab" looks like it fills a large gap but on reflection in the local context [it] may not do – a gap still remains for identification of substantial groups such as those from Afghanistan, Iran and parts of North Africa' (London Borough of Barnet). Whereas the Muslim Council of Britain said, 'The inclusion of "Arab" is fully supported ... Ideally Arab should be broken down to "Arab-North African", "Arab-Iraqi" and "Arab-Other" (because each of these groups are believed to be quite large – more than 100,000 in 2006, but there is little statistical information)' (2008: 20).

Some categories have been relocated, for example 'Chinese' to reduce confusion between the 'Other Asian' and 'Other ethnic group' categories. The categorisation of ethnic groups in 2011 will continue to include use of colour categories such as Black and White in order to identify patterns of discrimination against visible ethnic minorities. There is opposition to the use of colour terminology from some respondents and organisations as it is seen as out-date, stereotypical, inappropriate and offensive. However, removing this from the categorisation of ethnic group may hamper service provision and anti-discrimination efforts and may also confuse respondents and increase non-response and therefore it has been retained as one key marker of ethnicity. Overall, these changes will lead to an improvement of the data base on ethnic group, particularly for Gypsies and Irish Travellers where very little data existed previously. But the collection of ethnic group data remains controversial for individual respondents and communities with varying levels of ambivalence, confusion and opposition.

Inadequate enumeration of ethnicity remains a major problem as the small sizes of some of the groups means that survey samples cannot be meaningfully disaggregated (Walby et al. 2008). Grouping together some ethnic categories, such as Gypsy and Traveller groups, leads to a loss of potentially important distinctions. Additional boosts to the main sample composed of those from ethnic minority groups can be used, but this can introduce complexity and loss of transparency.

Inter-ethnic relations and conflicts

In the UK the leading government agency concerned with antiracism, racial equality and multiculturalism, the Commission for Racial Equality, was abolished in 2007. In its final summing up of the state of inter-ethnic relations it said:

Britain, despite its status as the fifth largest economy in the world, is still a place of inequality, exclusion and isolation. Segregation – residentially, socially and in the workplace – is growing. Extremism, both political and religious, is on the rise as people become disillusioned and disconnected from each other. Issues of identity have a new prominence in our social landscape and have a profound impact upon race relations in Britain. An ethnic minority British baby born today is sadly still more likely to go on to receive poor quality education, be paid less, live in substandard housing, be in poor health and be discriminated against in other ways than his or her White contemporaries. This persistent, longstanding inequality is quite simply unfair and unacceptable. (CRE 2007: 2).

It has been replaced by the new Commission for Equality and Human Rights with a much wider brief for different forms of social division. The Traveller Law Reform Project, along with many other organisations, thinks that the proposals will weaken existing protection for ethnic minorities, including Gypsies and Irish Travellers. They argue that Gypsies and Travellers benefited little from race equality legislation until the Race Relations (Amendment) Act was passed in 2000, that voluntary guidance does not work and that a focus on race equality is needed which may be lost in the harmonisation of equality legislation and agencies. In applying 'modernisation' and managerialist priorities to equality legislation, protection against discrimination and the statutory responsibilities of public authorities and agencies have been eroded through the principle of 'proportionality' ('no need to take any action which might be disproportionate to the benefits of that action'). This is a move back to voluntarism, allowing public services to only address issues of ethnicity, racism and related inequalities as they see fit (Gillborn 2008: 131-132). Here a school may wish to act to narrow achievement gaps, tackle racist bullying or encourage greater parental involvement, but there is no statutory obligation to do so. Despite public and media debate at the time, the moment has passed, and this issue will only emerge again on public and news agendas dependent on the mobilisation of minority groups and the success of the new Commission.

The EHRC's triennial review of fairness in Britain confirmed the extent of racial and ethnic inequalities, with African-Caribbean and Pakistani babies being twice as likely to die in their first year as Bangladeshi or White British babies (EHRC 2010). By the age of 22-24, figures suggest that 44 per cent of Black people are not in education, employment or training, compared to fewer than 25 per cent of White people. Five times more Black people than White people are imprisoned in England and Wales and there is now greater disproportionality in the number of Black people in prisons in Britain than in the USA.

As regards Gypsies and Travellers they currently fare very badly in many dimensions of equality including longevity, health, education, political participation, influence and voice, identity, expression and self-respect, and legal security. Particular conflicts have arisen over housing and sites, media coverage and wider hostility where anti-gypsy prejudice is often expressed with significantly less shame attached to expressing it than is attached to expressions of prejudice against other groups. Also the criminalisation of this group has been accompanied by many high profile case and conflicts including where they have been criminalised for being homeless (since those living on unauthorised encampments are very often legally homeless), criminalised for pursuing a nomadic way of life, and collective punishment for the crimes of specific individuals, whereby whole settlements are evicted because of the behaviour of certain of their members (TLRP 2007). Many Gypsy and Traveller families have been forced off the land they owned and found it increasingly difficult to find stopping places which has brought them into greater conflict with other people and local institutions. Reduction in local authority sites and growth in the GRT population means that now that over 30 per cent of this group live on unauthorised sites or having nowhere to stop they are sometimes forced to occupy public places, which overall has a huge detrimental impact on health, mortality, education and labour market position (TLRP 2008).

More broadly in the UK diverse and highly durable forms of racist hostility provide a constant source of tension and conflict including, anti-Gypsyism, Islamophobia, anti-Black racism and anti-Semitism. Despite significant developments in policy and procedures across many institutions there is a 'racial crisis' where increased understanding and evidence accompanies entrenched racism. Sources of inter-ethic and intercultural conflict in the UK are cultural, political and economic and include opposition to the recognition of difference and super-diversity, contested control of territory and land (particularly for GRT people) and disputes over access to social housing, schools and other resources. Newly articulated forms of hostility, hatred and grievance have been suffered by refuges, asylum seekers and other migrant groups to the UK. More widely everyday cultural ignorance, miscommunication and misrecognition of difference lead to offensive behaviour, affronts to dignity and lack of respect which have all lead to various forms of conflict (Hemmerman et al. 2007, Law 2008).

A continuing linkage between Blackness, violence, masculinity and dangerousness and the ensuing high profile misrepresentation of young Black men in the news media has been exacerbated by both government and media response to a series of shooting, stabbings and related violent incidents in the UK (Sveinsson 2008, Law 2002). National controversy over Black male youth has focussed on the problems of gangs and gang-related violent crime, under-performance in education and the labour market, school exclusions, over-representation in the criminal justice system, absentee fathers and low aspirations. In response, it has been argued that there are a large number of young Black men who have high conformist aspirations, strong aspirational capital (John 2008, Yosso 2005, Byfield 2008, Finney 2011) and who succeed, despite institutional racism in school environments including receiving harsher punishments, being over-represented in the lowest ranked teaching groups and being taught by less experienced staff, with lower expectations and entered for the lowest 'tiered' examinations (Rollock and Gillborn 2010). The need to rethink the construction of Black masculinities and multiple identities and move beyond the pathological, one-dimensional accounts of educational experiences is also urgently needed here

(Donnor and Brown 2011). National controversy over Muslim male youth has also been increasing. Muslim boys, often regarded as passive, hard working and law-abiding, have been recast in the public imagination in recent years with hostile images of volatile, aggressive hotheads who are in danger of being brainwashed into terrorism, or of would-be gangsters who are creating no-go areas in English towns and cities and preying on White girls (Shain 2011). Gypsies, Travellers and the Roma are still seen, portrayed and stereotyped as thieving scum, scroungers, gangsters and child traffickers (Leeming 2010). Media coverage of Gypsies and Travellers has historically been markedly hostile and, as noted above the most recently arrived Roma in the UK have been subject to highly visible media hostility and vilification (Craske 2000). This group probably receives the most unfavourable media coverage of any minority group, with headlines like 'Stamp on the Camps' being used by the Sun newspaper in calling for government and police action on Gypsy and Traveller sites (BBC News 11 March 2005).

Ethnic relations and education: policy and intervention

The present policy context is the result of an accretion of changing phases and themes, these have recently been mapped out by Gillborn (2008). Education has often been the most high profile policy field where changing national and local government priorities are signalled and implemented. From 1945 to the late 1950s racial discrimination legislation was seen as unnecessary despite strong popular racism. These issues and ethnic diversity were largely ignored in government policy. From the late 1950s to the late 1960s a cross-party political consensus emerged advocating strong racialised immigration controls and weak protection against discrimination to manage the perceived de-stabilising effects of minority migration. In education, assimilation was a key goal with a focus on dispersal and English language teaching. Cultural pluralism and integration came to dominate policy rhetoric into the 1970s with an emphasis on minorities changing and adapting to 'fit in'. Increasing community, ethnic and religious-based and antiracist protest led to the popularisation of multicultural and antiracist education across local education authorities through the 1980s, but schools had great freedom to ignore these developments should they wish, and many did. From 1986 onwards there was a weakening of these movements and a government drive to curb and push back these developments. The introduction of a National Curriculum which failed to acknowledge race and ethnic diversity is indicative of this position.

New Labour from 1997 onwards signalled a change of direction with a welcome explicit focus on the significance of these issues, but this more progressive stance lacked a fundamental understanding of racism and equity issues (Somerville 2007, Gillborn 2008). Following 9/11, government policy moved from 'naïve' to 'cynical' multiculturalism (in other words a move from promoting the values and organisations concerned with different minority cultures with little commitment to equality to a view that this was misguided and primarily led to increasing divisions between communities which then required action to promote social cohesion), and signalled a return to integrationist and assimilationist priorities with an increasing perception that multicultural policies had failed through encouraging greater ethnic division. In the wake of the urban disturbances of 2001 much policy discussion has focussed on the goal of community cohesion. To some extent this has replaced an earlier emphasis on social exclusion and inclusion, in part because some analyses of those events suggested that self-segregation of minority ethnic communities was a factor in undermining cohesion. Following the 7/7 attacks, the rights and perspectives of the White majority became increasingly asserted with calls for stronger intervention to improve integration, community cohesion, security and contemporary assimilation, summed up by Gillborn (2008) as 'aggressive majoritarianism'. In education this is exemplified by attacks on wearing the veil by Muslims in school in new guidance on school uniform codes which emphasised security, integration and cohesion which was quickly interpreted by the media as 'a school ban on veils'. Here, looking different is seen as a 'common sense' threat to national society and local community cohesion. This indicates a deteriorating policy climate and one in which it is increasingly difficult to prioritise fundamental race equality and ethnic diversity objectives and which shows greater concern for White racist sentiments. The attacks in the UK provided justification for increasingly punitive and disciplinary policies in a range of fields.

This overall stance has continued under the current Conservative/Liberal Democrat coalition government. The shift away from multiculturalism was firmly signalled by the current Prime Minister David Cameron in a speech in February 2011 which reverberated around the world where he made it abundantly clear that this approach had failed and that he rejected 'passive tolerance' advocating instead a 'more active muscular liberalism'. This move is also connected to a wider shift from the politics and law of identities to the politics and law of human rights symbolised in the harmonisation of equalities legislation in the UK. The wider climate of austerity and cuts in public expenditure together with these political agendas is leading to a dismantling of racial and ethnic priorities, policies and practices for example in the implementation of drastic cuts in the Traveller Education Service and to other educational services concerned with ethnic minority achievement in education.

Welfare, education and ethnicity initiatives

The closing of scores of Sure Start Children's Centres across the country driven by cuts of 22 per cent in 'early intervention' and childcare services in 2011 is reversing New Labour initiatives on improving opportunities for minority groups (DCLG 2007) which highlighted the creation of extended schools and Sure Start Children's Centres,[2] targeting disadvantaged areas and working to engage and provide high-

---

2   Children's centres are service hubs where children under five years old and their families can receive seamless integrated services and information. By 2010, every

quality, integrated services to children and families as important in reducing inequalities and offering high-quality support to people from all backgrounds, tailored to their individual needs. In the first phase (2004-2006), Sure Start Children's Centres were exclusively developed in the most disadvantaged areas in which minority ethnic communities were strongly represented (40 per cent) where parents can access up to 12.5 hours a week of free childcare for three and four year olds. The stronger regulatory framework for early education in the Childcare Act 2006 set in place important new general duties on local authorities to improve outcomes for all children and reduce inequalities between them. The Early Years Foundation Stage,[3] which was launched on 13 March 2007 and came into force in September 2008, sets out a comprehensive statutory framework for children's learning and development, focusing on the individual needs of children in early education and childcare settings, and is underpinned by an ethos of personalised learning and development for every child (DCLG 2007: 18). Providers of these services will be across all sectors, private, voluntary and public. The impact of closure of services in this field will have immediate detrimental consequences for minority ethnic families and their children.

Declining GCSE attainment for Gypsy/Roma and Traveller of Irish Heritage pupils is seen as being caused by family circumstances such as housing, income and health, as well as peer pressure, all impact on children and young people's performance in school, and the government aims to tackle these through a combination of mainstream and targeted programmes. Initiatives to improve minority ethnic achievement at school include the 'Aiming High' programme, the Ethnic Minority Achievement Grant (EMAG),[4] the Black Pupils' Achievement

---

community would have had a Sure Start Children's Centre, offering permanent universal provision across the country, ensuring that every child gets the best start in life. These services vary according to centre but may include: Integrated early education and childcare – all centres offering early years provision have a minimum half-time qualified teacher (increasing to full time within 18 months of the centre opening). Support for parents – including advice on parenting, local childcare options and access to specialist services for families. Child and family health services – ranging from health screening, health visitor services to breast-feeding support. Helping parents into work – with links to the local Jobcentre Plus and training.

3   The Early Years Foundation Stage (EYFS) brings together: Curriculum Guidance for the Foundation Stage (2000), the Birth to Three Matters (2002) framework and the National Standards for Under 8s Daycare and Childminding (2003), building a coherent and flexible approach to care and learning. All providers are required to use the EYFS to ensure that whatever setting parents choose, they can be confident that their child will receive a quality experience that supports their development and learning.

4   EMAG is provided by the DCSF to schools and local authorities for the support of minority ethnic pupils. EMAG-funded staff are frequently deployed to support the integration and achievement of new arrivals. Ofsted's report *The Education of Asylum-Seeker Pupils* recognised the vital role school staff funded by the EMAG played in supporting asylum-

Programme[5] and a cross-national programme to raise attainment among Gypsy/ Roma and Traveller pupils which was launched in September 2006, with 11 local authorities and 48 educational settings offered targeted support.

The New Labour government introduced a range of initiatives and projects many of which are currently under threat of closure:

- REACH, seeking to identify recommendations that would lead to real improvements in the attainment and aspirations of Black boys and young men. This is an independent group of practitioners who were tasked with identifying good practice by DCLG.
- ELAMP4, the e-learning and mobility project offer distance learning opportunities to children who travel during the school year, using laptops and data cards together with learning materials. This is DfES/DCSF project which provides funding to local authorities to employ outreach staff.
- Strategies to reduce the disproportionate exclusion of Black pupils, for example through mentoring and mediation schemes.
- Recruiting entrants to teacher training from minority ethnic backgrounds, currently 10 per cent.
- Online guidance for schools on tackling bullying related to racism, religion and culture ethnic groups, as well as specific groups such as Travellers, refugees and asylum seekers.
- Initiatives to improve support for parents.
- Skills coaching aimed at adults for whom a lack of skills is the main barrier to finding and keeping work, helping them to improve their employability, Leeds is one of the trial areas targeting minority ethnic groups.
- Improving funding for English for speakers of other languages.

Overall, the last Labour government's recognition that raising attainment and minority ethnic groups is a key component of national strategy is now seriously in question. Although initiatives and policy implementation were highly uneven, they are now likely to be substantially dismantled and racial and ethnic inequalities are likely to widen with particularly deteriorating outcomes for young people

---

seeking pupils and their families. Teaching was at its most effective where there was close collaboration, planning and support between class teachers and EMAG staff.

5   The aim of the programme is to work with Local Authorities (LAs) and schools to focus on raising the attainment of all Black pupils and by doing so raise overall attainment. The programme aims to:

- support schools to develop leadership (senior and middle managers') capacity to lead a whole school approach to raising achievement of Black pupils,
- develop knowledge and understanding of the specific issues facing Black pupils and equipping teachers with the skills to respond to them,
- develop LAs' capacity to support schools to raise Black achievement,
- work to mainstream issues around raising achievement within the national strategies.

from Gypsy, Roma and Traveller groups. The critical view that such inequalities are locked into the UK education system and that policy is not designed to eliminate this but to 'sustain it at manageable levels' Gillborn (2008) now appears inadequate and could be more usefully summed up as a policy environment where such inequalities will escalate at increasingly unmanageable levels.

The Traveller Law Reform Project (TLRP 2008) argued that the existing barriers of bullying and racism against Gypsies and Travellers that are common in schools and colleges contribute to their low attendance record. The endemic problem has been the reluctance of local authorities to respond to the needs of young people from these groups – for example the London Gypsy and Traveller Unit states that there has been no strategy on how to provide adequate, useful vocational training for the 14-16 year-olds whom the Government recognised were not benefiting from school. They argue that there is a need to oblige all local authorities to have a Traveller Education Service resourced commensurate with the population identified in Gypsy and Traveller Accommodation Assessments, without which many children would completely drop out of the system. The experience of TLRP member groups in London is that where no Traveller Education Service exists, very poor practice is common in schools, especially concerning bullying and discrimination (TLRP 2008).

In many local authority areas, despite conflict with residents and media hostility, efforts have been made on a variety of fronts to improve communication, social inclusion and provision of services to both settled and non-settled Gypsy and Traveller families. A recent evaluation of multi-agency partnership working to achieve these objectives in Scotland concluded with the view that many families had been helped towards the services they needed and a good number were able to describe how this had helped health and wellbeing. But, as yet these developments had not achieved a generalised impact across the Gypsy/Traveller Community as a whole (Macneil et al. 2005). Here, additional resourcing was seen as constituting positive discrimination and this was supported by many agencies given the clear failures of non-specific mainstream service delivery. So, the UK experience can provide a wide range of examples of innovative practice across different local authority areas as new ways are found to improve patterns of provision, but substantial inequalities remain and future prospects look grim. The new coalition government has already sparked protest (IRR 3 June 2010) from campaigners and academics over cuts and cancellations to progressive policies giving incentives for local authorities to develop Gypsy and Traveller sites in the Housing and Communities Agency (HCA) budget. The Conservative Planning 'Green' Paper in February 2010 also threatened to scrap Planning and Housing circulars which have started to give Gypsies and Travellers and Showmen a 'level playing field' in planning disputes with local authorities and planning inspectors. Also the Conservative Party, according to Eric Pickles, the communities and local government secretary, will revive elements of the 1994 Criminal Justice and Public Order Act that turns trespass from a civil into a criminal offence. This will mean that Travellers who refuse to move from land that is not privately owned by them could be arrested by police or forcibly evicted. Gypsy and Traveller Accommodation Needs Assessments has identified targets for sites for Gypsies and Travellers and yards for Showmen and progress was starting to be made. Matthew Brindley, spokesman for the Irish Traveller Movement was reported as saying that,

> Over a decade's campaigning work has been destroyed overnight by this coalition ... if the communities don't have stable accommodation, that impacts on the health and education of our children, and the health and employment of our adults. Accommodation is the overriding factor. It is a catalyst to all the other severe problems faced by this incredibly vulnerable community. (Hill 2010).

Ethnic inequalities, economic crisis and future prospects

Minority ethnic groups currently experience disadvantage in a variety of areas, including employment, education, housing, health, crime and political participation (Mawhinney 2010). These groups are at higher risk of poverty because of their concentration amongst those key 'at risk' groups including lone parent families, workless households and large families, but there are other factors at work here too. Other factors contributing to differences in poverty across ethnic groups include 'rates of employment, hours of work and pay, non-take-up of benefits and credits, numbers of adults in employment relative to dependants within the household, and lack of additional "buffers" such as savings, sources of credit or alternative incomes' (Platt 2009: 6). Two recent studies have also examined stark ethnic differences in poverty rates and there causes concluding that they are determined by a variety of factors including persistent discrimination, patterns of educational qualification, labour market outcomes, housing locations, disabilities and ill health (Palmer and Kenway 2007, Clark and Drinkwater 2007). The National Equality Panel report (NEP 2010a, 2010b) has summarised up to date evidence on some of these key factors in its analysis of contemporary economic inequality. In general terms, this report confirmed that:

> There remain deep-seated and systematic differences in economic outcomes between social groups across all of the dimensions we have examined – including between different ethnic groups. (2010a: 1).

Median total household wealth varies considerably by ethnicity, from only £15,000 for Bangladeshi households to around £75,000 for African-Caribbean, £97,000 for Pakistani households and £200,000 or more for Indian and White British households. Those from Bangladeshi and Pakistani households have a median equivalent net income of only £238 per week, compared to the national median of £393 (2010b: 233). In education although some ethnic minority groups do improve their test scores from below the national average as they move through compulsory schooling, but at 16, Pakistani, Black African and African-Caribbean boys attainment in England is still well below the national average. Children recorded as having Traveller or Gypsy backgrounds have a pattern of educational attainment that declines during the school years, resulting in much worse results than any other group with ethnic differentials steadily widening. This group, together with Black and Pakistani/Bangladeshi students are also less likely to go to more prestigious universities or to get higher class degrees (NEP 2010: 16). Despite Chinese, Indian and Black Africans having higher education qualifications than the White British population, nearly all ethnic minority groups are less likely to be in paid employment than White British men and women, and for some groups differences in unemployment rates are as great for the 'second generation', as for those who were born outside the UK. Pakistani and Bangladeshi Muslim men and Black African Christian men have an 'ethnic pay penalty', not explained by factors such as age, occupational classification, family circumstances and qualifications, earning 13-21 per cent less than White British Christian men (Longi and Platt 2008). Even one of the groups with the most successful educational outcomes, the Chinese, faced an 'ethnic pay penalty' of 11 per cent (NEP 2010b: 228). Evidence on current levels of racial discrimination in the labour market show that this persists at a consistently high level of 35 per cent in the private sector but this has dropped to 4 per cent in the public sector (Wood et al. 2009). Also the levels of discrimination were similar across all the ethnic groups studied, and applied equally to both men and women.

The relative vulnerability of ethnic minorities in a variety of market contexts means that the current economic recession and associated cuts in welfare are having and will have a greater negative impact on these groups. Almost half (48 per cent) of young Black people are unemployed compared to the rate of unemployment amongst White men (21 per cent) with mixed ethnic groups having the greatest overall increase rising from 21 per cent in March 2008 to 35 per cent in November 2009 (IPPR 2010). Lower employment means more poverty. Ethnic minority women experience higher rates of poverty then White women and a recent report has argued that the economic recession presents two major risks (moosa and Woodroffe 2009: 5). Firstly, that ethnic minority women will be locked into their destitution for the foreseeable future and, secondly, that anti-poverty approaches marginalise the needs of ethnic minority women through failing to recognise and address those needs, and that they are being pathologised and ignored. A focus on poverty at household level also fails to capture what is happening to individuals within intra-household relations and particularly women (moosa and Woodroffe 2009: 43).

The increased threat of financial exclusion facing ethnic minorities has also been recently highlighted in a series of reports by the Runnymede Trust (Kahn 2008, Mawhinney 2010). Some key findings from this work include the lower levels of savings, lower take-up of contents, health, buildings and life insurance, and poorer pensions amongst ethnic minorities, together with higher levels of debt and forms of direct and indirect racial discrimination in accessing credit both for ethnic minority small businesses and individuals. Even worse many people from these groups are also excluded from sources of advice including mainstream financial institutions and advice organisations. Many ethnic minority migrants do understand welfare benefits systems or tax and utilities systems, which can result in debt, in the form of unpaid taxes, utilities arrears and lack of take-up of benefits and tax credits (Mawhinney 2010: 5-6).

In the five years to 2003/04, both in-work and out-of-work child poverty fell for the only time in the last thirty years (Macinnes et al. 2009: 9). This fall did also include a reduction in racial and ethnic inequalities. Even before the economic crisis in 2008/09 child poverty was increasing with the overall picture steadily becoming worse in the last five years, and look sets to increase further. Current statements and policy indications from the new Conservative/Liberal Democrat government indicate that this will be the case. Immediately after the 2010 election a review of the national context of poverty and welfare was issued by the Government (Cabinet Office 2010). This confirms the worsening context with income inequality at its highest level since 1961, increases in severe poverty since 2004/05 and continuing differentials in terms of ethnicity.

Conclusion

This chapter has examined the development of ethnic diversity and ethnic relations in the UK. It has compared the situation and context of three selected ethnic minority groups whose educational experiences will be examined more closely in later chapters. It established that the African-Caribbean population tends to be economically disadvantaged and socially assimilated, in terms of cohabitation and marriage patterns, and with some significant degree of political incorporation. However five times more Black people than White people are imprisoned in England and Wales and there is now greater disproportionality in the number of Black people in prisons in Britain than in the USA (EHRC 2010) which indicates an enduring crisis in the relationship between the criminal justice system and Black communities. The Pakistani population tends to be in a position of greater economic marginality and poverty, with more social distinctiveness, due partly to social closure, and less political incorporation. Whereas the Gypsy and Traveller population appears to be in the most vulnerable position of economic, political and social marginality of any these groups, although data for this group is much more limited. A deteriorating policy climate has been identified where it is increasingly difficult to prioritise fundamental race equality and ethnic diversity objectives and one which shows greater concern for White working class sentiments of exclusion and resentment. This accompanies deteriorating prospects for Gypsy and Traveller communities and a wider context of increasing patterns of long-term poverty for ethnic minority groups (Tomlinson and Walker 2009). The Government's rejection of multiculturalism accompanies the rejection of the significance of racial and ethnic inequalities for policy making and provision and a new acceptance of the inevitability of worsening educational outcomes for ethnic minority groups.

Chapter 3

Education and Ethnicity in England

Introduction

This chapter will present an overview of ethnicity and the educational system in England which will be of particular value to readers from outside the UK. It will discuss key issues including the various types of school and their structural organisation, and some basic statistical data on schools, such as numbers of pupils in attendance at different institutions and how many remain in education after the compulsory schooling period is over. This chapter will also present an overview of how ethnicity plays a role in education in the context of New Labour policies, 1997-2010. It will discuss key issues grouped in four broad categories: the numbers of minority ethnic pupils in schools; law and regulations on schooling of minority ethnic youth; inter-ethnic relations in education; and ethnicity in public education. In addition it will present an account of the structures and mechanisms that maintain or reinforce inequalities in education. It will discuss major dimensions of social differences in education and will situate the role of ethnicity among them. It will also discuss differences in school performance according to membership of minority ethnic groups. How education of minority ethnic youth is framed in public discourse, how contested issues are put on the agenda of policy-making, and what kinds of policies are applied to respond to the claims will also be examined. Particular emphasis will be put on initiatives, policies and measures to combat 'minoritisation' in schools. Then a summary of the most significant research findings concerning the role of ethnicity in education with regard to the schooling, particularly of African-Caribbean, Pakistani and Gypsy and Traveller children will be presented, together with analysis of research on recent educational policies and initiatives designed to improve the educational achievement of the ethnic minority groups. Lastly, following on from the discussion in the last chapter, further consideration will be given to the changing educational policy environment and the climate of austerity and public expenditure cutbacks and their significance for ethnic minority groups since the election of the Conservative/Liberal Democrat coalition government in May 2010.

Types of school and their structural organisation

At a national level, the education system in England is governed by the Department of Education (DoE), which is responsible for policy on education, children and youth issues up to the age of 19 in England. There are two types of schools in

England: publicly-funded schools known as maintained schools; and public schools which are non-grant-aided and are often know as independent schools. At a local level, the responsibility for organising publicly-funded schools lies with local authorities (LAs), which have an obligation to provide quality assurance and to promote high standards of education. All LAs should have developed an Education Development Plan to provide information and guidance on key goals. Education Development Plans are produced in accordance with guidance from the Secretary of State for Education and Skills, and submitted to the Secretary of State for approval. In terms of the schools they govern, LAs vary in size, ranging from approximately 50 to 500 schools. LAs provide funding for schools according to numbers of student and staff. Those schools which are in danger of falling below the target floor levels for academic achievement are offered Targeted Improvement Grants, and schools in areas of high deprivation are provided with extra funding. This funding does not take into account differences in the financial circumstances of LAs.

LAs allow schools to take responsibility for their own management. Nevertheless, LAs retain a number of core functions which cannot be delivered by schools: support for special educational needs, school transport, school improvement and tackling failure, educating excluded pupils, pupil welfare and strategic management. Strategic management refers to the capacity to develop policy, allocate resources and draw up plans for delivery of education. At an institutional level, all schools have a governing body which includes representatives from a range of stakeholders – for example, lobby/interest groups; public and voluntary sectors bodies; commercial suppliers – and which is responsible for decision-making related to each institution. Within the context of LAs and their remits, all schools maintain a high level of autonomy. The legal framework for primary and secondary schools divides them into community, voluntary and foundation schools. The great majority of schools are community schools, established and funded by LAs. Foundation schools are owned by school governing bodies or charitable foundations, though are also funded by LAs. Voluntary schools were originally funded by voluntary bodies (e.g., churches), which retain some control over their management; however, voluntary schools are now generally funded by LAs.

Independent schools are secondary schools that are funded by private sources, predominantly fees generally paid by the parents of their pupils. Some independent schools, particularly the more traditional institutions, also have charitable status. The Independent Schools Council (ISC) represents 1,289 schools which collectively educate over 80 per cent of the pupils in the UK independent sector. Schools in England that are members of the ISC are inspected by the Independent Schools Inspectorate under a framework agreed between ISC, the DCSF and Ofsted. Independent schools are free to select their pupils, and the few parents who cannot afford the annual fees are offered means-tested bursaries. Independent schools have a better teacher to pupil ratio than mainstream schools (1 to 9 on average) and academic achievement is significantly higher. Quite a number of independent schools have boarding arrangements. Pupils can move between independent and mainstream schools, or indeed between any type of school, but entry would be dependent on normal practice in the relevant school's admissions policy. There has been a general increasing level of appeals and disputes over school admissions, with some highly controversial evidence of mainstream and faith schools charging parents for admissions, and of city academies using elitist selection methods. This has led to new government codes of practice and procedures for appeals being issued by the Department for Children, School and Families (DCSF) in 2007/08, with additional regulations being introduced for both faith schools and academies. Parental/school conflict and political controversy over school admissions has been increasing and appears likely to increase further with rising pressure from parents for the school of their choice.

Faith schools are schools which are partly funded by the state and which draw the remainder of their finances from either religious organisations or fees paid by parents of pupils, though some faith schools are now wholly maintained by the state. Additionally, there exist a number of city academies which are all-ability, state-funded independent schools established and managed by sponsors from a wide range of backgrounds, including high performing schools and colleges, universities, individual philanthropists, businesses, the voluntary sector, and the faith communities. City academies cater for all age groups; they follow the National Curriculum programmes of study in the core subjects of English, maths, science and ICT, and carry out Key Stage assessments and offer qualifications within the national framework. Academies are backed by LAs and are assessed by Ofsted (Office for Standards in Education, Children's Services and Skills). Academies were developed to tackle inner-city poverty, and retain a degree of flexibility to modify their curriculum to meet the needs of underperforming pupils as well as other pupils with specific needs. Academies are located in areas of social disadvantage and admit higher numbers of pupils with special educational needs and those eligible for free school meals than mainstream schools. However, since places in academies are oversubscribed, some sponsors have targeted the best pupils in their regions.

There are also special needs schools which cater for pupils with a variety of difficulties that may impact upon their educational performance in mainstream schools. These schools have staff trained to deal with the needs of such pupils and can provide education up to the age of 19 years old. Ratios of pupils in relation to staff at special schools tend to be kept as low 6 to 1. These schools also have specialised equipment suited to the needs of their pupils.

Quality control in schools is the responsibility of a separate, non-ministerial government department called the Office for Standards in Education, Children's Services and Skills (Ofsted). Following the Education and Inspections Act 2006, and since 2007, Ofsted's remit has included all state-funded learning outside of higher education, as well as independent schools. Ofsted assigns a category to a school after inspection: poorly performing schools are described as 'special measures' or 'notice to improve'; these categories contribute to the school's reputation (Leech and Campos 2003). Schools labelled 'special measures' receive support from LAs, additional funding, and reappraisal from Ofsted until the school is no longer deemed to be failing. Additionally, senior managers and teaching staff can be dismissed and the school governors may be replaced by an executive committee. Schools which are failing but where inspectors consider there is capacity to improve are given a Notice to Improve. All schools are inspected every three years.

There are approximately 24,600 schools in the UK, with just under 10 per cent being independent schools. Of the 21,000 state schools, about one third are faith schools of which the majority are Christian and with about 50 being non-Christian which comprise mainly Jewish schools with some Muslim, Sikh and (most recently) Hindu schools. Official statistics from the Department of Education (www.education.gov.uk) indicate that in 2010, there were 7.9 million children in 24,605 maintained and independent schools in England.

While existing data collection strategies enable the DoE to monitor the impact of specific schemes to improve pre 16 non-attendance, the lack of nationally available pupil-level attendance data has hampered any detailed understanding of the relative impact of such schemes on groups of pupils, or, indeed, of any comprehensive awareness of the relationship between attendance levels and pupil attainment. Data on 343 Excellence in Cities schools did show lower than average levels of authorised and unauthorised absence for Black, Chinese and South Asian pupils (Morris and Rutt 2004), whereas the opposite appears to be the case for Gypsy, Roma and Traveller pupils, although data here is very limited. Most recent data shows that across maintained secondary schools, city technology colleges and academies absence rates (authorised, unauthorised and overall) were highest for the Traveller of Irish Heritage (26 per cent overall absence); Gypsy, Roma (23 per cent overall absence); Mixed (White and African-Caribbean) (almost 10 per cent overall absence) and Irish (just over 9 per cent overall absence). The rate of overall absence for pupils of White and Mixed ethnic origin was above the national average; for pupils of Asian, Black and Chinese ethnic origin it was below the national average. The rate of overall absence for minority ethnic pupils was significantly below the rate for White British pupils. The overall absence rate for all pupils was around 8 per cent. Caution was recommended in interpreting the data used here for Traveller of Irish Heritage children and Gypsy, Roma children due to the small numbers recorded (DfES 2007). Parents, schools and LAs all have legal responsibilities to ensure children attend school. Policy and practice does vary across each LA area. In Leeds, an Attendance Strategy Team (AST) provides support to schools to manage and improve individual pupil and whole school attendance by working in partnership with parents/carers, pupils, schools and other agencies, and undertakes the statutory reporting to the DoE around attendance, and instigate legal proceedings against parents/carers for persistent non-attendance when appropriate. It also manages the process for the identification, tracking and re-engaging of Children Missing Education (CME). This Team works to remove barriers to regular attendance by using a wide range of interventions for example undertaking a Common Assessment, visiting the family, signposting to other support services, and liaising with home and school. Where there is a lack of improvement or engagement following the referral, the AST can consider a range of legal procedures against the parents/carers to secure regular attendance including Penalty Notices, Education Supervision Orders, fines, Parenting Orders, Community Rehabilitation Orders or a custodial sentence.

Drop-out rates of post-16 pupils has been notoriously high in the UK. There is a clear disparity between social groups, with pupils from lower socio-economic backgrounds more likely to leave school earlier. Financial measures such as the government's Education Maintenance Allowance allow pupils from low earning families to draw a small income as an incentive to stay on at school; students must apply for this allowance and are eligible if they are studying for specific courses and their parents have a low income. Research shows that staying-on rates improved by 5.9 per cent as a consequence of this scheme (www.education. gov.uk). Other schemes designed to improve staying-on rates are services that offer advice to pupils (for example, Connexions), learning mentors who address barriers to learning (bullying, trunacy, etc), Education Welfare Officers, and teaching assistants who work with individual pupils. Connexions is undergoing serious cutbacks and many related schemes are also subject to similar reductions and changes arising from expenditure cutbacks which indicate the likelihood of a future decline in staying-on rates.

Exclusion rates were in decline, being down to 7 per cent in 2008 from the previous year, with 8,900 pupils permanently excluded from school. Fixed rate exclusions, however, went up 4 per cent to 363,000, with the great majority being for five days or more. The most common reason for exclusion was persistent disruptive behaviour, while boys were more likely than girls to be excluded permanently and on a fixed rate basis (temporary suspensions from school attendance) by four and three times respectively. There are a number of alternative educational routes for permanently excluded pupils; these include reintegration in other schools and Pupil Referral Units which function as schools and are inspected by Ofsted.

Schooling of minority ethnic youth and New Labour policies, 1997-2010

This section will present an overview of how ethnicity plays a role in education. It will discuss key issues grouped in four broad categories: the numbers of minority ethnic pupils in schools; law and regulations on schooling of minority ethnic youth; inter-ethnic relations in education; and ethnicity in public education.

Attendance at school

In maintained primary schools the number of pupils (of compulsory school age) who were classified as minority ethnic origin increased from 20.6 per cent in 2006 to 25.5 per cent in 2010 – an increase of just under five percentage points. A similar increase was apparent in secondary schools with 16.8 per cent of pupils classified by minority ethnic groups in 2006 increasing to 21.4 per cent in 2010. These increases are largely born of demographic changes and increasing population sizes of minority ethnic groups in the UK. Data for numbers of minority ethnic groups in independent schools have never been provided, though analysis of student composition in higher education evidence suggests that Chinese and Indian groups are more likely to attend them (Tomlinson 2005)

This book examines the perceptions and experiences of school pupils and parents from Gypsy, Roma and Traveller, African-Caribbean, and Bangladeshi minority ethnic groups. In 2010, there were over 14,000 Gypsy, Roma and Traveller pupils, over 171,000 African-Caribbean pupils (including White and African-Caribbean pupils), and approximately 322,000 Pakistani and Bangaldeshi pupils in mainstream schools. Overall Caribbean, Pakistani, and Bangladeshi groups have lower average levels of attainment than Whites. Indians, African Asians, Chinese and Africans are more likely to have higher qualifications. These trends can be found in both lower and higher education (Modood 2005, Parekh 2000, Gallagher 2004). Gypsy, Roma and Traveller pupils experience the most severe educational exclusion of any minority ethnic group in the UK with levels of attainment being roughly a quarter of the national average.

Schooling of minority ethnic youth

These policies were current at the time fieldwork reported on in Chapters 4-7 was being carried out.

When New Labour came to power in 1997, the party pledged to commit to social justice and education as a means to create a just society. One of the first policies to attempt to pursue this goal was the 2000 Race Relations Amendment Act (RRAA – an extension of the original act implemented in 1976). This act requires LAs to eliminate discrimination and promote equal opportunities, as well as develop race equality policies in a proactive rather than a reactive way, as had previously been the case (Tomlinson 2005). Schools and teachers have responsibilities as part of the RRAA including having an agreed written statement of policy for promoting race equality and monitoring by reference to ethnic group, the admission and progress of pupils. Data from the annual Level School Census now enable schools and LAs to monitor achievement and to target support where it is most needed. Promoting race equality is a key part of the policies and practices of all schools and other educational institutions, not only those with Black and minority ethnic pupils. Ofsted must ensure that inspection teams look at the progress schools and local education authorities are making in terms of equality issues. The aim is to make such good practices fit effectively into the routine work of the school.

Among the strategies generated as a consequence of the RRAA was a Social Exclusion Unit, created partly to enquire into the high figures for the exclusion of Black pupils. Ofsted was also charged with a new framework for assessment that included issues relating to racial equality. The *Excellence in Cities* programme (2004) identifies action zones with the intention of combating urban disadvantage in these areas; the programme attempted to bring together local schools, communities and businesses, and offered support to gifted and disruptive children, who were given learning mentors (Tomlinson 2005). Another important intervention has been *Sure Start* for children under 4 and their parents in the most disadvantaged neighbourhoods in the UK, many of which are areas with high proportions of minority ethnic groups. Financial support for high quality provision of child care support and significant local control has been very beneficial in some areas, improving collective self-esteem and children's future chances at school. A department called the Ethnic Minority Achievement (EMA) Unit was also set up to provide money for LAs with a significant number of minority ethnic pupils. The previous New Labour government additionally provided an Ethnic Minority Achievement Grant of £155 million annually. The funding and encouragement of separate faith schools is also encouraged. The Ethnic Minority Achievement Grant (EMAG) is allocated on a needs-based formula. The formula is based on the numbers of pupils with a mother tongue other than English and numbers of pupils from nationally underachieving minority ethnic groups. Pupils who are both bilingual and from an underachieving group are only counted once. This number of pupils is then multiplied by the proportion of all pupils receiving free school meals (FSMs) in the authority to calculate what proportion of the national grant an LEA should receive. The EMA Unit provides support to LAs and schools in using funds effectively in this area and monitoring EMAG occurs primarily through financial management. The scheme itself has not caused national controversy unlike schools' concerns over coping with increasing numbers of foreign children, particularly from Eastern Europe, a situation described by the National Association of Headteachers as 'out of control'. EMAG is seen by the government as one useful source of funding to help schools cope with increasing numbers of migrants.

Despite these attempts to tackle problems involved in the education of minority ethnic groups, however, commentators have highlighted a number of difficulties relating to other issues which have impacted upon schooling, especially the marketisation of education. This process means the shift towards more devolved systems of provision with increased emphasis on parental choice and competition between increasingly diversified types of school sometimes run by a variety of different providers from public, voluntary and private sectors. Here, marketisation means the development of 'quasi-markets'. This involves the separation of purchaser from provider and an element of user choice between providers, and with the government regulating entry by new providers, investment, the quality of service and price (Whitty 2000).

According to Gallagher (2004), educational policies with commitment to social justice were largely driven by economic policies, and since education has become increasingly marketised (that is, the process of school allocation is now competitive, involving schools engaged in marketing strategies to attract pupils), parents are forced to compete with one another for school places, a process which does not ensure integration, justice and equity (Parekh 2000, Tomlinson 2005). Market policies in education continued to exacerbate the hierarchy of more and less desirable schools (Ball 2009), with the most desirable the least likely to be attended by minority ethnic groups. League tables have been made available to enable parents to compare the performance levels of different schools. This system where failing schools are placed on special measures has introduced a 'naming and shaming' policy for schools who may often have a large proportion of minority ethnic groups, which leads to further scapegoating and stigmatisation (Parekh 2000). Additionally, the failure to develop a curriculum which would educate people for a multicultural society does not mitigate ignorance and xenophobia (Tomlinson 2005).

Another problem relates to the choice mechanisms that were inaugurated by New Labour and which have been shown to disadvantage minority ethnic groups and to increase segregation (Gallagher 2004). Choice mechanisms involve parents possessing the right to select the school at which they wish their children to study (see Chapter 1). Evidence suggests that school diversity has led to a White 'flight' from schools with large numbers of minority ethnic pupils (Tomlinson 2005). Similarly, attempts to improve standards in school were at their height during their term of office, and this involves practices of selection which places minority ethnic students in lower ranking groups (Gillborn 2006). Explicit positive discrimination policies on grounds of ethnicity do not formally operate in UK schools. However, policies aimed at improving ethnic minority inclusion and achievement as discussed above do operate and these do constitute positive discrimination in a broad sense.

Inter-ethnic relations in schools

The Race Relations Act of 1976 made it unlawful to discriminate against someone on racial grounds, and asserted that segregation of a person is to be regarded as treating him or her less favourably. Segregation according to ethnicity in schools is of interest for several reasons. If children's performance at schools depends on peers, then higher levels of segregation will result in greater educational inequality in academic achievement and may even threaten social cohesion. Much research has shown that segregation in schools increased in England between 1994 and 2004 (Allen and Vignoles 2007, Goldstein and Noden 2003). Over the five year period of 1999 to 2004, there has been rising social segregation between schools in 60 per cent of LEAs and falling segregation in 40 per cent, school segregation has risen fastest in London. Other research has suggested that apart from in certain parts of Northern England and for certain minority ethnic groups, ethnic segregation is not increasing and has even decreased in some places. Interwoven social and ethnic segregation is evident in LAs which have a large South Asian or Black population such as London (Weekes-Bernard 2007).[1]

More recently, however, some commentators have voiced concern that New Labour's focus on parental choice with regard to their children's place of education has led to social and ethnic segregation. As Tomlinson (2008) suggests, choice policies can result in young people from different ethnic backgrounds being kept apart. Nevertheless, the role of parental choice is not regarded as the only or even a major reason for what segregation does exist, since many parents actually support moves towards more social cohesion (Weekes-Bernard 2007). Jenkins, et al. (2006) drew on data from 2003 and demonstrate that in England, segregation in schools is driven by the uneven spread of children from different social backgrounds. To this can be added the roles of increasing divisions of income and wealth, housing policies, patterns of immigration, levels of poverty and experiences of racism (Weekes-Bernard 2007). This can be seen as a major problem in terms of education, since evidence suggests that under New Labour the division of wealth was larger than it has ever been, with the potential for social mobility significantly reduced.

The level of ethnic segregation in England's schools is high. There is significant variation across LEAs and across ethnic groups, with segregation higher for pupils of Indian, Pakistani or Bangladeshi origin which coincides with the locations of urban unrest in the summer of 2001. School segregation does not simply follow income or housing segregation but arises from a complex interplay of factors in differing local contexts including geographical location, social class, the history of particular schools, the impact the quasi-markets and the emphasis on parental choice (Burgess and Wilson 2004).

Organisational structures and practices in schools create patterns of social relations which can be viewed as contributing to ethnic divisions. Tracking tends to lead to ethnic pupils being placed in lower sets which have a reputation for behavioural problems. Additionally, it can be argued that there is a White bias in terms of the curriculum with exam questions often reflecting a White cultural perspective (Singh 1987). Some schools have recognised the multi cultural nature of its catchment and responded to it. For example, the variety of languages spoken in school resulted in the creation of the Ethnic Minority Achievement Forum (EMA). Some schools give pupils the possibility to translate their knowledge of another language into taking GCSE qualifications and therefore offer the choice to learn community languages such as Urdu too (Edwards 2001). There are English as an Additional Language (EAL) Reading Programmes. School may forge close links with study support and mentoring groups which aspired to combat poor achievement. For example, in Sheffield this would include Somali Education

---

1 Some of the confusion regarding the degree of segregation that exists may be linked to different ways of categorising pupils; some studies use free school meals as an indicator of poverty, and others use socio-economic information from such sources as the National Census 2001; no single method is wholly accurate.

Breakthrough, Reach High Two run by the Kashmiri Education Trust, Roshni, and a Yemeni-led group. This is a positive step since evaluation of the impact of participation in after school study support on the academic attainment, attitudes and attendance of secondary school pupils has been shown to be effective with children speaking of feeling more comfortable and secure in their own community groups (Macbeath 2001).

While served with the best intentions, the cumulative effect of these activities highlight the fact that race is 'a signifier of relational identity politics' (Luke and Carrington 2000: 5) which does shape school experiences. While such activities could be seen to thwart the ethnocentrism of the school curriculum through circumventing bounded 'islands' of racial and cultural distinctiveness, the boundedness of the school's organisation of cultural diversity contradicts the open natured of multi-culturalism. Although these activities carried a firm conviction of racial identities, they work by differentiating pupils in terms of racial identities, a mechanism that always has the consequence of creating 'outsiders'. The critical point becomes the racial/cultural boundary that defines the group, not the cultural nexus that it encloses (Barth 1969). While acknowledgement that different cultures have different values and different ways of life is important, there is a danger that we carry on the tradition of exoticising them. McLeod and Yates (2000) would view some schools' practices as the omnipresence of Whites being positioned at the centre, 'around which a carnival like array of multicultural difference is displayed for their enjoyment and sampling'. Cultural issues stemming from racial identities may impinge on school practices. For example, arrangements like prayer rooms may be made for Muslim pupils during Ramadan. Pupils who are fasting during this period may be feeling drowsy or headaches due to dehydration, so schools may plan less strenuous activities during PE. Alternatively pupils could have short levels of concentration which would mean avoiding setting exams in this period. Lupton's (2004) research unpicks some of these issues in detail. She notes tensions in value systems between home and school, 'parental restrictions and enforcing these with punishment were viewed by staff as uncomfortably authoritarian accustomed to a more liberal culture.' The Race Relations (Amendment) Act 2000 imposes upon schools, education institutions and LAs a duty to promote good relations between pupils of different racial groups. Bullying and harassment in schools is well-documented, and these problems are frequently exacerbated when pupils belong to different minority ethnic groups (for example, the experience of Gypsy, Roma and Traveller groups – Children's Society 2007). A new scheme announced by the government in 2007 was the *Safe to Learn: Embedding Anti-bullying Work in Schools*, which sought to provide guidance to schools for tackling bullying.

However, in multi-racial schools many teachers are still unprepared to deal with the antagonisms they encounter among pupils of different groups, with White teachers particularly finding it difficult to get involved in issues of race (Pearce 2005). Mac an Ghaill's (1993) ethnographic study looked at the interaction of White teachers and two groups of anti-school male students – the Asian Warriors and the Afro-Caribbean Rasta Heads – at an inner city secondary school in an English city. He found that teachers tended to stereotype on the basis of pupils' ethnic group,

> There was a tendency for Asian students to be seen by teachers as technically of high ability and socially as conformist. In contrast Afro-Caribbean students tended to be seen as of low ability and potential discipline problems. (Mac an Ghaill 1993: 152).

This suggests an educational self-fulfilling prophesy whereby a mutually accepted stratification system arises from the social interactions between pupil and teacher which impacts on expectations of performance. Mac an Ghaill (1993) found that the Rasta Heads perceived the school language as a major instrument of their own deculturisation and in response, they asserted themselves by speaking Creole within the classroom, using language as a 'mechanism of White exclusion'. This is an important and visible symbol of defiance of what pupils perceive to be the dominant White culture of the school. Focusing on how the Rasta Heads' perceived school, Mac an Ghaill came to see their disaffection as a legitimate mechanism opposed to the school's institutional racist practices.

Awareness of racial difference has become perhaps more profound throughout the world following 9-11. This has filtered into school as Lemos' (2005) research shows how Muslim, Asian, Afghan and Iraquic pupils were considered to be potential terrorists by their classmates. Nevertheless, some minority ethnic groups have developed their own strategies to promote inter-ethnic relations. A project based in Slough involved Sikh, Hindu and Muslim communities and trained teenagers to deal with conflict; later the project was expanded to the Polish community in the town (Salman 2006).

One issue in which segregation has become a central concern was New Labour's focus on encouraging the role of Faith Schools in education. Faith schools seek to provide an alternative to the state education system by the creation of communities which provide instruction in one religious faith. Of the 20,704 schools in England in 2007, the majority were of no religious character (13,861 schools). However, there were over half as many Christian faith schools, including 6,642 Church of England schools, 2,038 Roman Catholic schools, 26 Methodist schools, and a further 88 other Christian faith schools. Non-Christian faith schools are represented by 37 Jewish schools, 7 Muslim schools, and 2 Sikhs schools. There are also approximately 700 madrassas in Britain unregulated by the state, and attended by approximately 100,000 Muslim children. Madrassas are after-school clubs run by mosques, to teach children about the Koran and how to speak Arabic. Although they are obliged to follow the laws set down by the Children Act 1989, no single body such as Ofsted monitors their performance and they are accountable to no one. Some madrassas educate up to 500 children. The Muslim Parliament of Great Britain has voiced concern over the risk of physical and sex abuse in these schools and has called for national registration.

The great majority of Faith Schools are partly funded by the state and draw the remainder of their finances from either religious organisations or fees paid by parents of pupils, though some faith schools are now wholly maintained by the state. Most of the Christian Faith Schools are primary schools, though of the 37 Jewish schools, 28 are primary and 9 are secondary schools; of the 7 Muslim schools, 4 are primary and 3 secondary schools; and the 2 Sikh schools includes both a primary and a secondary school. Faith Schools follow the same national curriculum as state schools.

The issue of Faith Schools has led to some controversy. New Labour granted maintained status to a number of minority ethnic Faith Schools (on the basis that since Christian faith schools exist, it would be hypocritical to do otherwise) and claimed that schools with a strong individual identity were a sound basis for improvement in standards. Others have claimed that schools which treat all pupils exactly the same, regardless of religious faith, may lead to serious misunderstanding and anger on behalf of Muslim pupils and their parents. However, other commentators – for example, Sir Herman Ouseley, Former Head of the Commission for Racial Equality – argue that Faith Schools can lead to the separation of communities, and significantly some Muslim leaders have criticised faith schools for the same reason. Recent attempts to forge legislation which makes it legal for Faith Schools to provide a multicultural agenda in their curriculum has failed to be implemented, and there is no guarantee that Faith Schools will teach universal human rights vales as distinct from particular group values (Tomlinson 2008).

Ethnicity in public education

A number of policies that were implemented by the previous New Labour government to improve the education of all young people included the DCSF's *Aiming High* scheme, a national strategy for young people and their development; the DCSF's *14-19 Programme*, a scheme that offers young people more opportunities in their educational pathway; and monitoring guidelines for schools to assess the profile of their pupil population in terms of educational standards, needs and targets; and improved processes of monitoring teachers through school self-review processes. A school census is also completed three times a year for all pupils and covers issues such as personal characteristics, achievement records, attendance, exclusions, and special needs. There was additionally a focus on citizenship, conducted via compulsory modules.

Major educational changes for 14- to 19-year-olds were introduced from September 2008 which were aimed at raising the education and skills levels of students by delivering a curriculum which gave them life and social skills, set stretching and challenging targets, and better prepared them for a fast-changing world. Curriculum changes have prioritised improving core skills; English, Maths and ICT. Three main qualification routes have been established although there is some flexibility. At age 14 pupils can choose the Diploma, GCSEs or a young apprenticeship. At age 16, in school or college, they can take the Diploma, A Levels or an apprenticeship. A further option at 16 is to be in work, with time set aside for training. At age 18, young people should have the qualifications to carry on in education or training, or to go into skilled work. Differential steering of these groups into these different pathways is likley to have significant effects on both patterns of educational achievement, future incomes and labour market position. It is likely also that a sustained focus on those young people who are not in education, employment or training (NEET) is resulting in reductions in their numbers in the majority of local authorities, and this may be of particular significance for Gypsy, Roma and Traveller young people.

LAs and schools under their remit have responded to this legislation in a variety of ways, a selection of which is detailed below. The Aiming High scheme has a component dedicated directly to the schooling of minority ethnic groups which advocates strong leadership, high expectations, effective teaching and learning, and parental involvement in education. There has also been a drive towards recruiting teachers from minority ethnic backgrounds, as well as programmes designed to assist White teachers to effectively teach minority ethnic pupils, particularly with regard to difficulties born of different languages.

Within this policy context, several LAs have developed their own systems for teaching minority ethnic groups within their schools. One London LA uses a group-based mentoring programme aimed at reducing the exclusion of African-Caribbean students. Group-work was aimed at encouraging young people to direct their attention towards what they could get out of school (Warren 2005). This was also directed at developing a different approach to being Black through a critical exploration of Black history. Warren (2005) argues that this provided the minority ethnic youth with a language to construct a cultural politics of race which takes them beyond individual resistance. Some schools in their attempt to overcome prejudice and discrimination take time to talk to both students and parents and are prepared to consider and debate values and strategies to overcome inequity (Gilbert 2004).

With Asylum Seekers, one school devised its own Welcome Packs aimed at helping new families to settle by using pictures of local amenities and school activities, accompanied by key words in English (Whiteman 2005). Bilingual teachers or teaching assistants to help with language barrier have been employed in Birmingham and Bradford; aspects of the curriculum are taught by bilingual teachers who give a priority to the origin of some ethnic minorities (Gokulsing 2006). Asylum seeker pupils are sometimes paired off with another child of the same language. Pupils are encouraged to learn and use their first language as well as English. Other schools also use anti-bullying workshops as a way of communicating about issues surrounding race and ethnicity (Whiteman 2005), and others make use of the recourses provided by the *Ethnic Minority and Traveller Achievement Service*, which provides support for both schools and pupils in the form of guidance and funding (ibid.). Some schools used a 'Red Card to Racism' scheme as a way of promoting tolerance (ibid.).

Nevertheless, in terms of broad critiques of the system, many commentators point to several unaddressed problems in LA and school strategies to combat racism. More concerted efforts towards conducting ethnicity monitoring in schools are also needed (Parekh 2000). There is a severe lack of minority ethnic teachers (Tomlinson 2005, Wilkins 2001), while a change in institutional ethos is required with a teacher education curriculum based on a critically transformative notion of education (Wilkins 2001): teachers need to see themselves as agents of social change (ibid.). Citizenship needs to be tackled as a contested notion that confronts issues of social inequality head on, and there needs to be a structured educational framework which discusses racism and other forms of oppression, rather than passing reference made in the curriculum (Singh 2001). Cultural diversity should be valued and reflected in the curriculum (Gokulsing 2006) and Gundara (2000) proposes a 'curriculum of recognition'.

Inequalities in the educational system

This section will present an overview of the structures and mechanisms that maintain or reinforce inequalities in education. It will discuss major dimensions of social differences in education and will situate the role of ethnicity among them. It will also discuss differences in school performance according to membership of minority ethnic groups.

Differences in school careers

Research conducted on the school careers of pupils of different backgrounds has focused predominantly on three broad issues: gender, socio-economic factors/ social class, and ethnicity.

It is a well-documented (if rather oversimplified) observation that girls outperform boys in schools. For instance, At GCSE, girls continue to progress more than boys. The difference between boys and girls attainment (5+ A*-C) in GCSE English is as much as 14 percentage points. It has been suggested that the reasons for this difference in educational achievement include an 'anti-achievement culture' among some boys, male peers disrupting schoolwork, the low expectations of boys, teaching styles that prioritise girls, a loss of motivation in boys engendered by a decline of traditional masculine jobs, and the way that pupils are grouped in lessons. Research on the effects of social class predictably reveal that those who come from disadvantaged backgrounds are more likely to have a lower level of academic ability when starting primary school and make less progress than the national average while there (with particularly poor numeracy and literacy skills); this pattern is likely to be repeated in secondary school, with the result than they are generally ill-prepared for adult employment (see below for examples of performance indicators reflecting differences of social class). This failure to achieve what their socially advantaged peers manage has been ascribed variously to low expectations, poor parenting, involvement in crime, poor provision in schools for children with special educational needs, and poor school attendance records.

This problem is compounded when such socially disadvantaged pupils also belong to ethnic groups with similarly poor educational achievement records, particularly those who are not fluent speakers of English and have problems with engaging in everyday school life. Indeed, members of the poorest ethnic groups – such as African-Caribbean, Pakistani and Bangladeshi pupils – unsurprisingly have low educational achievement records (see below).

The interplay of these three broad pupil characteristics in terms of how they impact upon school careers is complex. Recent research conducted by the Equal Opportunities Commission (EOC) suggests that social class is the biggest factor affecting attainment in education. It is argued that understanding its relationship with gender and ethnicity is central to reducing the gap between success and failure in schools. As mentioned above, girls on the whole perform better than boys in education. However, research factoring in social class and ethnicity reveals a more nuanced picture. For example, the analysis of England's 2006 Key Stage 2 results (for 11 year olds) reveals that while girls are significantly outperforming boys in English, disadvantaged girls trail behind their wealthier male peers. While ethnicity and gender remain major factors in the achievement gap, social class appears to be the biggest factor determining success, a conclusion endorsed by Gillborn and Mirza (2000) who show that social class is the largest determinant of variations in educational achievement, followed by ethnicity and then by gender. Drawing on analyses of the percentage of children who achieve Level 4 or above in English (this is the national attainment level at ages 14-16, which is Key Stage 4 and this encompasses Levels 4-8), the EOC research reveals that:

- Social class is twice as important as gender in English, with an achievement gap of 22 percentage points in children receiving free school meals compared to those not doing so. Boys' achievement levels are particularly affected by social disadvantage: those who receive free school meals trail 24 percentage points behind their wealthier male peers.
- Girls outperform boys across the board in English by 10 percentage points. In mathematics and science, however, there is no gender gap, with boys and girls performing similarly.
- Taking into account social class and ethnic background (among broad ethnic groups), White boys receiving free school meals had the lowest level of performance compared to boys from other ethnic groups. Similarly, White girls receiving free school meals had a worse level of performance than girls from other ethnic groups. Researchers ascribe this to a correlation between eligibility for free school meals and socio-economic deprivation.
- Social class can reverse the gender gap, however: girls receiving free school meals are falling behind boys of the same ethnicity who do not receive them.

- Overall, the group with the lowest percentage in achievement of Level 4 English were White boys receiving free school meals. Researchers ascribe this to socio-economic deprivation and 'anti-achievement' culture among White boys.
- There is also a large difference in performance across Black and minority ethnic groups, with a 16 percentage points' gap between the highest and lowest achieving ethnic groups in English results.

In order to tackle these complex gaps in gender, socio-economic status and ethnicity, the EOC report recommends a school-wide approach to achievement involving strong leadership from the head teacher, high expectations for all pupils, and effective partnerships with parents and in the community (Skelton, Francis and Valkanova 2007). To some degree, moves towards this end have already begun. When analysing all three dimensions simultaneously, Gillborn and Mirza (2000) show that between the years of 1988 and 1995, all groups improved exponentially in terms of achievement at GCSE level, and that this largely due to improvements in strategies of providing education. However, some groups continue to struggle, and White boys from a low socio-economic background are currently a major concern for policymakers. In the case of minority ethnic groups, further analysis of the role of social class and gender is complicated by differences between groups, and we shall turn to this issue now.

Differences in pupil performance of minority ethnic groups

Pupil performance in schools is assessed in several ways: by academic progress made between the four Key Stages, by class banding in terms of ability, by achievement at GCSEs and A-level, as well as by attendance and exclusion rates. Another indicator of achievement is entry to higher or further education. Recent research on the performance of minority ethnic groups has revealed a complex picture in terms of educational achievement. These are summarised below:

- African-Caribbean, Pakistani, and Bangladeshi groups have lower average levels of attainment than Whites. Indians, African Asians, Chinese and Africans are more likely to have higher qualifications. These trends can be found in both lower and higher education (Modood 2005, Parekh 2000, Gallagher 2004).
- Some ethnic groups such as Pakistanis and Bangladeshis are very internally polarised, with both highly qualified and unqualified individuals. In 40 per cent of LAs, Pakistanis are more likely than White people to attain 5 grade A-C GCSEs (Modood 2005). Bangladeshi pupils made considerable advances in the 1990s and in some areas outperform White pupils (DfES 2006).
- Research with African-Caribbean pupils tends to show that the relative performance of high starts to decline in Key Stage 2, tails off badly in Key Stage 3 and is below that of most other ethnic groups at Key Stage 4.

While African-Caribbean children begin school as the same standard as the national average, by the age of 16, the number of students who have five GCSE passes is less than half the national average (DfES 2006).

- African-Caribbean women were much more likely than their male counterparts to have higher qualifications (Modood 2005).
- In second and third generations, most ethnic groups have made significant academic progress, as have their White peers. The exception is young African-Caribbean males who do no better than their elders (Modood 2005).
- All ethnic groups, with the possible exception of African-Caribbeans, have increased their share of higher education admissions since 1990 (Modood 2005).
- All minorities, with the exception of African-Caribbean males, are escalating in terms of their representation in further education and some groups now exceed the government's target of 50 per cent participation (Modood 2005).
- Around 70 per cent of African-Caribbean and 60 per cent of Pakistani and Bangladeshi students pursue their degrees in new universities which were formerly polytechnics. Only 35 per cent of White pupils do so (Modood 2005).
- African-Caribbean pupils are considerably more likely to face disciplinary action and exclusion from school; there has also been a recent increase in exclusions of Bangladeshi, Pakistani, and Somali pupils (DfES 2006).
- Permanent exclusion rates are higher than average for Travellers of Irish Heritage, Gypsy, Roma, African-Caribbean, Black Other and White/African-Caribbean pupils (DfES 2006). African-Caribbean pupils are more likely to be excluded for physical assault than for persistent disruptive behaviour (DfES 2006).
- African-Caribbean pupils are one and a half times more likely than White pupils to be identified as having behavioural, emotional and social needs (DfES 2006).
- Gypsy, Roma and Traveller pupils experience the most severe educational exclusion of any minority ethnic group in the UK with levels of attainment being roughly a quarter of the national average: 13-15 per cent of Gypsy, Roma and Traveller pupils obtaining five A*-C GCSE passes compared to a 60 per cent national average. In addition, patterns of attainment at this level are declining, which is markedly different from other minority ethnic groups where there is evidence of some improvement (Children's Society 2007).
- Asylum seekers are making new demands on LAs and schools. Asylum-seeking children suffer significant racial harassment born of a 'rabid discourse' which construes them as proto-terrorists and 'benefits-scroungers' (Gillborn 2006). Refugee children suffer three times the national average for psychological disturbance (Whiteman 2005), and LAs do not provide

sufficient information for schools with regard to these children (ibid.).

New Labour highlighted the improvements that had been made and ascribed these to the success of policies designed to promote the educational needs of minority ethnic groups (Department for Communities and Local Government 2006). However, as we can see above, certain minority groups are still failing in school, despite existing schemes intended to help them. Indeed, research conducted on the reasons why other minority ethnic groups are succeeding points towards other factors than school initiatives.

Explanations for these trends have tended to focus on African-Caribbean males. It has been shown that African-Caribbean males have the most confrontational relations with teachers, and that teachers feel threatened by them. This leads to low expectations, as well as teachers interpreting certain behaviour more negatively than in the case of similar behaviour exhibited by White or Asian pupils (Connolly 1995). Additionally, it has been claimed that African-Caribbean males bring to school an anti-school attitude born of street culture, which allows them to resist racism but which also results in underachievement (ibid.). Another factor may be that African-Caribbean, Bangladeshi, Pakistani and refugee pupils are disproportionately educated in schools with lower levels of resources, which are less able to attract the best quality staff. Additionally, the implication of looking at levels of attainment is that racial categories are seen as relatively uniform and stable although the concept of race as a collective phenomenon does not adequately capture the range of identities within racial groups. Blakey, Pearce and Chesters (2006) sought to capture the voices of 'minorities within minorities'. They found cultural and social tensions in Bradford's South Asian community, reflecting caste, gender and generational hierarchies deriving from place of origin. These hierarchies were often severely limiting in terms of social mobility since judgements on the basis of caste were still being made by some young people born in the UK.

These explanations are undoubtedly important reasons why certain minority ethnic groups underachieve in education, but they are not without their shortcomings. For instance, if racism leads to victims being turned off school, why do Asian males and females have high staying on rates? Modood (2003) suggests that too much research has focused on why African-Caribbean males underachieve, and not enough on why Asian groups do make progress. One explanation for progress in education is that some minority ethnic groups manifest a strong drive for qualifications. Modood (2005) points to the *self-concept* of a minority ethnic group which involves striving to achieve higher status and prosperity, aware of the fact that the 'dice are stacked against them'. This issue is exemplified when issues of gender and social class are considered in relation to minority ethnic groups. Research suggests that cultures which are portrayed as opposed to educating women seem to be producing growing cohorts of highly motivated young women (Ahmad et al. 2003), while Pakistani and Bangladeshi families – generally among the poorest minority ethnic groups, with large households, more dependents and less money – are nonetheless making significant progress in terms of academic performance.

It has been argued that parental social class is a major factor in determining university entrants. Modood (2003) provides evidence showing that offspring of parents with non-manual jobs exceed those with manuals jobs by a large margin. This is certainly the case with African-Caribbean ethnic groups, but in the case of Indian and Chinese groups, university entrants are as likely to come from manual working parental backgrounds as non-manual. However, Modood (2003) suggests that in the case of Indian and Chinese migrants, employment may not reflect their social class and capital; members of these groups may have suffered downward mobility upon migration, and may actually value education more than White workmates. They may also foster high expectations, give encouragement, maintain discipline, etc. Therefore, it can be claimed that certain ethnicities compound class disadvantage, while others counteract it when it comes to academic achievement.

Indeed, racial discrimination has meant that minority ethnic groups have been particularly dependent on qualifications for jobs and educational progression. Surveys of employers show that they would much rather recruit from the older universities (Parekh 2000). There is strong evidence that, when applying to old universities, minority candidates face an ethnic penalty (Modood 2003). Qualifications can therefore be argued to have more value to certain minority ethnic groups in that they serve as a way of progressing economically. In short, the government's claims that many minority ethnic groups have more recently made significant improvements in terms of academic achievement can be seen to mask a situation complicated by which ethnic minority group is being referred to, as well as gender, socio-economic status, and structural problems relating to entrenched racism in society (Tomlinson 2008).

Education of minority ethnic youth in the light of public debates and policy-making

This section will present an overview of how education of minority ethnic youth was framed in public discourse, how contested issues are put on the agenda of policy-making, and what kinds of policies are applied to respond to the claims. Particular emphasis will be put on initiatives, policies and measures to combat 'minoritisation' in schools.

Public discourse and representation

More recently, in the wake of New Labour's attempts to tackle racism via the education of children, there have been a number of issues debated in the public arena. At the heart of these issues is the notion of what it means to be British. Although these debates have been prevalent in British public debate in previous generations, more recently many no longer regarded Britain as a cohesive society, rather a fragmented one in which the problems engendered by multi-culturalism were perceived to be something that needed to be immediately addressed (Tomlinson 2008); this fracture was ostensibly a consequence of the presence of minority ethnic groups and the arrival of more migrants and refugees.

In 2004, the editor of *Prospect* magazine sparked a debate by attacking progressive liberals for supporting diversity. He suggested that ethnic groups must adopt the 'history of their new country' (Goodhart 2004 – cited in Tomlinson 2008) in order to avoid diverse groups leading to tensions. This view was supported by the Chair of the Commission for Racial Equality, Trevor Philips, and then endorsed by MPs, journalists and other leading spokespeople. Indeed, these concerns were escalated after the suicide bombings in London in 2005: the men responsible had been born and educated in Britain, and consequently some schools came to be regarded as potential training houses for terrorists. Riots among minority ethnic groups in major cities occurred in 2005, together with a continuing trend of racially motivated stabbings and killings. Other commentators have claimed that maintaining diversity can lead to ethnic integration. In the context of education, research has discovered that White children in all-White classes had no appreciation of the difficulties ethnic minority children can face. They were also less likely to make friends across ethnic divides (Weller 2008).

As a consequence of all this unrest, New Labour claimed that terrorism and immigration were the public's main concern, and MPs targeted the Muslim community's unwillingness to respond to pleas for integration. A nationwide discourse of 'Islamophobia' quickly developed. An emphasis was placed on extremist members of minority ethnic groups, particularly Muslims, and a plea was made to moderate membership of such groups to defend British values. Tony Blair, the Prime Minister at the time, claimed that 'the right to be in a multi-cultural society was always implicitly balanced by the duty to integrate and accept British values' (Blair 2006 – cited in Tomlinson 2008). Other commentators, however, have claimed that multi-culturalism remains a workable concept. A representative of the Runnymede Trust claimed, 'we need also to ensure people are treated fairly and their identities are not denigrated or subsumed into some sort of non-identity because that gets rid of all the benefits of diversity.'

One case related to education that was debated keenly in the public arena concerned the hijab – a traditional headscarf worn by many Muslim women. In 2005, Muslim women protested in London against the proposed law banning the wearing of religious symbols in French schools. However, in Britain the school teacher Shabina Begum successfully overturned a court ruling, allowing her to wear the hijab in school. This debate was set within the wider context of the tensions between liberal and multicultural political visions (Ward 2006). This case was representative of broader tensions regarding minority ethnic relations with British *mores*.

New Labour responded to these tensions by commissioning a review related to diversity and citizenship. The *Ajegbo Report* (2007) made a number of recommendations with the aim of promoting community cohesion among different groups, including several aimed at schools: school twinning, extended school activities to include parents from different communities, 'buddy' schemes to help second language speakers, citizenship education, a review of the religious education curriculum, and involving local employers and voluntary groups in the 14-19 curriculum (Ajegbo 2007).

Nevertheless, despite a rhetoric of concern, tensions remained. One example was in 2006 when a university lecturer argued on the basis of IQ tests that Black people were intellectually inferior to Whites, and this view was endorsed by a paper published by another academic that claimed that poverty and ill-health in Africa could be ascribed to lower intelligence. Researchers from voluntary organisations and university student unions have protested against these conclusions, claiming that low IQ levels are born of a lack of education and that this kind of thinking could retrigger debates about eugenics. Soon after, another attempted bombing was made in Glasgow airport by educated (medical and technical) minority ethnic men who had originally entered Britain as refugees; these acts were associated with whole Muslim communities, and the public fear remained that schools and universities in which segregation was manifest could be 'breeding ground' for terrorists. The role of education was again at the heart of publicly debated concerns with regard to multi-culturalism. Muslims are particularly targeted as potentially dangerous ('Islamophobia'), though this discourse maps on to existing patterns of racism with many other minority ethnic groups suspected of anti-Western rhetoric.

Inequality and poverty were overlooked in the debates (arguably the most plausible source of unrest – see above), as was genuine academic progress on the part of many minority ethnic youth (see above); Tony Blair angered community activists by claiming that violence involving minority ethnic groups (including killings) was caused by Black culture which involved absent fathers and a lack of positive role models – certainly a problematic conclusion that does not reflect existing data on minority ethnic achievement in schools (see above). With regard to the persistent academic failure of African-Caribbean youth, activists located the problem within government indifference and institutional racism, while the government continued to suggest that the problem was in fact born of a lack of community cohesion. The onus has been repeatedly shifted on to Black communities, individuals, parents and schools to deal with what are almost certainly structural issues relating to house, educational and employment (Tomlinson 2008).

Policy making

As mentioned above, when New Labour came to power in 1997, the party set out to tackle the challenges presented by an increasingly multi-ethnic society by focusing on education as a way of inculcating anti-racist attitudes among a new generation of children. However, we have also seen that New Labour's strategies have been regarded by many commentators as problematic. At the heart of New Labour's policies concerning the education of children with regard to issues of race is the notion of citizenship. Citizenship education as advocated by *The Crick*

Report (1998) covers social and moral responsibility, community involvement and political literacy; citizenship studies were made compulsory to all children in 2002. Some interpret the introduction of citizenship studies in schools as the government's (deeply inadequate) response to the *McPherson Report* (1999), which, following the failure of the police to charge anyone for the death of a Black teenager, Stephen Lawrence, said all public institutions must deal with their 'institutional racism' (Gillborn 2006). The report's inadequacy is seen to be an attempt to promote universal values but without an understanding of difference; it is also seen to contribute to a trend in educational policy of 'deracialisation' – that is, of reducing racism to individual ignorance and prejudice.

Other problems with this approach include an absence from *The Crick Report* of any direct mention of racism, either personal, institutional or structural. The targets set for citizenship education do not include ethnic equality, international and global issues, conflict resolution and anti-racism. When *The Crick Report* does talk about ethnicity and diversity it makes no mention of inequality or power imbalances, nor of anti-racism; it also regards ethnic minorities as a homogenous mass. The report states that minorities must 'learn and respect the codes and conventions as much as the majority', implying that minority communities are outside current conventions in a way that White people are not; this also reflects the move by the former Home Secretary to create a 'citizenship test' for all those acquiring British nationality. Finally, when racism is mentioned in citizenship educational literature, it reduces it to a matter of personal prejudice.

Some of the applications in schools of other New Labour policies have led to further problems. The Education Act 2005 obligated local authorities to set targets for schools to meet with regard to promoting 'community cohesion'. This resulted in additional pressure on schools, which were regarded as accountable and blameworthy if their application of these measures failed. Community cohesion is also promoted by the Neighbourhood Renewal Unit, a government strategy for facilitating conflict resolution, though owing to New Labour's focus on education as the principle way of addressing multi-cultural tensions, schools still bear a great responsibility for this. Additionally, schools were given more powers to exclude pupils and make their parents responsible for them; this latter measure impacted particularly on Black parents (Tomlinson 2008).

New Labour's focus on parental choice with regard to the schools that children attend served only to exacerbate these difficulties. Headmasters became reluctant to promote race issues in case the school became branded as 'radical' and puts off potential pupils (Tomlinson 2008). White parents attempted to segregate their children from schools in which there were a large number of minority ethnic children. As detailed above, Faith Schools were not obligated either to accept a considerable group of children not raised in that faith or to teach human rights common to all groups as opposed to faith-based values; this remained a problem despite Ofsted inspection (Tomlinson 2008). A study carried out by the University of Lancaster revealed that segregated White pupils held more stereotypical attitudes about minority ethnic groups than those who attend mixed schools

(Tomlinson 2008). The relationship between ethnic segregation and racism is not clear, closer contact may bring increased conflict not necessarily understanding and lower hostility. Lack of contact may bring less conflict and not necessarily greater hostility.

In short, it can be claimed that schools are expected to compensate for deeper, structural problems in society (Tomlinson 2008). At the heart of New Labour education policies in this period is an assumption that the problems engendered by multi-culturalism are the central concern and that schools are the place where these can be best addressed. However, many commentators suggest that it is actually wealth and social class issues which are more important in terms of explaining the differences in academic achievement among children (see above), and that ethnic status merely exacerbates this problem in some cases: for example, the poorest households are often Muslim and Indian (Tomlinson 2008). Additionally, New Labour's move away from institutional racism – that is, a collective failure on the part of social organisations to tackle racism – and towards racism as a personal failing of individual people is regarded as a refusal to affect the changes needed at a local, national and international level (Arora 2005).

This problem is in fact encapsulated in schools. A study by Warren (2005) draws on post-colonial theory to look at racism in schools, arguing that it is less a case of institutional racism than deeply embedded cultural assumptions that have emerged out of an historical context of empire and colonialism (Warren 2005: 244). The 'normal' pedagogical processes or circuits of power in schooling are self-consciously colour-blind and produce consistently racist effects. He and others conceptualise these as instituting practices of racial formations and particular racial imaginaries. In this sense, schools represent institutional forms of struggle attempting to construct a racial settlement in a post-colonial context.

The state of the art in research on minority ethnic youth in education

This section aims to provide a summary of the most significant research findings concerning the role of ethnicity in education with regard to the schooling of the three minority groups selected to participate in the present study. It will give an insight into the issues investigated and discussed by the scholarly community more recently. It will also present research on recent educational policies and initiatives designed to improve the education achievement of the selected minority ethnic groups.

The schooling of Gypsy, Roma and Traveller pupils

As detailed above, Gypsy, Roma and Traveller groups experience the most severe educational exclusion of any minority ethnic group in the UK with levels of attainment being roughly a quarter of the national average. Additionally, patterns of attainment at this level are declining, which is markedly different from other minority ethnic groups where there is evidence of some improvement. The consequences of missing out on an education include an inability to find employment and exclusion from society at large (Bhopal 2004). This particularly a problem for Gypsy, Roma and Traveller girls (Children's Society 2007).

Research conducted to discover the basis of underachievement in Gypsy, Roma and Traveller groups has shown that their regular mobility is only one factor which contributes to difficulties in attending school. Other factors may be the perception of school as being unsupportive of Gypsy, Roma and Travellers' lifestyles; parents being fearful of what their children will experience at school, despite otherwise valuing education; a less than positive first experience in schools which leads to a cycle of non-attendance (Kendall and Derrington 2003).

Much government policy fails to take sufficient account of Gypsy, Roma and Travellers' educational needs (Bhopal 2004), and as a result there has been a decline in attendance of Gypsy, Roma and Traveller pupils at secondary schools, with only one third of such children now in mainstream education and an average drop-out age at 11.49 years (Children's Society 2007). Nevertheless, traditional hostility to schooling among Gypsy, Roma and Traveller parents has shifted more recently, and with new distance learning programmes and the use of technology, many pupils can combine a nomadic lifestyle with effective education (Bhopal 2004).

With regard to the Gypsy, Roma and Traveller children who do attend schools, there remains the problem of bullying and being alienated (Children's Society 2007). Gypsy, Roma and Traveller children have no problem in identifying themselves as such, but do object to disparaging and offensive ways in which other label them (ibid.). A major issue is the degree to which it is possible for such children to achieve integration in mainstream schools while also preserving their cultural identity. Okley (1997) claims that entry into mainstream education can lead only to assimilation and that participation should be resisted by Gypsy, Roma and Traveller communities, with learning, rather than formal education, taking place within community and family groups. Indeed, this may be one of the main reasons why Gypsy, Roma and Traveller parents are reluctant to send their children to school. Research has also shown that parents worry additionally about racism, the moral welfare of teenage girls, sex education, drugs, and potential damage to the family network (Save The Children 2001). Indeed, family is regarded as important among Gypsy, Roma and Traveller children and any policies directed at helping them enter mainstream education must take into account familial networks involved in these communities (Children's Society 2007).

Education among Gypsy, Roma and Traveller children has recently generated a good deal of public attention, with major reports published by the Commission For Racial Equality (*Common Ground: Equality, Good Race Relations and Sites for Gypsies and Irish Travellers*, 2006) and The Department for Schools, Children and Families (*The Inclusion of Gypsy, Roma and Traveller Children and Young People*, 2007). Nevertheless, much work needs to be done in order to reverse some of the declining trends among Gypsy, Roma and Traveller children, both in terms of their attendance at mainstream schools and their educational achievement record. Here, appropriate research would be concerned with identifying key barriers and constraints to inclusion and evaluating the impact of interventions that have been established to address these problems so far. Different barriers are likely to operate in different local contexts and with varying impact across different Gypsy, Roma and Traveller groups, so identifying specific contexts, key intervention mechanisms and outcomes is required in evaluation research. Further current research is addressed in Chapter 4.

The schooling of Pakistani pupils

As shown above, although Pakistani pupils show on average a lower educational achievement rate than the national average, there is in fact an internal polarisation within this group, with both highly qualified and unqualified individuals. Recent research has focused on this central issue, along with the growing cohort of highly motivated young females in education.

Abbas (2007) conducted an empirical study with Bangladeshi, Indian and Pakistani pupils from independent and secondary schools; he focused on issues of social class, ethnicity and culture. Qualitative interviews with pupils and parents revealed that certain working class South Asian parents possess strong middle class attitudes towards education and that this is unrelated to their ability to facilitate them in terms of financial or social capital. Many middle class parents were also motivated to focus on education as a crucial part of their children's development, yet they did possess the relevant financial and social capital. In conclusion, Abbas claims that social class was the most important factor in pupils gaining entry to their selective schools.

Nevertheless, Crozier and Davis (2006) warn against an individualised approach which focuses only on pupils' parents. They claim that the division between highly motivated parents and those who are ostensibly indifferent is more subtle than it initially appears. They argue that in South Asian communities, it is also important to take into account the extended family's attitudes towards education. Parents who are ostensibly indifferent to their children's education may be compensated to some degree by a broader family focus on the importance of schooling.

In another paper, Crozier and Davis (2007) argue that South Asian parents who claim not to care about their children's education are regarded by teachers as 'hard to reach'. Although research (with Pakistani and Bangladeshi communities) shows that some South Asian parents know little about the education system and do not get involved their children's schooling, it is not the case that these parents are 'difficult' or 'indifferent' – terms that, the authors argue, the phrase 'hard to reach' implies. This research suggests that schools often inhibit accessibility for certain parents, and that their inference about these parents being 'hard to reach' merely pathologies them.

Another siginificant phenomenon emerging from South Asian communities in the growing cohort of highly motivated young women. Shain (2000) studied and theorised the experiences and strategies of young women of Pakistani, Bangladeshi and Indian descent and identified the following issues:

- With many of the young women she interviewed, there was the perception that they were unequally treated by White staff.
- Pupils were responded to particularly negatively when they deviated from their race/gender stereotype (of the timid and passive Asian female).
- When pupils disassociated themselves from solely Asian groups and adopted western attitudes and modes of dress, this was met with a positive response from both White students and teachers.
- Many pupils appeared to have internalised racist ideologies, which became apparent when talking about other Asian pupils.
- Religion was identified as an important mediating factor in their experience of racism. It often provided a vehicle for resistance against teachers.
- It is not simply that colonial relations are reproduced, but that its ideologies are being reworked in the shifting relations of late modernity.
- Rather than being passive recipients of oppressed cultural practices, Asian women were actively involved in interpreting these practices, choosing which ones to reject and which ones to accept. Young Asian women are involved in creating new identities and meanings that involve conscious strategies of survival.

A study by Dale et al. (2002) shows that young Pakistani and Bangladeshi woman face an even more complex situation than South Asian young men with regard to education. Although their parents may have the same aspirations with regard to their children's schooling, there is additionally a risk of young Asian woman jeopardising the family's honour by their academic achievements. Nevertheless, Dale (2002) shows that these young Asian woman see academic qualifications as a way of gaining paid work, and that paid work results in independence and self-esteem. The growing numbers of South Asian young women in full-time undergraduate education reveals a desire to combine employment with family life.

The schooling of African-Caribbean pupils

As revealed above, African-Caribbean pupils are less likely to achieve acceptable standards in education, and this is particularly true for African-Caribbean boys. Much academic research has been carried out on this community with regard to schooling, and what follows are the central issues.

Haynes et al. (2006) indicate that the common sense explanation for why African-Caribbean pupils fail in education is to do with identity problems, low self-esteem, impoverished socio-economic backgrounds and low teacher expectations. These reasons map on to the fact (discussed above) that social class tends to be the most powerful predictor of academic success, particularly among minority ethnic groups. However, there is no conclusive reason why underachievement should persist in African-Caribbeans while it has improved in other minority ethnic groups.

It is argued by many anti-racist commentators that schools display differential treatment in the case of African-Caribbean pupils, while apolitical commentators argue that such pupils only receive such treatment because they are more likely to misbehave (Pilkington 1999). Research by Warren (2005) found that African-Caribbean young men engage in performainces of opposition but do not in fact resist what school offers: they do not reject school but rather the inequality of respect they experience. Teachers have strong preconceptions about pupils, and teaching practices are problematically racialised. In her research on African-Caribbean pupils, Youdell (2003) looked at the discursive constitution of identity within schools, and particularly how identity traps are produced. The moment when African-Caribbean students constitute themselves in terms of student subculture may be the same moment the school constitutes them as a challenge to authority: the very success of their street cultural identities entrap them.

There are clearly subtle factors at work with regard to the schooling of African-Caribbean pupils. However, the central issue is whether schools should readdress their institutional policies with regard to African-Caribbean pupils or whether this is not necessary because the problems exist elsewhere. Nevertheless, the debate remains contentious and is unconcluded.

One possible route out of this impasse is to look at how some schools are succeeding in improving the educational performance of African-Caribbean pupils. Demie (2005) reports on good practice at 13 schools in Lambeth. Findings from the study show that African-Caribbean pupils have improved achievement records in Key Stage 2 and GCSE results. Among the features that contribute to this success are strong leadership which aims at improving standards for all pupils; the use of performance data for school self-evaluation and tracking pupils' performance; a commitment to creating a culture which allows teachers to use creative intuition to maximise their pupils' learning; a highly inclusive curriculum that meets the needs of African-Caribbean pupils; a strong link to the community and the involvement of parents in school issues; well-coordinated support for African-Caribbean pupils via learning mentors and role models; a commitment to equal opportunities and a strong focus on racism. In the case of schools discussed in this research, academic achievement among African-Caribbean pupils was far superior to the national averages.

It would therefore appear that under-achievement among African-Caribbean pupils has a number of complex causes, but that sensitive and appropriate practices at schools can be effective in terms of improving their performance in education.

Recent policies and initiatives relating to the selected minority groups

In this period New Labour developed a number of policies and initiatives in order to support schools in their tuition of minority ethnic groups. *Aiming High: Raising the Achievement of Minority Ethnic Pupils* (2003) is a key scheme designed to help young learners (particularly those who do not have English as their first language) get the best from their education. Other schemes include courses for teachers to achieve accredited training in English as an additional language, while the *Making the Grade: Key Stage 4 Project* aims to help teachers understand the needs of bi-lingual pupils. There has also been a drive towards recruiting more teachers who belong to minority ethnic groups.

Three initiatives designed specifically to help children belonging to each of the minority ethnic groups selected for the present study are as follows:

- The *Aiming High* programme seeks to provide good quality materials about Gypsy, Roma and Traveller history and heritage, to employ regional advisors at both primary and secondary school levels, and to provide a website about bullying with a dedicated section for Gypsy, Roma and Travellers.
- Part of the *Aiming High* programme is a Minority Ethnic Achievement Project (2004) designed to support pupils of Bangladeshi, Pakistani, Somali and Turkish heritage at Key Stage 3. The project was developed in consultation with Muslim organisations and is concerned with improvements in teaching and learning.
- In 2003, the *African-Caribbean Achievement Project* was launched in both primary and secondary schools. The aim has been to emphasise in schools strong leadership, high expectation of success, mutual respect and intolerance of racism, recognition of cultural diversity, active participation of parents and the wider community. The *Black Pupils Achievement Programme* has been especially effective in tackling issues relating to African-Caribbean pupils, helping teachers understand their needs and promoting race equality issues, as well as providing support for such children and their parents.

These initiatives were targeted on schools in urban areas with high numbers of pupils from the relevant minority ethnic groups and are voluntaristic rather than compulsory, relying on local awareness, uptake and commitment to specific programmes. Coverage in schools is therefore patchy and uneven across the country, with relatively little impact of these programmes in non-urban areas.

Nevertheless, despite policies and initiatives designed to improve the educational achievement of all minority ethnic groups, it was admitted by New Labour that much work needs to be done to achieve parity and progress among all groups. The children of Gypsy, Roma and Travellers, Pakistani and Bangladeshi pupils from poorer backgrounds, and African-Caribbean children (particularly boys) are among those most in need of help (DfES 2006).

Education, ethnicity and the Conservative/Liberal Democrat Coalition, May 2010-

Cuts in public expenditure and ramping up the neo-liberal agenda of choice and competition in education, developed under New Labour, are the two key drivers of current government policy on education. Expansion of the academies programme, creation of 'free schools' and severe budget cuts mark out some of the central actions of the new government in this sphere. The further re-structuring of secondary education in this way is likely to have a detrimental impact on ethnic minority groups, as in Sweden (see Chapter 7). Cuts are leading to the dismantling of the complex raft of policies, initiatives and programmes concerned to address ethnic minority achievement and address issues of racial and ethnic diversity in schools. In a recent survey of half of all local authorities in England about the current position of Ethnic Minority Achievement Grant (EMAG) services 80 per cent of respondents had experienced or were expecting to experience restructuring and/or the reduction of posts through forced or voluntary redundancies in the near future and nearly a third of authorities had already completed or finalised plans to delete or reduce their Ethnic Minority Achievement Services (NUT/ NALDIC 2010). Common negative impacts on schools included a reduction in pupil support; a reduction in availability and a rise in costs of valued additional school based work such as interpretation or home school liaison; a shortage of knowledgeable specialists when demand is rising and a disproportionate impact on less well funded schools in which ethnic minority pupils are concentrated. The biggest deterioration reported was in the quality or availability of support for ethnic minority pupils and students.

The attempt to scrap the education maintenance allowance (EMA) by the government was partially reversed but still substantial cuts will be made and this impacts differentially on ethnic minority students as a much higher proportion of some minority groups had received this support, 43 per cent of all 17- to 18-year-old full-time students received EMA whereas 67 per cent of Black African and 88 per cent of Bangladeshi students were in receipt of this allowance.

The move away from prioritising issues of racial and ethnic equality in educational policy is clear in the silence on many of these issues from the Department of Education and reflects the explicit rejection of multiculturalism and policies to address ethnic diversity by the Prime Minister. The Department of Education website (accessed 7/4/11) now contains practically no information or guidance for schools on matters of ethnic minority achievement which is very different to the mass of reports and guidance made available to schools under New Labour. Overall, this new climate of muscular majoritarianism and strengthening neo-liberalism resulting in the decimation of progressive interventions marks a political acceptance of increasing racial and ethnic inequalities, an indifference to the racialisation of education and hostility to race and ethnic specific policies and programmes. There are strong parallels here with trends in Central and Eastern Europe and these are discussed further in Chapter 7. The next chapter introduces new evidence from local fieldwork with Gypsy and Traveller communities.

Chapter 4

Gypsies and Travellers, Perceptions and Experiences of Secondary Education

Introduction

The Gypsy and Traveller population of the UK is in the most vulnerable position of economic, political and social marginality of any minority ethnic group and formal secondary education for many from these groups is not working (Cemlyn et al. 2009). Non-participation, particularly in secondary education, by pupils from these groups, is the most serious problem of ethnic segregation in this field. This is compounded by increasing levels of poverty and immiseration, high levels of racial hostility and the limited scope of constructive interventions. This chapter highlights the complex and multidimensional causes of this educational outcome including school inaction, difficulties in attending school because of poverty and poor health, perceptions of school as being unsupportive of Gypsy and Travellers' lifestyles, parents being fearful of what their children will experience at school, despite otherwise valuing education, and a less than positive school experience including bullying and discrimination which leads to a cycle of non-attendance further exacerbated by peer pressure. Norms and values within these communities are also tending to reinforce traditional roles and occupations for young people and depress educational aspirations. But, there is evidence that targeted inclusion work with recently arrived has been successful in substantially increasing school attendance, particularly at primary level but it is unclear yet whether this will impact at secondary level. More generally across UK society Gypsies, Roma and Travellers are still seen, portrayed and stereotyped as thieving scum, scroungers, gangsters and child traffickers (Leeming 2010).

This chapter presents new information on the experiences of Gypsy and Traveller children and education in Britain, providing both an assessment of current patterns of social and educational exclusion, and evidence from fieldwork with schools, parents and community groups in a Northern City. The names of the cities, schools and respondents used in this book are fictitious to preserve anonymity and this was explicitly confirmed to research participants. This is a common research strategy in educational research and is particularly important in this research due to the sensitive nature of the subjects addressed and the age of the participants. Welfare outcomes are particularly poor for this group, for example they have higher levels of infant mortality and lower life expectancy due to difficulties in accessing health services than most other groups, life expectancy for men and women is 10 years lower than the national average and Gypsy and

Irish Traveller mothers are 20 times more likely than mothers in the rest of the population to have experienced the death of a child. In education, as well as some of the lowest levels of educational attainment, some schools are refusing to admit children from this group, imposing discriminatory conditions on admission or delaying registration. Also, of those that do get access to education, at least half of Gypsy and Traveller children in England and Wales drop out of school between the ages of 8 and 16. This is indicated by recent data on pupils: 2,840 Travellers of Irish heritage and 7,190 Gypsy and Roma children are in primary schools, but only 1,090 Travellers of Irish heritage and 3,620 Gypsy and Roma children are in secondary schools (DfE 2010). So there are less than half the number of children from these groups in secondary education compared to primary education, whereas for White British children there are more in secondary than primary. Furthermore, there is increasing evidence of almost total failure of access to higher education for this group which will be confirmed with release of 2011 census data.

One main issue in considering the identity of these young people in relation to education was that education itself was not seen as a key issue by many families. Despite the fact that educational policy has emphasised that these children are the most at risk in the education system, this sense of urgency has not been translated at local level and educational urgency and high educational aspirations are also not necessarily strong core community values. The reason is simple. What is at the forefront of the minds of many families is the importance of daily management of everyday life, being strong and maintaining family cohesion in adverse circumstances.

Following consideration of research sites and methods, this chapter is structured into seven sections. The first section examines identity as a source of pride and discrimination. This dual focus emphasises the complexities of ethnicity as a lived experience. The second section looks at gender roles and the significance of family. Gender was closely entwined with cultural identity which as well as denoting a clear sense of self, also constrained individual potential. Remembering that identity is not a fixed unwavering root, the third section considers the changing nature of identity. The fourth section looks at how the policy context is currently failing these children. Lastly, perceptions and perspectives on education are examined.

Research sites and methods

This section introduces both the fieldwork sites and methods used for this study presented later in Chapters 5 and 6, as well as those used for research presented in this chapter. General patterns of ethnic inequality in education determined the selection of minority ethnic groups for this project, as identified above, these were Gypsies and Travellers, African-Caribbeans and Pakistanis. Two cities in the North of England were chosen as sites for the research. Northcity was the main site and here a quantitative survey of 434 Year 10 pupils in three multicultural secondary schools was firstly carried out in 2008-2009. This city has over half a million inhabitants and a fairly typical pattern of ethnic diversity with an 11 per cent Black and minority ethnic population of which the Pakistani and African-Caribbean groups were the largest. All the three schools had about one third minority ethnic pupils but varied widely in their intake from inner city areas (from 93 per cent, 68 per cent and 23 per cent respectively) and hence their socio-economic profile.

The quantitative survey both provided background data and information on key aspects of inter-ethnic relations as perceived by the pupils. This was followed up by qualitative research which included focus-group discussions and in-depth personal interviews with students, school-personnel and parents, further interviews with community and educational informants, classroom observations, case studies of schools and minority ethnic groups and ethnographic fieldwork into youth and community cultures. The purpose of this stage of the research was to investigate the factors and motivations behind varying school performances and diverging educational careers, the impact of ethnicity on everyday life in school, experiences of being 'othered' and perceptions of identity.

Very few of the Gypsy and Traveller Year 10 pupils on school rolls were in school and hence included in the quantitative survey, also the local population was fairly small and access hard to achieve. For these reasons, a different city location was chosen for a qualitative community study of these groups. This second city location also has a fairly typical pattern of ethnic diversity. It also contains over half a million people and over 500 Gypsy and Traveller children have been identified here. In researching these groups access was initially difficult, and building trust and working relationships with people who were known and trusted by the community was key. The local authority service concerned with educational achievement amongst these groups operating in the selected Northern city in the UK, identified 574 Gypsy and Traveller children aged 5-16 in their census in 2004, and it has worked with over 1,000 children from these groups recently. Access for qualitative research was facilitated through this service which has a well-established reputation for identifying and facilitating educational inclusion for children from these groups. This chapter draws on, and is informed by, formal and informal interviews with key informants (11), Gypsy and Traveller parents (19) and young people (17) and ethnographic fieldwork across both locations, with a particular focus on the experiences of Irish Travellers. The fieldwork interviews were all carried out by Sarah Swann between April 2009 and March 2010.

Gypsy and Traveller identity as a source of both pride and hostility

In interviews, respondents tended to frame their ethnic identity in two ways, firstly as the object of hostility, discrimination and prejudice, 'If we can't use the word racism, what can we use?' (Traveller mother) which points to some of the ambiguities of policy in Britain and some of the inconsistencies in managing ethnic diversity. Despite Traveller being a distinct ethnic identity, respondents felt their White skin impeded recognition of the issues they faced. Reclaiming racism was one way this community accounted for the inequalities in housing, employment, education and access to government services. Predominantly this was through attention to skin colour which provides a critical standpoint from which to unpack racism. Ethnicity and racism is recognised by skin colour and since Whiteness is not popularly equated to ethnic minorities, Gypsy and Traveller identity remains 'invisible' and a form of culturelessness which serves to disadvantage and exclude. Chapter 3 showed how other writers have sought to explain culturelessness as the 'omnipresence of Whites' being positioned at the centre, 'around which a carnival like array of multicultural difference is displayed for their enjoyment and sampling' (McLeod and Yates 2000: 3), but this is not the case for Gypsies and Travellers. Their culture simply is not acknowledged. They are not included as visibly targeted minority ethnic groups but are rather placed unnoticed on the periphery of 'normal' Whiteness.

Daily inconsistencies in managing diversity with inclusion policies creates many layers of understanding that constitute how Gypsies and Travellers learn to understand the world and themselves. In informal conversations, respondents drew on a number of examples which 'proved' their inferior social standing in race relations. Dialogue around the subject of racism often highlighted inter-ethnic competition with other minority ethnic groups for resources. Recently settled communities such as Eastern Europeans were perceived as getting a better deal with housing and benefits. Collections for Haiti invoked the response, 'charity begins at home'. One conversation contrasted the high profile coverage of Black murder victims Stephen Lawrence and Damilola Taylor with Johnny Delaney, a 15-year-old Irish Traveller who was killed in a racist attack in 2003 which has been scarcely mentioned or discussed.

Understanding ethnic identity and social self-positioning involved emotional work. Specifically this meant how they positioned themselves in relation to others and how others positioned them. Overall identity was seen as being rooted in lower social class status,

> Because we as society like to put things in to little boxes, which forces people to fall under classes, and once you've been branded a class it is hard to progress from that ... the government make it harder by keepin' lower classes together, so all they are gonna know is what they are around. That's the Government's aim. "Dont Teach Them, Phase them out"... (Traveller man).

Everyday life invoked belonging to a lowly social status. In a mistake over change in a shop, a Pakistani shop keeper told one mother, 'You Travellers can never add up'. Her response was to say that 'Pakistanis only got out of Pakistan because of Travellers'. Attitudes are complex. Such interaction shows the significance of ethnic boundaries in demarcating social status but in doing so it demonstrates more of an artificial prejudice where one group claims higher ethnic social ranking through the putting down of another group. In this sense ethnic groups are being located in centrifugal circles of worth around a White middle class centre. Gypsies and Travellers view themselves as being at the very outer circle. Significantly though, how larger society chooses to identify you then has implications. It creates prescriptive social norms which serve to marginalise and subordinate the community's interests. Being perceived negatively resulted in a complex and ongoing struggling sense of personal ethnic identity. Sometimes community members exercised complicity and sometimes resistance which links back to the reticence Gypsies and Travellers have in publicly acknowledging their ethnic identity.

Discussion of discrimination referenced daily experiences of unfair treatment which evoked strong passions. This often included a high police presence on sites and being targeted in public spaces, for instance being followed by store detectives around shopping centres. The image of the Gypsy and Traveller and its otherness also brought opportunities from time to time. For instance a television company wanting to achieve a 'faithful' interpretation of *Wuthering Heights* had approached one Traveller community for an actor to play Heathcliffe. Although in some ways it represents a positive opportunity for an individual person, there was also the sense that it exploited ethnic stereotypes as the fictional character is an untamed, volatile and wild man set against society at large.

A chameleon identity was often used as a coping strategy for fear of harassment. Much was said about being adaptable and hiding their 'true' identity in order to fit in. This was made possible by having White skin and tweaking aspects of physical appearance. For one young Traveller woman shopping for Miss Sixty jeans, she abandons those things which have cultural significance by altering her style of dress and wearing less jewellery so she does not stand out. One young Traveller man was participating in higher education at college but in order to succeed he felt he had to act like a *gorja* (a member of the settled community), which 'made me feel a bit disappointed in the whole system to be honest, and that I was keeping what was truly me back'. His strategy worked until his gran died and he asked for time off to grieve. He was faced with a lack of understanding so came clean about his identity and from this point people treated him differently,

> They came out with the typical stereotypical (comments) "rubbish spongers, ain't gonna do anything with this ... why is he bothering? They're difficult" (…) they have to ask the stupidest of questions like have I been locked up and so on (…). You just laugh it off, take the piss back and you get on. It's harder to deal with when it comes from the people who should know better, and who you are looking to for help. (Young Traveller man).

Responding to insults in everyday life through jokes and banter was a strategy which enabled him to build friendships with peers which were sustained after day to day institutional contact, 'most of the people I went to college with I still talk to and meet up sometimes to catch up'. This was at some personal cost but he was most negatively affected by the responses of lecturers whom, placed in positions of power, he felt he was supposed to respect.

It was felt that discrimination had been going on so long that it was almost inevitable. As one Traveller female parent says, 'I believe we are victims of hate and ignorance. (….) How long have Travellers been in England? 400, 500 years? If we haven't got rights now, when will we?' Discourse frequently drew on a collective heritage memory and the long history of racism linked to world events (in particular the Nazi Holocaust) which invoked struggles to survive against centuries of persecution. The need for equality and equal treatment are frequently emphasised as the general consensus appeared to be that Gypsy and Traveller identity is not respected,

> Travellers should be able to get treated like everybody else and they should have really good jobs like everybody else not just because they are Travellers, we are all human beings, we haven't got 50 heads, we have only got one head like every other person, just because we live in a trailer what is the difference? (Traveller mother).

Racial discrimination is perceived here on the basis of life style rather than skin colour. Simultaneously ethnic identity brought about strong feelings of pride which was not as apparent in discussions with other minority ethnic groups. Pride seemed to stem from a shared sense of who these people were and where they came from, in other words identity, traditions and heritage, and a shared sense of cultural imagination. The influence of mass media was very much evident among young people and their use of social networking sites like Facebook and Youtube emphasised pride in the community. It was a way of connecting to other members of their communities. For instance Facebook hosts groups like 'we are loud and proud to be gypsy'. Being Gypsy and Traveller meant being resilient, self reliant, adaptable and showing initiative which were the qualities which had enabled them to survive. Being a person from these groups was understood as something primordial, it was in the blood and etched into the psyche. It was not an instrumental choice but something you were born into, an ethnic category.

Like all other ethnic groups Gypsies and Travellers have customs and cultural values which mark out their way of life. Family members often had the tendency to draw comparisons with the White settled hegemonic 'Gorja' community. This process of 'ethnic othering' highlighted a number of policy relevant facets. First was a strong sense of boundary between childhood and adulthood, each having established norms. Life within the community revolved very much around the family which provides social and psychological security. Children are very much the centre and it is the sole role of the family to raise children. The centrality of family serves as a great source of solidarity and stability in a world of instability. Parenting being very much the responsibility of the family, contrasts with the institutionalisation of children in school where responsibility is left to professionals.

Adult attitudes revealed strict age boundaries which unambiguously demarcated the shift from child to adult, and which contrasted with the settled community where there are no clear markers,

> Once you become 10 years old you are seen as a totally different role model in life. You have to basically get up and do things for yourself, you are not a child, and you are not a baby no more. Gorjas, they are still swinging out of their mother and father's bank accounts at 21 to 22 years old. (Traveller mother).

This was reflected in dress where girls changed from wearing pink and glitter to wearing miniature versions of adult dress. Being educated to become independent from a younger age has implications for secondary schooling where the statutory school leaving age is currently 16 with a proposed increase to 18. Travellers took pride in independence at a young age which is highly significant and has implications for secondary schooling.

Gender roles and the significance of family

Many marry young and family life comes first. In the family traditional patterns were still very much forged around traditional gender roles which young people tended to follow,

> The man has a role and the woman has a role. In my eyes it's a bit like 1960 ways of life. The men go out and work to provide money for food and things like clothes for their children. (....) the men are the providers. Women are meant to look after the children, cook, clean and provide a nice home. (Traveller mother).

Gender roles reinforced a strong work ethic based on separate spheres which has enabled the community to survive. The women took great pride in the cleanliness of their homes. Descriptions of Gypsy and Traveller men tended to be rooted in hegemonic masculinity with qualities like physical toughness being valued. The focus was very much on the man taking responsibility for his family and this was taken very seriously,

> If a man can't get up off his computer and stop playing on the games all day and on Facebook all day and on the Play Station and all the Game Boys and go out and provide money for a living for his family then he may as well go kill himself to be honest. (Traveller mother).

These gender roles gave a clear and proud sense of identity but this asymmetry had deep roots within the community and distribution of power was unequal. Men are viewed as 'much higher than a woman' (Traveller mother) and gendered power relations shaped all relationships and structured daily life. Incidents of domestic violence, on one Traveller site, were prevalent but were accepted as normal,

> Women are very isolated and won't ask for help. I have seen the cycle repeat itself over and over again. Many women is not realising what is domestic violence. (Traveller mother).

Women had often suffered for prolonged periods as talking about suffering abuse was stigmatising. Divorce is extremely rare in the community as Travellers have traditional views on marriage and a woman leaving would be ostracised by her community.

The significance of gendered power relations seeps through all levels of social interaction and some demonstrate the possibility of multiple positions and alternatives which bring resistance. For instance, in online discourse on a social networking site,

> Boys Are Like A Deck Of Cards, You Need A Heart To Love Them, A Diamond To Marry Them, A Club To Smash Their Head In, And A Spade To Bury Them :) your husband is limping around bleeding outside what do you do..? stay calm take a second reload aim FIRE!!

Here the use of humour demonstrates some resistance to gender inequalities in interactions with men in the form of counter-positioning. By creating and making visible an aggressive female identity, some small transgression of gender roles is achieved. Men tend to follow traditional employment options like scrap metal dealing but the problem is that these traditional types of work are not so easily available. As such life is one of uncertainty requiring adaptable identities,

> You have got to think about your children, because when they grow up the world is not going to be like it is now, it is going to be harder. Travelling life is going to change. (Traveller mother).

This brings about ambiguous views. In one sense the future is education since it is necessary to adapt to cope with modern life and a changing economic climate. But this is an instrumental goal rather than an aim rooted in improving individual talents, aspirations or personal fulfillment. Education simply is not viewed as developing individual potential. Rather education as a concept is seen as irrelevant and meaningless mainly because it is associated with assimilation to the detriment of one's cultural identity.

The changing nature of Gypsy and Traveller identity

There was evidence of changing community lifestyles and values although this was often achieved at some personal cost. For the older generation there was the feeling that the old way of life was being threatened through a general breakdown in cultural values and beliefs which were a great source of pride. Although the majority of women do not work there is some sign that women's roles are changing. One inclusion worker was from the Traveller community and lived on the site. When she first began her role she faced resistance from other women who implied that working in a professional role would be to the detriment of her domestic duties,

> ....they would say, "how come you can work I don't know how you do it? I don't know how you see to your children?" And I would say, "well simple as my children won't want for anything". (…) It was a bit of jealousy, because the women think, "well how can K. do that? She has got four children and family, a house to clean; how does she do it?" To be honest with you I do it because if I didn't I would go mental. (Traveller mother).

Within the community women's responsibilities towards home and family weighed over gaining employment or career aspirations and the satisfaction this might bring. One Traveller mother had undergone some internal rebellion to undertake paid employment as at first it felt like abandoning her community. She was talked around by the manager of a project who wanted to recruit from within the community it served.

> So she said, "I could really do with a person like you", so I said to her, "my reading and writing is crap but I will help you". She said, "no I need you to start working with me properly and get paid for it". So I said, "well no not really because we are not allowed to work". (…) I said, "honestly, no matter how much money you offer me I am not going to come out of my culture for any organisation." (Traveller mother).

Initial trepidation was combated to a large extent by the fact she worked for a community led organisation which aimed to improve the prospects of these groups.

> But then I saw what they were doing and I thought "well maybe if I mix that in with the culture". Keep the culture, you can still keep the culture and this is one thing we have to learn as Travelling women. You can still keep your culture and work, although other women don't think that. (Traveller mother).

She obtained job satisfaction because her work was suited to her interests. This Traveller woman herself provided a valuable resource for her community, not only through the role she performed as inclusion worker, but through exposing other women within her community to the possibility of having a career.

However, to a large extent undertaking structured learning or training meant becoming a Gorja. One Gypsy man had taken the choice to enter higher education in his late 20s. His motivation was to follow an interest in music. A Gypsy or Traveller person with a higher education is rare. But while he did not define himself as an unconventional Gypsy/Traveller man he was viewed as a Gorja by his community. He had the stance of someone who does what feels right rather than what is expected of him. As such his path could be viewed through a capability and resilience framework where personal qualities of autonomy enable him to move more fluidly in the wider world.

Policy context is currently failing Gypsy and Traveller children

We must pay attention to the institutions and codes that define the particular local and national context which works to limit Gypsy and Traveller lifestyles. The rationale to justify the Every Child Matters framework is one of equity, that all children and young people have a democratic right to be healthy; stay safe; enjoy and achieve; make a positive contribution and achieve economic well being. Education is a key component of this but at the root is poverty and one must turn to local level to explore how this fails in practice. Consideration must first be drawn to living conditions where policy has worked to physically and socially separate Gypsy and Traveller families from the mainstream. In one of the city locations the Traveller community was housed on two adjacent sites. The first site initially housed 20 families and a second site was built a few years later. Residents did not want the second site to be built so close as they felt it was too big and unsettling. However it is directly next to the original site so in practice it amounts to one large authorised site. The site is situated in a very remote and isolated location on the outskirts of the city, close to a motorway in an industrial area with problems of traffic pollution. Basically it is an area where no one else would want to live. Residents cannot access mainstream services without a car. There are no shops within walking distance. The community is therefore physically placed in parallel from the rest of the city. Physically, since it represents disorder, the site is hidden from public view. It is approached via a long winding drive which obscures the trailers. In terms of the shift in policy brought about through government pressure for councils to provide sites, it can therefore be seen as containment rather than exclusion which results in the further marginalisation of its inhabitants.

This site currently consists of over 40 pitches. Residents provide their own trailers which are situated on pitches. The overall site is self funded through rents collected from residents. At the time of the study residents were paying £170 a week in rent which is more than local authority housing. Technically the rent is a pitch fee and on top of this, residents pay for their own trailer and for gas, water, electricity and all other charges. Residents perceive that these are also substantially more expensive than the rates people in local authority housing pay. Overall the benefits trap is perceived as a particular issue within this community which provides severely constraining circumstances. As one interviewee commented, 'It's a poverty trap' which was defined by the means testing of social benefits which culminated in strong economic incentives discouraging paid employment. Simply put, living on the site is not affordable for those not on full housing benefit, 'When I got my job I wasn't earning enough to keep the plot on and I was in arrears for the first time in 30 years. The city council advised me to give up my job'. Labour market inclusion is intrinsically linked to social participation and citizenship. It implies empowerment by being involved in public life but the way the benefits system works in practice reinforces a cycle of benefit dependency among this community.

Social exclusion among the community stems mainly from feeling trapped on a site on the physical periphery of a city where no one else would want to live. The layout of the site is poor with a lack of adequate accommodation and basic amenities. It is overcrowded and residents feel 'packed in like sardines' (Traveller mother). Over 100 children live on-site and are equipped with a 'play area' which in practice consists of a large empty tarmacked space. There are no communal facilities. Overall the site is fenced off from the rest of society by metal fences which make you feel enclosed. In one respondent's words,

> It is an acre of land with a shed and it is like Beirut. It is an eye opener. You would think "what are these people doing to be living here?" It is not that we are blind; it is not that we have nowhere else to go, but it is either that or basically the roadside, getting moved up and down 24/7. (Traveller mother).

Although living conditions on the site are poor, families living on the roadside face worse conditions. They are evicted on average every two weeks and have no basic infrastructure such as a water supply and sanitation. The poverty trap arises when different forms of deprivation are connected. The lack of education and qualifications within the community result in unstable job opportunities which limit regular financial income. This is reflected in the poor quality of accommodation which in turn results in high rates of depression.

The site's layout and architecture also significantly structures social relations. As with pretty much all of Gypsy and Traveller sites, at the entrance of the site there is an office, which is not for residents' use but is solely for the use of 'managers' who are responsible for site management. This is very visible and functions like a panoptic structure. The managers can see who enters and who leaves the site. On one occasion one manager exerted power by refusing entry to a photography student who had come to work with residents on a project because he did not know who she was. As such it feels like it is the site managers rather than the residents that run the site. The lived dynamics of living on the site and control of social space is epitomised by a large rock outside the office which has been graffitied with the word 'war'.

The constraints of a panoptic structure stretched further out than living on the site. There was considerable tension and distrust of the police, 'No policemen's good. They're not there as … they make conflict'. Complaints were targeted at one police officer in particular,

> He's proper 1960s. The way he goes on, he's like Hitler. "You're shit and I'm it". That's the sort of man he is. (…) Why don't you think the CCTV equipment works Sarah? I think it's fucked. They've done something to the equipment. (.) You have to be sly. You have to have people in high places. (Traveller mother).

A Gypsy Liaison officer had been employed to build wider awareness and understanding of the community and promote good relations but he never came on site. This was mainly because his role was treated with some contempt within the organisation, 'He's getting stick from his colleagues. A lot of stick to be honest with you'. This created a constraining environment which puts these families in a poor position to take equal advantage of opportunities.

Ambiguous perspectives on education

It is useful to begin by considering the connotations the concept of education brought about. Possibly as a result of limited knowledge of what schooling entailed as well as doing without it for so long, education simply was not viewed as having an instrumental value. Discussion with community members did not emphasise the narrow 5 A*-C GCSE attainment target concerns that drive much policy. Neither did it mean anything much to do with schools as institutions. Rather education meant actively promoting a better image of Gypsys and Travellers and challenging stereotypes. This was not one-sided but was framed as a process of mutual integration, 'it's about educating Traveller people and Gorjas alike' (Traveller man).

Only a few Gypsy and Traveller children and young people were in secondary school at the time of the research. Some young people had home education but this was only for a couple of hours a week. A number of reasons were given for young people's non-participation. There were examples of tensions stemming from a culture clash between home and school. Traveller pupils were often found to respond to racist name-calling by fighting back, which teachers tended to attribute to behaviour problems rather than recognising it as a racist incident,

> I remember getting called Gypsies by other school pupils and me sticking up for myself. And I am the one seen as being violent because I was sticking up for myself. (…) If you are telling them one thing and the school is telling them another thing then what do you do? We don't have bullying and that is one thing; our community doesn't like bullies, our community will go up to the bullies … I will be straight and honest with you, we will go up to the bullies, we will go and get people. (…) Because we were always taught don't wait for anyone to be the victim, don't be the victim, do not be the victim, if you want to be anyone

then you get up there and you give it back to them, don't you ever be a victim. We were never allowed to go home and say, "Mum, Dad, this boy hurt me", you were never allowed to say that. (Traveller mother).

Racist bullying has tended to become normalised as White against Black in school. As such racism against Whiteness is not acknowledged. Parents' own negative experiences with school provoked social distancing in the present day for their own children,

> Even now I don't blame my own children. I know my children and so I don't believe their teachers sometimes because of the experience of my own education. I know if my child is lying and I know when he is telling the truth and I am sorry to say but if my child tells me something and the teacher is saying something I will believe my child. (Traveller mother).

This was not helped by the fact that attention received from school was negative '...they were contacting me that many times, "he is not doing this right; he is not doing that right..." I was sick of them contacting me to be honest with you'. Memories of school were rooted in experiences of attending schools with very low proportions of Gypsy and Traveller children. These experiences had tended to emphasise ethnic 'difference' separating them from the 'normal',

> Travelling children I do not think get as much encouragement from schools when they are in education. I felt very much excluded from school when I was young and I feel this is still the case today. They don't feel like they are being made welcome and feel left out. When I first went to school I was taught in a separate classroom from the other children. This I think made it harder for myself and the rest of my cousins to fully communicate with the other children in school and outside in the playground. (Traveller man).

Specific structures such as specific classes or 'outreach workers' or 'inclusion workers' were being used but most were ineffective because of the patronising tone these took, 'No one knows the people better than ourselves. ... the workers are not Travelling people and they don't fetch Travelling people in'. Previous and current policy frameworks have had a negative impact and built a wall which continued into adulthood. Jonathan who returned to college in his late twenties continued to feel isolated within a single large institution,

> ...a few people found out I was a Gypsy. That was when all the typical stupid questions started. When some of my lecturers found out I was a Gypsy they definitely acted different towards me. I didn't receive as much encouragement as I did before they found out... and it was like they lost interest in what I was trying to do (Gypsy man).

These communities were very child-centred and very protective towards their children and extremely concerned about moral welfare. This brings about anxieties about the impact of social mixing in school. School with the presence of other children presents risky terrain for a number of reasons. Confrontation with a wider social mix could have negative effects on children's behaviour,

> You put two children together; one Gypsy and one from a council estate and that Gypsy child will talk like that council estate child within a week (…) the language of the children that do go to school is like, for example, "dickheads" is a big no go area, you just don't say "dickhead" in our community It is totally disrespectful (…) It is a horrible language. (Traveller mother).

Attending school meant cultural beliefs were compromised. Gender codes were compromised by school trips for instance and the teaching of sex education within school clashed with the cultural belief that unmarried teenagers should not be sexually active. There was also a sense of resentment about having to conform to the compulsory nature of schooling which imposes institutional rules which lie in direct contrast to the freedom of choice the community.

Finally Gypsy and Traveller parents suffered a lack of confidence in understanding the curriculum,

> I am very supportive of his education and I want to make sure that he is educated (…) Why would you give a child big boxes of homework to bring home when he is struggling with his homework. I just write on the letter "too hard, my child cannot do this". (…) Do you think I can read or write? Do you think I can do miracles? I am only barely starting my self, do you know what I mean? I am not confident. I can do it but I am not confident. You need more confidence. (Traveller mother).

For more recent migrants a similar pattern of issues has quickly developed. Families from Bosnia, the Czech Republic and Slovakia have arrived in this region in recent years and similar patterns of difficulty in making ends meet and non-attendance in school were evident. Action by Achievement Services and local Early Years Outreach Teams have been successful in boosting primary school attendance from almost nil to up to 70 per cent in some areas. Transforming inclusion at secondary level may prove much harder to achieve. Pride in their culture helps to protect these families from the shame and indignity of racist hostility in the street and racial discrimination in the labour market, but poverty and very low levels of employment are likely to persist for these families.

Conclusion

The study has shown how the non-participation of children from these groups in education is complex and multidimensional and related to a broad range of factors. This brings about a number of implications for policy and practice. First housing and site provision is a central issue which needs improving. The provision of good, safe and secure accommodation with facilities is viewed as one essential which would go some way to creating a strong sense of security and ease tensions. Second is to allow the community to decide for themselves what is appropriate to their needs. Parental engagement is vital and the provision of community led education would go some way to encourage more parents to become more involved.

Formal secondary education provision is simply not working for many children from these communities and an alternative curriculum may help to engage learners which relates to their own lives. This could be achieved through a flexible curriculum which reflects Gypsy and Traveller culture, history and lifestyle. A strong focus on remembering and sharing is empowering since it ensures culture is recognised, celebrated, valued and accepted. Expanding upon this there should be career development activities which specifically recognise that they have been successful in entering a range of professions and occupations.

There is a wealth of experience and skills within these communities which are not formally acknowledged through qualifications. Despite the potential skill base, the reality is that insufficient education within the community causes difficulties in accessing employment. With a supportive mentoring programme in place encouraging more people from the community to work in schools serving areas where there is a Gypsy and Traveller presence would go some way to tackling negative stereotypes bridging the gap.

Increasing the participation of Gypsy and Traveller children in secondary education must be an educational priority. The continued failure to arrest declining educational attainment requires a new creative national campaign to address literacy and generate aspirational capital amongst these communities, led by these communities with government, local authority and school support. Some local initiatives have shown that entrenched patterns of school non-attendance can be substantially transformed with effective outreach programmes but they remain marginal and insecure and it is vital to build on the success of targeted initiatives like the Achievement Service programmes and Early Years Outreach teams and also that schools show positive leadership and do not turn away these children due to concerns over absence figures. Empowerment of Gypsy and Traveller community organisations, adult mentors and securing involvement of families and parents is also vital in achieving this objective and overcoming 'deprecatory and antagonistic attitudes' towards education which are particularly prevalent amongst Gypsy and Traveller men (Levinson and Sparks 2003). Gypsy and Traveller parents' concerns about cultural erosion, safety and security of children and young people and their risk-avoidance strategies also need to be taken into account in the formation and development of educational interventions (Myers et al. 2010).

Chapter 5

Young People's Lives in Northcity: Gangs, Homes and Racism

Introduction

Gypsy, Roma and Traveller children are mainly not in secondary schooling, and the previous chapter looked at their experiences both inside and outside school. This chapter and the chapter to follow focus on African-Caribbean, Pakistani and White students and the role and significance of ethnicity in their everyday lives, how some students 'perform' their identities and how they see their lives and social worlds in Northcity. This city has over half a million inhabitants and a fairly typical pattern of ethnic diversity with an 11 per cent Black and minority ethnic population of which the Pakistani and African-Caribbean groups were the largest. This chapter draws on findings from the quantitative survey of 434 Year 10 pupils in three multicultural secondary schools in 2008/09 and the qualitative community studies carried out in 2009/2010 (Swann and Law 2009, 2010). The quantitative survey was carried out by Sarah Swann, who also carried out the bulk of the community study fieldwork. All the three schools had about one third minority ethnic pupils but varied widely in their intake from inner city areas (from 93 per cent, 68 per cent and 23 per cent respectively) and hence their socio-economic profile. These schools have been named Tannery Rise School, Proposal High and Jubilee School for the purposes of this study. The qualitative research included focus-group discussions and in-depth personal interviews with students, school personnel and parents, further interviews with community and educational informants, classroom observations, case studies of schools and minority ethnic groups and ethnographic fieldwork into youth and community cultures. The purpose of this stage of the research was to investigate the factors and motivations behind varying school performances and diverging educational careers, the impact of ethnicity on everyday life in school, experiences of being 'othered' and perceptions of identity.

This chapter begins with an introduction to the Northcity fieldwork location. The next section examines the significance of neighbourhood identities, postcode street gangs and the influence of 'gangsta' culture on school life. Focusing on the way particular neighbourhoods are layered with social meaning and social significance allows us to contextualise both the material conditions that have shaped students' individual identities and their perceptions and experiences of school life. The third section of this chapter explores young people's perceptions and experiences of home environments. Lastly this chapter examines the strength and significance of racism and racial stereotypes and the ways in which this external environment shaped school life.

Northcity

Due to its historically parochial setting the neighbourhood in which you live in Northcity is deeply associated with particular identities. This urban setting is shaped geographically by the hills and valleys which give a strong sense of spatial boundaries and separate communities and a series of urban villages, each having distinctive ethnic and social class characteristics. Northcity expanded and evolved at various periods with waves of new developments. Many neighbourhoods developed from villages and townships which were absorbed as Northcity grew in size. This physical environment goes some way to structuring social divisions and inequalities in poverty and wealth within the city. However it is important too to recognise that physical manifestations of social division are not static, but work in a dynamic process of flux as its residential populations shift through this urban ethnoscape. Unlike patterns of social segregation in other cities, Northcity cannot be so easily summarised as a dirty picture (socially deprived poor inner city areas) within a golden frame (affluent middle class suburbs lying on the outskirts). While this was once the case, Northcity in the twenty-first century looks broadly more asymmetric with affluent White middle class owner occupied households located in the south-west and social deprivation predominating in the north-east areas.

Recent studies have shown a broad understanding of 'neighbourhood effects' and how spatial concentration of disadvantage impacts on overall life chances (Buck and Gordan 2004, Burgess, Gardiner and Propper 2001, Thomas et al. Dorling 2009). In Northcity statistics from a number of sources reveal stark differences between the wealthy south-west areas and the deprived north-east. National Health Service (NHS) data shows a wide disparity between neighbourhoods in a number of health indicators such as smoking, life expectancy, breastfeeding rates, low birth weight babies and teenage pregnancy. Voting patterns also show differences in political allegiances by neighbourhood. Average price of properties for sale in the postcode area of the schools selected for this study differ vastly with similar residential properties in the south-west being on average three times as expensive as those in the north-east. Overall Northcity's residents are living in separate spheres and different worlds with different norms and different values, aspirations and goals. From this perspective Northcity is a microcosm of the social divides which run through British society at large. Although the cityscape does not appear to show a coherent divide as studies of other cities have implied with a distinct 'faultline', Northcity remains highly segregated along socioeconomic and ethnic lines and its residents have a deep understanding of where physical (as well as psychological and social) boundaries lie.

There is not sufficient space to set the scene of the city as a whole here, rather that has been done in some depth elsewhere (Swann and Law 2010) so focus shall be on the key areas where the pupils of the study lived. In the north-east lying close to the city centre is the district of Brunsmere which has a high concentration of Black Minority Ethnic (BME) groups. Approximately 40 per cent of the residential population is in owner occupation. The area provides social and rented housing stock predominantly to low income groups including asylum seekers and immigrants before they move on to other areas and has significant levels of deprivation. Brunsmere feeds into all three schools and is widely viewed as a risky and unsafe neighbourhood with its associations of drug-dealing and shootings. The concentration of a Safer Neighbourhoods[1] team, community wardens,[2] the presence of drug and domestic violence support projects and CCTV contribute to the stigma. There is a small number of White middle-class residents who have self-selected to live in Brunsmere and this is contrasted further on in this chapter with the White middle classes of the south-west.

The physical geography of Brunsmere in the 1800s plays a significant factor in the development of its social geography today. The north-east was suitable for heavy industrial development because it was a flat area of land close to a river. In response to international demand giant new factories were erected in the east of the city which had a startling effect on the landscape. Reports on the conditions of Northcity at this time show social and living conditions for the working classes were extremely harsh. Like all Victorian industrial towns of the period it had a reputation of being grimy and unsanitary on account of the dense smoke which enveloped the city. Industrial activity required cheap labour and slum housing was built to accommodate the factory workers. These were tightly packed rows of houses adjacent to the factories and situated in close proximity to the noise, smell, smoke and dust. The worst sort was 'back to back' housing which saved space and building costs. These houses were arranged around yards with communal outside toilets. Half of the houses faced on to the yard, the other half directly onto the street. Living conditions were intolerably cramped. Some of these had just one room downstairs which functioned as kitchen, living room and bathroom. Overall poor living areas and the absence of ventilation resulted in epidemics of disease. Affluent visitors who wrote about their time in Northcity were scathing viewing it as a filthy, stinking and savage place.

The period following World War 1 marked the beginning of progressive planning and house building nationally. In Northcity there was large-scale postwar slum housing clearance from the inner city and this replaced slum housing in the 1950s

---

1   Safer Neighbourhoods teams were established to tackle 'local' problems of crime and disorder in particular neighbourhoods. Teams consist usually of a sergeant, constables and police community support officers.

2   Community wardens are ordinary citizens who have been appointed to provide a uniformed presence on the streets, parks and open spaces of particular areas. They do not have the same powers as the Police but deal with low level crime such as antisocial behaviour, criminal damage and noise and neighbour nuisance. See Johnston's (2003) discussion of the scheme.

and 1960s with burgeoning low density satellite housing developments dispersed in the suburbs. Spreading out from Brunsmere are areas of social (council and housing association) housing including Tannery Rise. These are semi-detached houses with gardens to the front and rear. They are arranged in geometrical patterns, with circles and crescents and parallel streets. The aspiration of these developments was to create a strong sense of community through the 'garden suburb' ideal with wide open spaces.[3] Many of these developments have easy access to municipal parks and green spaces which physically is the polar opposite of the earlier suffocating industrial landscape. Public perceptions of these areas however remain highly negative associated with White lower class problems of high rates of unemployment, a reputation of anti-social behaviour and poor school performance. This is unsurprising as most people can identify a council estate by its layout so it becomes an emblem of low social status (Hanley 2007). The council estates gradually disperse into more affluent middle class suburbs and furthest afield in the north is the old parish of Endswood which set in open countryside has in parts a traditional rural character.

The south-west forms the catchment for Jubilee School and is composed of the wealthiest suburbs in Northcity. Covering the rural fringe it has a diverse choice of property ranging from large detached nineteenth-century mansions to modern flats. The neighbourhoods within this district are marked out in varying ways. The oldest and wealthiest neighbourhood of Bramsford is marked by classical architectural style buildings made from stone. Although most of the south-west is leafy, the mature trees in both streets and gardens of this suburb serve to differentiate it from the younger suburbs and terraced housing areas (which would have once housed the Victorian middle class clerks). Although the south-west is mainly an affluent White middle-class residential area there are distinct pockets of deprivation. For instance at the bottom of The Golden Mile lie dilapidated tower blocks which paradoxically directly face a prestigious development of luxury apartments and a Waitrose[4] supermarket.

Interest must also briefly turn to how this privilege is codified in White people's perceptions in Northcity since White middle class students are the 'ideal' materials for schools in providing high academic attainment levels. The focus here is on the White middle-classes in the south-west of the city since some of the neighbourhoods here provide the catchment for Jubilee School. In the early 1800s the factory owners (the newly formed middle class) were practical men experienced in local trades whose social ambitions were to appear important. They named their factories after volcanoes or significant mythological figures and built fine large houses in the higher south-west facing slopes of the city

---

3   Much of the developments planned in Northcity as well as policy at regional and national level today has replicated these same notions. Twenty-first century rhetoric talks about creating 'sustainable communities' which are well connected.

4   Waitrose is a brand popular with the middle classes. It is associated with high quality groceries and has a reputation for being expensive.

upwind of the pollution from the smoke stacks of the east and close to beautiful natural surroundings such as ancient woodland. Wealthy middle class residents concerned with the lack of public open space bought land and made it into formal botanical gardens with glass pavilions which remain there today. The middle class perception of the time was to find 'rational recreation' activities which would improve and make respectable the lower classes by thwarting their times in pubs. The idea of a healthy mind in a healthy body was promoted through activities designed to improve contact between the social classes through pride and competition although it is likely these were '...tinged with the patronising air of Lady Bountiful' (Fraser 1980: 468).

The legacy of the formation of the White middle classes in Northcity and with it an anxious sense of class consciousness in the Victorian era remains today. A high proportion of White middle class residents in the south-west are employed in public sector roles and some of what happens today can be seen to replicate the moralistic notions of the Victorian middle classes especially in terms of widening access to education and cultural interests. For instance, BookStart[5] is a national charity primarily aimed at 'hard to reach' families with the aims of enhancing literacy skills, developing imagination, and curiosity. Although the aims are those of social justice, there nonetheless remains a distinctive moralistic White middle class undertone.

The south-west of the city remains the greenest in the city with well managed, safe parks and woodlands hosting many events and recreation activities. These tend to be White and middle class in nature, for instance the 'music in the gardens' event plays hosts big band, jazz, classical and opera. Jubilee Park hosts a traditional duck race which is promoted as a fun family event. Proceeds raised went towards the restoration of a locally-based water wheel, a remnant of Northcity's past before industry. Some BME communities have become involved in these events. For instance at the local farmers' market the stall-holders were predominantly White, selling organic fruit boxes, local farm produce, and local ales but there was also a Pakistani food stall and art sold by Brunsmere art group (predominantly African-Caribbean women). When there is significant 'ethnic' input, the tendency is for it to have an 'on trend' focus. For instance world music equates to Cuban, which stems from the scene of Cuban bars in the city centre.

This differs from the small group of White middle class residents who lived in Brunsmere. Much like the White middle-class parents described in Crozier et al.'s study (2008: 261), these parents too were, 'caught in a web of moral ambiguity, dilemmas and ambivalence, trying to perform "the good/ethical self" while ensuring the "best" for their children'. In discussions they tended to emphasise the positive points of Brunsmere in terms of a collective neighbourhood of 'diversity' which brought benefits. In doing so, they conceptualised their choice of living in Brunsmere in terms of moral and political principles but tension arose from the existence of 'outside' negative perceptions of Brunsmere. For instance one parent

---

5   http://www.bookstart.org.uk/Home.

described how angry he felt when he tried to advertise a room in his house to rent to students at the university and he was refused on the grounds that it was an 'unsafe' neighbourhood.

In recent years and consistent with national trends,[6] a number of markers signal a return to traditional White England and the values it represents. Play performances in the park are Shakespeare and literary classics such as The Railway Children. There are also quintessentially 'English' activities like a 'picnic in the park' event. Alongside the hairdressers aimed at the fashion conscious on the Golden Mile there remains traditional Barber shops with the red and white striping. The café in Jubilee Park displays a copy of one of the mass produced vintage posters popularised in merchandise[7] and a couple of children have been seen wearing the 'Keep Calm and Carry On' T shirts. New social spaces have arisen through local knitting groups, cake decorating classes and book clubs. In consumer production, antique shops sell distinctive statement pieces which have been renovated using traditional crafts or 'antiques in a modern world'.[8] The use of allotments have grown in popularity which is shown in the fact that the ones located close to Jubilee School have a year-long waiting list. Many south-west neighbourhoods host traditional street parties, which traditionally used to happen to commemorate major events but now are used as a way to get to reclaim a (lost) sense of community. This is viewed by some commentators as a response to the recession and a backlash against traditional capitalism with individuality and uniqueness over conformity and uniformity. The word subversive was used earlier because although the White middle classes of Northcity tend to view themselves as proactive agents tinged with eccentricity, they are startlingly alike in their claims for individuality. Their endeavours towards 'grow your own' and 'make do and mend' are to some degree the projections of the austerity of the war years, but symbolic too of something deeper which has been felt to be lost. Running in parallel to this White middle class identity is also a European flavour which offers a wider sense of 'culture'. The Golden Mile, which is a main artery road running from the edge of the centre to the suburban outskirts has French cafes, Italian coffee houses, trendy bars, boutique shops stocking Italian high end designers and patisseries. While it holds traditional values close, it also shows emerging progressive values which is seen in the new formation of fathers' baby groups.

---

6   The trend is apparent in heritage fashion. Vogue ran an article entitled 'Homing Instinct' documenting how 'in an unexpected style shift, a feel for the familiar is weaving its way through catwalks, interiors and furniture' (2010: 314). Cultural events like the 'Not the Knitting you Know' exhibition use traditional knitting and crocheting techniques to create art pieces.

7   A World War II propaganda poster devised by the Ministry of Information in 1939 was discovered in a bookshop and has since been used in various merchandise. See B. Lewis' (2004) discussion.

8   This probably stems directly from Kirsty Allsop's 'Homemade Home' show which was a popular television series.

Seen from a sociological perspective and spending time immersed in Northcity's south-west neighbourhoods show middle-class White tastes and the cultural attitudes these embody are muddling. First the emphasis is on uniqueness but as Lawler (2005: 429) states this 'is only achieved through an incorporation of collective, classed understandings'. These choices conjure up notions of sentimentality which is crucial to the White middle-class negotiation of class difference. Despite the emphasis on ethical consumerism much of middle class White-identity perpetuates capitalism. Mass consumerism and wealth is on show in the form of the 'yummy mummies' wearing babies in papooses and pushing Quinny or Mamas and Papas prams. Children wear Croc shoes, polka dot raincoats and striped jersey tops. It also capitalises on ethical food choices so fair-trade, organic produce and healthy choices are the norm.

Postcode gangs and gangsta culture

Neighbourhood location, postcode gangs and masculine 'gangsta' culture were imported into everyday school life and undermined educational attainment. The quantitative survey showed that pupils perceived bullying to occur mainly between pupils living in different neighbourhoods. This was the case for 50 per cent of African-Caribbean pupils, 33 per cent of Pakistani pupils and 36 per cent of White pupils. On this measure, there was variation between schools. Pupils attending Proposal High were least likely to report any bullying between pupils living in different neighbourhoods at 21 per cent. Jubilee School and Tannery Rise School which had a higher pupil catchment from Brunsmere scored 37 per cent and 42 per cent respectively. Bullying between pupils of different social backgrounds was most apparent at Jubilee School with 43 per cent of pupils perceiving this as a problem compared with 18 per cent at Proposal High and 28 per cent at Tannery Rise School. This can be explained by the fact Jubilee School had by far the most diverse social class intake so difference on this basis would be more stark.

Overall pupils saw their neighbourhoods as an important context and unpacking respondents' perceptions and experiences of where the boundaries around particular places lie emerged as an important identity activity. Neighbourhoods are made up of people and communities in places and there is great stability and cohesion in familiar settings. At Tannery Rise School, Pakistani respondents felt uncomfortable being in Tannery Rise after school hours because this meant waiting at the bus stop which brought about the threat of physical and verbal abuse from the White community. This shaped their decisions about whether to stay for after school clubs. How respondents felt about their area depended on knowledge, experiences and acquaintances. At different stages, the meaning of places seemed to change considerably. For instance, Shauna, an 11 year old girl attending Proposal High, enjoyed the freedom to explore her neighbourhood through streets and open spaces whereas her mother saw this as being unsafe, dangerous and unpredictable.

There was a tendency for parents to view the neighbourhood as an important factor in constructing their children's futures. This was explained by the social composition of particular areas. One Pakistani mother who was an active member of the Parent Teacher Association (PTA) distinguished between 'good' parenting and 'bad' parenting,

> I think it is the areas. I am not saying there are not any problems at the other side of Northcity, yes there are problems everywhere but there are a lot more problems in the inner-city areas because of the behaviour and the parents not spending enough time with their children, not communicating with them enough. They need to interact more with the children and get to know them more. I am on the PTA at the school and at the school there must be well over 300 pupils and at the PTA there are 14-15 parents of children that turn up to that meeting. I know language is a barrier but we have done our best to try and get parents in. (Pakistani mother).

The social composition of the wider neighbourhood was often reflected in the local schools. The expected factors influenced parents' choice of secondary school: GCSE attainment, distance and reputation. The first thing which stood out in the parent interviews was the extent of education literacy. Parents who had themselves been through the British education system understood more about the distinctions between schools. Those Pakistani parents which had had negotiated entry into the 'better' schools had relied on information gained from other family members. These parents made a strong distinction between inner city schools characterised by behaviour problems and the schools situated in the affluent south-west of the city which were characterised as safer places. One Pakistani parent described the experiences of her younger daughter who attended a local Junior school in Brunsmere,

> ... I am not very happy with her teaching because half of the time is spent on sorting out children with behaviour problems. Until about 10 o'clock in the morning the teacher spends time on the children with behaviour problems so my child and other children that aren't misbehaving are missing out on that valuable education, that is what I get most upset with. That when you go to the Head of the School, "Yes but this certain child's got problems". Everybody has got problems but things need to be done; that child shouldn't be in that environment; they need to be in an environment that is suitable for that child (...) My daughter... at the school that she is at... she has been pushed down the stairs, slammed in to a door. She has been pushed down the stairs, slammed in to a door... She has had those big block things that they play with in the playground thrown at her... (Pakistani mother).

She contrasts this with the experience of her son who attends Jubilee School,

...where my son goes is fantastic, good communication, they let you know everything and anything. I have only ever once had a problem and that is when a child actually punched my son because he got him mistaken for somebody else. They rang me straight away, they called the other child's parents straight away and they excluded that child.

The idea of certain schools presenting risky terrain was a common feature of interviews with both parents and pupils. One high achieving girl reflected on the prospect of attending the low achieving Brenton School in the south east of the city. Although it was nearer to her home, the school represented disorder which made her feel vulnerable,

That has a really bad reputation. They have changed their name to Academy[9] and they are trying to get better, but I really didn't want to go. I mean most of my friends went there and one of my friends did get hurt by someone there and then it made me feel that I did not want to go ... I definitely didn't want to go there. (Pakistani Year 10 girl).

Presented with the option of enrolling at the high achieving Jubilee School in the south-west of the city she went because it 'is quite high in education and it is good and I didn't want to get a bad education so I agreed to moving'.

Choice of school also resulted in wider educational opportunities such as exchange visits to France and Germany. There was a difference in how Pakistani parents viewed these experiences. Among parents who were active in school life, they were positive opportunities,

...it is independence for them and it is inner-growth for them as well for them to be independent because I am not going to be around forever for my children so they need to be self-reliant as well. (Pakistani mother).

Another analytical strand of identity and place lay with belonging and memory through public sites. This gave an interesting angle on how ethnic identities mesh and intersect with spatial location. The material culture of Northcity's industrial past seemed to resonate with Pakistani respondents as interviews and conversations often highlighted their family's individual, and also the collective input that the Pakistani community had in Northcity's past. For one high achieving Pakistani girl her connection to Northcity was deeply rooted in narratives of her grandfather's working life in heavy industry. When shopping in the shopping centre in the east of the city, her presence in Northcity today was materialised through a statue

---

9   Academies were introduced to target long term patterns of underachievement and behavioural problems specific to certain schools. Independent of local government control, schools with Academy status are funded by sponsors. The introduction of Academies did meet with opposition from a number of people including politicians, teachers and teachers' unions.

which for her reanimated her grandfather's past life and created for her a sense of meaning,

> It's like my Granddad came and he was a worker in Northcity Works. And you know in (names local shopping centre) where they have the statues of the iron men and we walked past there and my Auntie goes, 'that's your Granddad there', and the reason why she said that is because people that came from hot countries and middle eastern countries, like India, Pakistan and Bangladesh, they could stand in heat like that so that is why most of them jobs were given to Asian people. (..) Yes most of them jobs were for Asian people because Asian people could stand that heat of working in an area of humidity like that, so that is why. (Pakistani girl).

A statue memoralising workers from Northcity's industrial past contextualises this girl's ethnicity identity and her presence in England in a positive way. The forms that connect pupils to neighbourhoods, to cities, to England then may seem trivial at surface level but the underlying thread of belonging is significant. Here we see how her aunt instigates this dialogue with a seemingly innocuous object. The family plays an important role in preserving a sense of rooted connection and 'cultural imagination'.

The physical divide between neighbourhoods was entrenched further through the existence of postcode gangs in the wider community. An important part of identity for both African-Caribbean and Pakistani pupils and particularly for boys was bound up with allegiance to area, 'It's basically if you live in Northcity4 you are with Northcity4, if you live in Northcity3 you are with Northcity3'. It was physically evident in graffiti around the schools which as an act prompted competition,

> ...there is 'Northcity4' and 'Northcity5' written all over, then someone writes across 'Northcity3', then some people put threats up, then someone crosses that off and puts 'Northcity4'. It's all over. (African-Caribbean Year 10 girl).

Outside school pupils would also wear coloured bandannas to symbolise their allegiance. This was not permitted in school and was more of an issue at Prospect High and Tannery Rise School. At Jubilee School, pupils living in the south-west of the city were not involved in it. The issue of postcode gangs frequently emerged in discussions with both boys and girls. An African-Caribbean girl explained what would happen if she walked into rival gang territory,

> So if I walked into Northcity3 with a green bandanna on, I would probably get knocked out for wearing a green bandanna in a Black bandanna area. And if a Black bandanna came into a green bandanna area the Black bandanna would get banged for wearing a Black bandanna in a green bandanna area and same with all of them. (African-Caribbean girl).

Trying to ascertain whether postcode gangs were linked to ethnicity got mixed responses. For some it was associated with ethnic minorities only. It was something between Pakistanis, Somalis and Yeminis. White pupils were often viewed as posing empty threats, 'I don't think there are any White people involved (there are people in Tannery Rise) that joke about it but they won't actually (go ahead and fight)' (African-Caribbean Year 10 boy). White pupils at Tannery Rise School did however align themselves to the Northcity3 gang.

Overall much of this was bound up with ideas of 'hard' masculinity and involvement in gangs marked the transition to adulthood. It was a way to assert identity but the seriousness of the implications of this can however not be underestimated since there had been shootings in Brunsmere linked to gang wars. Visual reminders of this were very much evident, 'If you walk past the barbers now when the shutters are down you can see the bullet holes'.

The seriousness of the implications of this can however not be underestimated. A Pakistani boy, reflected in depth about a boy he had been close to in the early years of secondary school who had chosen a different path to him. The seriousness of the implications of this can however not be underestimated. This boy was the oldest in his family with a cousin whom he looked up to who he described as 'kind of a geek' and who influenced him to go down the academic path. The other boy's life had gone down a different route. He was a regular drug user (cannabis).

> Yes now with the postcode thing people are fighting more. That guy, (..), who got shot I knew him and he basically forgot about his school work (…) He got shot outside the barbers. If you walk past the barbers now when the shutters are down you can see the bullet holes. (Pakistani Year 10 boy).

Pupil's involvement in postcode gangs cut across disaffected and conformist identities within school. Schools were sensitive to the issues surrounding postcode gangs and some had taken a clear stance of zero tolerance,

> One of my friends got in to a fight with this other guy because he lived in Northcity4 and he lived in Tannery Rise so they just started to fight and the head teacher told them both, "if anything like this happens again you are both going to get kicked out". (Pakistani Year 10 boy).

Seeing what happened provided pupils with a sense of a protective identity buffer,

> …most of my friends they don't want to go down that path, they want to do well, they have got big ideas for their lives. So when you think about that and you think about how stupid it is and how you can lose your life. (Pakistani Year 10 boy).

It served as a stark reminder of what a Pakistani mother said, 'If you have not got your mind over matter you can get pulled in to things but it is your choice (…) you go the right way or the wrong way'. However the potential for a shooting retaliation remained,

> Yes but in some ways like I know that his cousins are wanting to get revenge (..) I am not scared because I know that I have got friends who live in the inner-city or are in the gang but I don't fight for anything. (Pakistani Year 10 boy).

Much of this seems to be a pathway into adulthood. Involvement in gangs marked the transition to adulthood. It was a way to assert identity and masculinity. Girls were not involved to the same extent. Much discourse drew on references to knives. Discourse was highly animated drawing on action. Everyday talk referenced 'knocking' or 'banging' people 'out'.

> My cousin knocked all of them out, one punch and knocked all of them out. Then one guy when he was on the floor, my cousin was punching him and he stabbed him and was about to die, blood was coming out of him. (…) He was still punching him and he said, "stop, stop he is going to die". Then in the next few weeks the guy's brother … because he told him and he chased them in to his house, his brother came out of the back garden, he ran in to his back garden and my cousin ran in to his back garden to bang him out. He went home, called his sister and his sister had a baseball bat and tried to hit him and my cousin knocked him out. Then they were all trying to hit my cousin but my cousin jumped over the wall and tripped and after they had machetes and everything. Then after they have been looking for that guy but they haven't found him. … They were all Somalis and then another day they came back with knives, there was lots of Somalis and my cousin was with them and none of the Somalis stuck up for him, only one Somali stuck up for him and there was about 200 of the other guys. Then after they were fighting my cousin and none of the Somalis stuck up my cousin, they all backed out and just the one Somali helped him. My cousin got stabbed and this other Pakistani was wiping my cousins' head and he was saying, 'come on you are going to die, you are going to die', and my cousin was still there punching them and he hit all of them and one guy just stabbed him with a knife. Then my brother was going to bang one out, my brother came to pick me up, he said, "you stay in the car", I said, "I am jumping in with you". (Pakistani Year 10 boy).

Chaotic home environments

Family life is becoming unstable due to long-term social and cultural change. As such people's lives are complex carrying an array of potential emotional, social and psychological baggage not only on individual pupils but on families as a whole. The diversity in family structure was difficult to capture in the design of the questionnaire as expressed by one informant, 'You've not given enough Q's for if you live with two families. You dunno which one to choose to write about' (White Year 10 boy).

Overall, the majority of respondents in the survey lived with both their biological parents which was more than the general statistics would indicate which may loosely connect with the fact more pupils assessed their home situation as 'rather good'. This was the case for 78 per cent of Pakistani and 57 per cent of White pupils. 40 per cent of African-Caribbean young people in the sample lived with both parents. 25 per cent lived with only their mother and 10 per cent split their time between families, which sometimes included half-siblings or step siblings. The inner city areas where African-Caribbean pupils predominantly lived had a high proportion of single parent families which has a direct bearing on income.

28 per cent of inner city pupils had parents who had divorced compared with 19 per cent of those living on the outskirts. African-Caribbean pupils were by far the most likely to have parents who had divorced, but surprisingly one seventh of all Pakistani pupils had divorced parents. This compares to 23 per cent of all White pupils. At 34 per cent Tannery Rise School had the highest proportion of pupils whose parents had divorced (compared to 27 per cent at Proposal High and 17 per cent at Jubilee School).

Results from the survey indicate that the occurrence of some events is in association with the family's social situation. At a basic level, the number of pupils reporting a devastating experience varied by school and pupils' residential area. Jubilee School which had the most privileged catchment tended to come out 'best' overall in dramatic measures. To provide a brief snapshot 8 per cent of those living in the inner city areas were forced to leave their home. This was more likely to happen to African-Caribbeans at 17 per cent, followed by Pakistanis at 11 per cent. This was most likely to happen to pupils at Tannery Rise School with 15 per cent compared to 9 per cent at Jubilee School and 5 per cent at Proposal High.

Pupils living in the outskirts were more likely to have a parent who had been made unemployed (16 per cent compared to 8 per cent of pupils in the inner city). At 11 per cent more White pupils had parents who had been made unemployed than Pakistani (7 per cent) and African-Caribbean (7 per cent) pupils. This was more of a common occurrence at Jubilee School with 12 per cent compared to 9 per cent and 10 per cent at Proposal High and Tannery Rise respectively. This may be a consequence of the fact unemployment in the UK as a whole has increased dramatically in recent months and this is said to have had a greater impact on middle class white collar workers unlike the 1980s recession which mainly affected manufacturing jobs.

7 per cent of pupils living in the inner city compared with 11 per cent living on the outskirts had a parent who became ill or disabled. Debt featured equally among all ethnic groups, with an average of 7 per cent of respondents saying this was a problem. 5 per cent of pupils in the inner city had suffered a bereavement

of a close family member compared to 2 per cent living on the outskirts. This was nearly five times more likely for Pakistani pupils.

Do these factors affect educational outcomes? Unemployment does not significantly appear to have an adverse effect. Pupils scoring throughout the level bandings was relatively equal. Divorce does in the sense that pupils achieving the upper echelons of attainment – levels 7 and 8 – were significantly more likely not to have been exposed to divorce. Perhaps this is because unemployment is viewed as a temporary issue whereas divorce can have a detrimental impact on young people's lives for years to come.

The community study yielded a richer tapestry of pupils' life worlds beyond school. Among the African-Caribbean community there was felt to be a generation divide. The first generation of African-Caribbean immigrants were now grandmothers and grandfathers. They often lamented the loss of respect among youth in society overall. They had raised their children under strict rules. This stemmed from the traditional structures brought from the Caribbean. The expressed anxiety and insecurity about their own children's future.

Similarly some Pakistani parents were anxious for their children to hold on to cultural traditions. Throughout the community religion was an integral component of this but the extent to which this dictated a family's way of life was on a continuum. At one level some parents viewed Muslim religious instruction as taking precedent. Their children went to mosque every day after school. This resulted in limited free time. Many interpreted the rules strictly and did not allow their daughters to go on trips (for instance on one residential course two Pakistani girls were fine but the coordinator needed to spend considerable time persuading the father of a Somali girl). The trip also coincided with exams at mosque which could not be missed.

The majority of pupils and parents interviewed lived in areas of high social deprivation and the circumstances of some families were extremely complex and difficult, for example hard pressed White mothers living on council estates with absent Black fathers not on the scene. One interview with an African-Caribbean girl highlighted socio-economic disadvantage and indicators of poverty through the life history narrative. A number of risk factors were revealed which seemed to both emerge from and contribute to the emotional and economic climate within the home. Louise[10] lived between homes, sometimes with her maternal grandparents and sometimes with her White mother. Her mother had been a heroin addict for a number of years and had worked as a prostitute. She had spent time in respite centres. As such Louise's childhood was extremely chaotic with a host of detrimental experiences which she felt directly impinged on her receptiveness to schooling and education.

---

10   Psuedonyms have been used throughout the report to preserve the anonymity of respondents.

> She used to be a prostitute. I used to see all the different … I used to see some
> right rubbish. One time she had this guy look after me and he wouldn't let me
> go to the toilet so I was like … I had to do a wee in the corner of my room so he
> rubbed my face in it. So then when my Mum came back I told her. And then I
> saw this guy just knocking her about in the kitchen, because there was only like
> that much space between to two cupboards, so this guy had just got her head
> going 'bang, bang, bang' against the two cupboards, it was mad, it was weird,
> proper crazy. (African-Caribbean Year 10 girl).

Growing up in an environment with frequent exposure to domestic violence
brought about intense feelings of frustration and helplessness. Some of these
problems meant that Louise was taking on adult responsibilities from a very young
age such as making meals. Recollection of memories brought about a sense of
grave sadness,

> I used to have to make my own breakfast and stuff when I was three I was making
> cups of tea and stuff, but yeah I spilt Rice Krispies and milk once and I got a
> right slap for it. One time my Mum was drugged out in bed with a Black man
> and I was three. And I knew my Nan's address, phone number and everything. I
> had one shoe on and one sock on the other foot. I had my pram with my doll in
> my pram, the doll was more wrapped up than me …. (African-Caribbean Year
> 10 girl).

There was a tendency for some disaffected girls to mark the transition to adulthood
in harmful ways as other studies have reported. In Louise's case, there were a
cluster of complex interconnected issues, but in her words, 'I kind of like did all
my adult stuff, like ages go when I was thirteen'. At the age of 12 she had a 23
year old boyfriend.[11] By 16 she had two police cautions. One was for carrying
a weapon in a public place. The other was for aggressive behaviour. At the root
seemed to be the intense sense of loss of her mother which she often experienced
as rejection. In her interview she described two mothers, almost a Jekyll and Hyde
characterisation. On one hand was her 'ideal' mother who engaged her in family
times,

> Off drugs she was just amazing. When I used to go see her on Saturdays and the
> first time I saw her I was like, "I don't want to go". I was only allowed to see
> her for an hour. And then when I went to see her and everything it was just like
> …, she was healthy, she looked healthy, she was cooking meals everyday. (…)So
> she would just take us like … one time we went swimming, one time we went
> to the fair, one time she took us to the pictures, it was awesome, it really was.
> (African-Caribbean Year 10 girl).

---

11   School was fully aware of home circumstances and she was on the Child Protection
Register.

The other side was the drug addicted mother who 'from being a kid she was just horrible to me'. Although she recognised that her mother's behaviour resulted from the effects of drug abuse, it caused huge emotional stress within Louise and investing her energy resources in work at school simply was not a luxury she could choose. One of Louise's teachers whom she had worked with since Y7 in the inclusion unit, confided that her behaviour problems had always increased when she lived with her mother. There were no firm boundaries in place so she and her younger sisters were allowed to stay up until as late as they liked listening to music and drinking alcohol. Extended family however provided some structure and protection. Louise went through periods where she felt relief and stability and experienced consistency as a result of living with her grandparents,

> When I was five my nan got a residence order for me! I had finally got away. My mum was sent to prison and I had got a home where I knew I could be myself and didn't have to worry about random drug addicts, who my mum used to let look after me so she could go and get money for her next fix, and the police knocking on the door. (Extract from Louise's English coursework).

She framed her grandparents as functioning through traditional gender role stereotypes so her grandmother is described as fulfilling the role of nurturer. In Louise's words she described her nan as 'one of them old wise owls (…) She knows what to say at the right times … she knows me page by page, she really does'. Her grandfather is described as a source of patriarchal power through his predictability of routine which served as an irritant but also as a source of protection,

> …my Granddad's right grumpy (laughs). He's proper one of them old fashioned, old men. "Shush the televisions on; I'm watching my programmes".(…) "Shush I am on the phone", but when I'm on the phone he can talk, it's right annoying. And "be in for half past ten because I am locking the gate, lights are going off …" the curtains get closed at half past six. (African-Caribbean Year 10 girl).

Her grandparents had set boundaries but these were simple and deemed reasonable by Louise, '…the only rules I've got is; respect my Nan and Granddad, be in when they tell me to and just go to School. Not bad really is it?' Sticking to these rules was a way of showing her grandparents respect. However dealing with ongoing problems and coping with a host of different stresses, meant that Louise started truanting heavily in Year 9. Before long she was in a cycle where the more she missed school, the harder it would be to catch up,

> I was like "I can't be arsed to go to School", too many people were coming up to me saying "oh why haven't you been in School.?" Do you know what I mean I don't think I could have coped with it? (…) That's what I thought there is no point in even trying to go to School because I am so behind with everything, I had missed like two years. (African-Caribbean Year 10 girl).

The reality was that by escaping the humdrum reality of school routine Louise was making herself more isolated and less integrated into social networks with peers. Her truancy lasted for two years and she returned in Year 11, a crucial academic year which sets post-16 pathways. Despite the personal constraints she had to battle through during this period, emphasis was very much placed on the role of individual agency rather than placing blame on mitigating circumstances. In her interview Louise stated simply that 'I messed it all up' which projects the belief that she has caused her own educational failure. From this statement it is possible to see how education is inextricably bound up with self worth and confidence.

Gaining some understanding of young people's identities requires examining their social and emotional worlds. Another White mother was worried that her youngest child, a daughter aged 11 was already going off the rails. Shauna refused to listen to her mother. She would throw everything from her bedroom down the stairs including a large mirror. Her mother felt hugely overwhelmed and felt she had lost control. As a single mother, the impact of Shauna's behaviour had affected the extended family. One of Shauna's brothers refused to visit when Shauna was there as he did not like the way in which she treated their mother. She had got psychological interventions from Child and Adolescent Mental Health services (CAMHS) but none of these had proved ineffective. Shauna and her mother had been exposed to violence from her father although he had died two years previously. The legacy of the abuse was very much evident with the mother. In her interview the mother stated, 'she's just like him', referring to Shauna's father. She had come to understand Shauna's behavioural problems as innate through the mechanism of projection. Imagining that Shauna had inherited the attributes of her father is a classic defence position which functioned to mask her own feelings of 'failing' as a mother. She reflected that even as a toddler Shauna was 'different' from her two older sons.

While it would be simple to blame single mothers and the absence of fathers, this alone does not explain diverging pathways in education. Young people participate in a range of social and emotional worlds through which they form and reform their identities. Although the word 'loneliness' was never used, the underlying feeling was that some people felt a deep sense of disconnection from family, community and the bigger world. They were locked in a web of tangled constraining circumstances. Although the focus is on African-Caribbean and Pakistani communities, it is important to recognise that the problems are also apparent in White working class and middle class communities. For instance the issue of parents going through a painful divorce came up a couple of times among White middle class girls when conducting the survey.

This chapter considers how pupils respond to the social boundaries that collective ethnic identities create and in doing so sheds light on subjectivities. Respondents differentiated identities through a number of means. Ethnic identity connected strongly with roots. When asked about what he wanted to do in his adult life one Caribbean boy said,

> Set up here and then move to the Caribbean. Then I would set up a business in the Caribbean. That is my heritage I think. (African-Caribbean Year 10 boy).

The Caribbean was innately connected to identity and this was about connecting with their family's place of origin. The Caribbean appealed to pupils' imaginations. With its tropical climate, reggae, rastas, national flag, and national food it inspired exciting folklore. They had heard about it through family stories and also in the curriculum. Year 10s and Year 11s were covering the 'Poems from Different Cultures' segment for their GCSE exams and there was a poem called 'Island Man' (Grace Nichols) which is about a man from the Caribbean who has moved to London. The poem is extremely visual in its imagery. In this sense ethnicity provided a core part of identity. One dual heritage mother speaking at the Caribbean community meetings in Brunsmere said she had been raised with a White mother and Black father. Her White mother was proactive in helping her understand her roots by cooking Caribbean food at home such as ackee and salt fish. This she equated to her mother's middle class social positioning.

On the other hand, parents' actions had very damaging consequences for some young people. Louise, whose mother was White was very aware of the impressions people had of her as a result of her White mother's past,

> People say to me "oh I feel right sorry for you, your Mum's done this" and everything and I just say "well at the end of the day I don't need you to feel sorry for me, yeah all that has happened but I have come out a better person". I want to do everything that my Mum didn't. I want to prove to all them people that said I was going to grow up to be like my Mum. People on my road used to say it from me being like seven "oh she's going to turn out like her Mum". I am going to prove it to everybody that I am not just...don't...what's that word? What's that word? Stereotype, yes, don't stereotype me, do you know what I mean? Just because my Mum is how she is it doesn't mean I am going to be like that. I am going to prove to all them people that I can do it, I am going to do it and they were wrong, all them people that said "she's not going to make it" and I am going to prove them all wrong because one day they are going to see me and they are going to be like "well done her, she did it, we were wrong and she did the best for herself." (African-Caribbean Year 10 girl).

Challenging the perceived self-fulfilling prophecy went some way to reclaiming power.

A key issue with dual heritage Caribbean pupils who had one White parent and one Black was how to reconcile the two. All dual heritage pupils within this study identified themselves as Black. A 'typical' response was 'I would say I am Black really. (...) I don't know why, it is just I have always said that really' (African-Caribbean girl, Proposal High). Some sought to clarify their response by locating themselves in terms of exposure to other family members,

> I don't know it is just like because I don't really know my dad's side of the family because I only go see my dad's mum like twice a year. But because I have grown up with my mum's side if the family it is all Black people so that is just how I have been brought up. (African-Caribbean Year 10 girl, not Louise).

What became clear however was the separate distinction between White and Black. Dual heritage pupils never identified themselves for instance as being both White or Black, 'But I don't class myself as not being White it is just that I am more…' Sometimes pupils sought to justify their response with a defence,

> It is not as if I have got a problem with White people, obviously I haven't. And then it is like all these people who are racist … I am not really bothered because I am White and Black, so when people are racist I just laugh at them, because it is just stupid really isn't it? (African-Caribbean Year 10 girl).

What they occupied was an uncertain territory to some extent. This was apparent in rendering race and ethnicity invisible, 'But I don't get involved with race, like people laugh with each other, you know like White and Black people, so we just have little laughs with each other'.

Louise had never known her Black father who had moved to London from Jamaica. She had been brought up mainly by her White maternal grandparents yet still identified herself as Black. She has recently met her father but this had been a major disappointment, 'I didn't really like him; he is a bit of a knob to tell you the truth'. Underlying this was a deep sense of rejection, 'My Dad doesn't pay attention to none of his kids; he doesn't care about none of us. There's about eighteen of us and he couldn't care about none of us'. She said that she was 'not too bothered' about this as he had not lived up to her ideal image of what her father would be. Her ideal father had existed as a physical image which collapsed upon meeting him for the first time,

> I was like … because last time they told me he had got dreadlocks and I was like "oh he is going to be right chunky and he is going to look like me and he is going to be right mad" and when I got there he had got a skinhead, right skinny, he was right horrible … complete opposite to what I wanted. (African-Caribbean Year 10 girl).

Louise discovered that she had a brothers and sisters. She admired one brother in particular who was training to be a professional rugby player. 'He's proper protective, he's right cool', which seemed to be an extension of her image of the ideal father. When describing her brother she said,

> We just look like each other. But he looks more like his Mum. So we have got the same sort of features but he has got his Mum's features and I have got my Mum's features; that's the only thing that is different.

In terms of personality she said,

> Kind of the same but he is a bit sensible, obviously because he is passionate
> about sport he is more on the sensible side and I'm not that sensible. I'm like a
> bit crazy and he is like, 'you're mad' and I'm like 'you're sensible'. (African-
> Caribbean Year 10 girl).

Ethnicity was not something which appeared to be discussed at home with family
members. When asked whether she thought her brothers would say the same,
another African-Caribbean girl replied, 'I'm not sure because I have never talked
to my brothers about anything like that, so I don't know to be honest. I think two
of them … I don't know'.

In focus group discussions, pupils saw the role of parents as exceptionally
important. Distinctions were often made between Black and minority ethnic parents
and White parents on 'correct' social values of respectability and reasonableness,

> It starts with the adults. Because the kids they don't care. If I went round
> throwing rocks at people's houses my mum wouldn't stand for it but their
> parents don't mind, they don't know where their kids are anyway. It goes back
> to family values. If my brother had a fight with someone my mum would go to
> their house and talk to their parents but here if my brother did that in a White
> persons' area then they would have a row, my mum couldn't have a conversation
> with their parents … (Somali Year 19 girl).

This was quite a widespread view among the Pakistani community of all ranks.
The coordinator of Pakistani Study Support said that the community did not
suffer the same problems of teenage pregnancy and crime as the White working
classes. The Pakistani community was different from the African-Caribbean and
White communities but similar to the Gypsy community in the sense that most
pupils lived in a traditional 'stable' family structure of married parents, siblings
and extended family. Strong family ties and cultural values potentially gave a
stronger sense of identity. Living in predominantly Pakistani neighbourhoods also
potentially gave a stronger sense of community. Unlike the experiences of African-
Caribbean pupils, Pakistani pupils never brought up the issue of racism as a matter
affecting their own lives and some parents also shared this perception. On one
hand, all parents felt that life in England offered their children better opportunities
than living in Pakistan. In Pakistan, one's social positioning and future situation
was very much determined by the rigidity of 'what you're born into, what you
inherit' (Coordinator) with little hope of mobility. Social class distinctions seemed
to matter less in England because 'Everyone has food, clothing and shelter …
everyone enjoys the same benefits' (Coordinator). When asked whether she felt
any discrimination as someone from outside England, the mother replied,

> Sometimes we felt this as we didn't know the language but that was our own fault because we didn't learn the language. Generally we have never felt like outsiders as everyone treats us right in this country. (Pakistani mother).

When asked whether she had ever confronted racism she stated, 'Never, and may Allah protect us from it'. This may have been because this woman was rarely exposed to situations where she may confront it. She lived in Cliffeton which was a predominantly Pakistani area with deep networks of kinship. There was a deep sense of gratitude stemming from having basic human needs met. Beliefs in institutional racism did correlate with informants' levels of education however. While those that had never been through the British education system felt that things were fair, those that had gone through schooling and progressed through further and higher education in England did feel that the system was weighted against them, 'All experiences, you know like in work settings you have to try triple times harder than what any other person would have to that is not ethic minority' (Pakistani mother). In discussing whether she would like her children to proceed through further education she answered,

> Yes I would like them to have further education to better themselves. Because it is a lot harder out there for people from different ethnic backgrounds because their colour, religion and race, everything comes in to it, so they have to try a lot harder than what any other person would. (…) I have achieved it yes, but it was hard, very hard. When you are at University and you are the only brown face in the class, it is hard. If you have not got your mind over matter you can get pulled in to things but it is your choice (…) you go the right way or the wrong way. (Pakistani mother).

'You go the right way or the wrong way' encapsulates the social reality completely. The study revealed that patterns of disaffection and underachievement are set very early for children. This was displayed on one particular education programme. Pupils tended to organise themselves by gender and ethnicity so all the Pakistani girls sat together and all the Somali boys sat together. Students participating within the Fellowship programme tended to demonstrate varying trajectories. One group of Somali boys was led by one displaying high status masculinity through disruptive behaviour. By secondary school, these patterns continue so at all three schools there were examples of disaffected pupils. In brief they violated rules, used foul and abusive language, assaulted, teased and bullied other pupils, caused damage to school property, were rowdy, talked excessively in class, disrespected teachers' authority and openly ignored lessons. They had apparently no fear of the sanctions, and in fact seemed to purposely flaunt their identities in opposition to them which resulted in them being in continuous friction with the school's 'disciplinary apparatus' (Foucault 1977: 328). In short, their identities were in direct opposition to the pervious and compliant 'subject' position expected of pupils.

The Pakistani girls were hard working and employed traditional gender roles. They all worked hard, and there was often an underlying sense of competition in who was achieving the highest levels. One girl in particular, Safiya consistently achieved level 6. She was an only child and had a high level of confidence. She was allowed on the residential trip. Her best friend Haleema was also hardworking but much more introverted. She was the youngest daughter of seven children. One of her sisters who was a student at the university often used to collect her from the sessions. There were other pupils who were floaters, not belonging to any group. The only Afghan boy elected to sit alone every session keeping himself physically and socially separate from the rest of the group. However, unlike other studies of quiet or invisible children in school (see for instance Gwent TEC, 1997), he was despite his self-exclusion extremely hard working and engaged in class activities. The only two African-Caribbean pupils, a boy and a girl, in a class of predominantly Pakistani pupils, both actively sought to distance themselves from the rest of the group. Corey preferred to sit by himself, always by the window where he would day dream but would easily slip in to conversations with the Somali boys when he wanted. Shauna sat with three Pakistani girls but she placed herself in a peripheral position through defence mechanisms like 'keeping to herself' and was extremely reluctant to participate, often to the point of sullenness. The emphasis here was not on maintaining peer group social relations

The danger here is that we may make unrealistic, essentialist generalisations from these examples and narratives. But, it is not possible here to generalise about whole communities with differing patterns and strategies being pursued by young people and families across these communities. This study does however confirm that many of these young people were living in difficult and chaotic home environments and felt disconnected/detached from family, school and community social worlds and felt lonely and locked into a tangled web of constraints.

'Messing up your life': gangstas, drug dealers and terrorists

African-Caribbean and Pakistani groups were strongly aware of negative and hostile stereotypes and attitudes and were able to identify the main features of constraining stereotypes for these groups. This is a point which featured in equal measure across all three schools. Since stereotypes have social implications and can provide a picture of how different groups are perceived, it is useful to consider how pupils believe they are seen. These young people had learnt and were exposed to the fact that people occupy different structural positions in society. For Pakistanis, their choices were limited to working in the service industry, 'working in a take-away or being something like a taxi driver. Or owning a shop on a corner' (Focus group interview, Proposal High). For some pupils limited ethnic stereotyping of their identity provided the motivation and internal resistance to 'prove *them* wrong'.

> Because you know when people look at you ... they just look at you and you can prove them wrong basically because they are like "oh he is going to be working in a take-away" or "oh he is going to be a taxi-driver". Something like that, so it is just proving them wrong and achieving what you can. (Pakistani Year 10 boy).

The stereotype for African-Caribbeans was viewed completely differently. Unjust stereotyping of the African-Caribbean community arose frequently in discussions with African-Caribbean pupils and with it a sense of outrage,

> Black boys get stereotyped, "Oh they are Black..." Yes Black boys do stupid stuff, so do White boys, so do Asian boys. (African-Caribbean Year 10 girl).

Stereotypes for African-Caribbean boys in particular were highly negative and fraught,

> Either being drug dealers, criminals, being in jail or...
> Not getting any GCSEs.
> Yes that's right or just not getting any GCSEs.
> Yes you just mess up your life. (African-Caribbean boys in focus group discussion).

The detrimental impact of these perceptions cannot be underestimated given the negative picture of achievement by African-Caribbean boys demonstrated by national statistics. Often the only portrayals young people are offered are of these types rather than the educated, professional identity achieved through social mobility which the goal of education attempts to endorse. Society's expectations of African-Caribbean boys were felt to be extremely low even to the point of being dangerous,

> He sells drugs, he uses knives and guns, he is not a very nice person, be scared of that person, you will get your phoned robbed. (African-Caribbean Year 10 girl).

Similarly at Proposal High a focus group discussion described much of the same,

> And yes if you are a Black person with a hood they straight away assume that you are a criminal.
> Yes a gangsta and everything.
> If you see a Black guy with a hood on then you are just going to walk the other way aren't you? (African-Caribbean boys and girls in focus group discussion).

All these show awareness of behaviours which demarcate ethnic identity. Blackness is perceived as symbolically threatening with its associations of drug culture, crime and therefore danger, which means that African-Caribbeans should be avoided or shunned in public spaces. Although there is a sense of empowerment which comes from being conceived of as a dangerous entity, this also functions a form of disempowerment. African-Caribbean girls considered the masculine stereotype in terms of actors in romantic relationships which also presents a negative image,

> He is a woman beater, he is a man slag, he cheats on his girlfriends. That is the typical Black guy. (African-Caribbean Year 10 girl).

There was a tendency for exaggerated displays of masculinity among African-Caribbean boys which leads us into a discussion of social gender identities. For instance in a focus group discussion of social groupings at Proposal High one boy said 'I am a pimp' which he defined as 'you are just chilling and cool (…). (You) have a lot of girls on your side; make them buy you a milk shake'. Having a lot of admirers seemed to validate his identity as an attractive male and thus enhance self esteem. In a similar way as the White chavs of Nayak's (2006: 813) study, African-Caribbean boys too 'accrue a body capital that has a currency and a local exchange value within the circuits they inhabit'. This embodied capital however contributes to the production of gender inequalities in the social world of school. The interviewer turned to the girls who had been quiet during this exchange and jokingly asked, 'Have you ever bought them a milkshake girls?' The girls smiled and said no, to which one boy replied with, 'No not these, these are dry man'. Boys tended to cast female peers in roles of attractiveness. It was unclear if gendered expectations were confined to ethnic location but 'dry' meant geeky, frigid and undesirable. But boys (and girls) also called girls 'slappers' so basically girls could not win.

African-Caribbean girls shared some of the same stereotypes,

> She's a bitch, she's right hard, she'll bang you, don't mess with her. Do you what I mean? Do you know how many times that has happened to me? It's unbelievable. (African-Caribbean Year 10 girl).

This girls' belief was drawn from everyday lived experience and during the course of her interview, she cited a number of examples,

> ...these girls, they were on the corner and I could hear them saying something and I thought, "Oh I'll leave it". So then I had gone in the shop and I came back out and I heard them saying something again. And they were like, "Hey there" and I turned round and I was like, "Have you got a problem?" And then I walked off and one of them was like, "Oh she's Black, she'll bang you, shut up", do you know what I mean? (African-Caribbean Year 10 girl).

All modes of identity construction are placed outside the 'norm' and with this came discrimination. Pupils drew on a number of examples of unfair treatment but these stemmed from experiences in the wider world,

Do you know what does my head in about people these days and it is racism (and the) Police. It happened the other week, there was a group of White lads, on two different days though, there was a group of White lads on the City Gardens and the Police drove past, they all had the hoods up and everything and the Police drove past. There was a group of Black lads with their hoods up, there were about twelve of them. The Police stopped asked to search them and brought twelve Police Officers. (African-Caribbean Year 10 girl).

Suspicion was directed at these boys because they were wearing 'hoodies'[12] but it was perceived that preferential treatment was given to White boys, who were also wearing hoods. The message that is received is clear. Black boys wearing hoods are more likely to be trouble causers than their White counterparts. Complaints focused on the excessive use of resources, 'twelve police officers'. The assumption is made that racism explains differential treatment between groups. This way of seeing the world is constraining in the sense of holding people back from fulfilling their potential,

What we have noticed today in fact, we was on about it today at the shops, I'm not racist obviously but there was a group of White people, a group of Asian people and then a group of Black people, it was right weird. (...) There was me, my boyfriend and his brother and we are all Black, and Cara who is White and then there was Jordan, Aaran and a few other people and then Lorrell who is Black so we were like the mixed group and then there was a bunch of Black people, a bunch of White people, a bunch of Asian people. (African-Caribbean Year 10 girl).

Despite being hyper aware of ethnic groupings within school, pupils displayed ambivalence about why they occurred. Probing into why these groupings occurred always received a uniform, 'I don't know'.

But, pupils attempting to cross these designated social (and ethnic) markers (also known as boundary crossing) were looked upon in a disparaging way. At Jubilee School there was limited evidence of White middle class boys incorporating hip hop style. They had patterns or 'borders' etched into their hair. This was done specifically at an Afro hair salon on Station Road. Their efforts were it seemed successful. However at Proposal High such displays were mocked among African-Caribbean boys. For instance in a conversation with a Pakistani boy and a African-Caribbean boy attending Jubilee School, they discussed White pupils who try and act 'Black'. White pupils who tried to emulate these styles were pejoratively branded 'wiggers'. They were White so wearing that style was deemed inauthentic.

---

12 A hoodie is a hooded sweatshirt. In Britain the hoodie has become emblematic of young people and street culture with its associations of crime, aggression and drugs. David Cameron, now the Prime Minister led a 'hug a hoodie' campaign as leader of the Conservative party in 2006.

This perhaps signals the structural constraints imposed. Middle class White boys at Jubilee School seemed to have more freedom to cross racial boundaries.

There was no evidence of White pupils emulating Asian styles however. This may be because the influence of American rap culture was so strong. The quantitative survey showed that Whites and African-Caribbean pupils seemed largely to get on, whereas Pakistanis remained more on the periphery, and that differences in acceptance are then reflected in which styles White pupils emulate. But, the reverse was also the case. Pakistanis at Jubilee School trying to fit into a more alternative identity similarly were looked at as deviants,

> There is one boy in our class and he is Asian like me and his hair was really short when he first came, he was new to the school, but now his hair is really big and everyone is like, "you have got to cut your hair, it doesn't look nice", and he is like, "well I am trimming it everyday" but it doesn't look any different. (..) it's just like a big flop on the top of his head. (Pakistani Year 10 girl).

In reality, ethnicity as a social identity is ascribed by social norms. Deviation from those norms resulted in different reactions which seemed to depend on class status. Taking on different ethnic markers labels pupils' identities as subversive and pupils were often unsure how to 'interpret' them. With the White middle class boys at Jubilee School, they dressed in gangsta styles that were tweaked but did not attempt to 'act hard'. Among the African-Caribbean community, White working class attempts to emulate Black styles and hard behaviours resulted in pupils being viewed as an object of mockery.

These styles strongly relate to ethnicity yet pupils, and White middle class pupils in particular, felt extremely uncomfortable discussing ethnicity. White middle class pupils stated they did not perceive or articulate ethnic difference at all and in fact took extreme offence to the mentioning of ethnicity as a marker of identity. Likewise Black African-Caribbean middle class parents also did not see ethnicity as a problem. At a Raising Boys' Achievement event, one educational professional speaking as a mother said that she felt ethnicity was often 'just used as an excuse'. She went on to say she had progressed successfully through the British education system and had done alright. It did become apparent that the term 'ethnic' meant being Black. Pupils would state ethnic meant 'anyone not Caucasian'. Ethnicity was therefore not a social marker like gender where everyone belonged to a category but rather was a status delegated to the 'Other' which stood in opposition to White middle class 'culturelessness' being unnamed. Analysis therefore had to take place through the above tribal categories pupils assigned each other. The head teacher at Proposal High commented that ethnicity was more of a 'hot potato' at Jubilee School. This gives an insight into the everyday tangles of the social reality of the school and also perhaps uncovers the need to tackle the issue of ethnicity explicitly.

Conclusion

Four key findings emerge from the evidence presented in this chapter. Firstly some of these young people were living in difficult and chaotic home environments. The majority of pupils and parents interviewed lived in areas of high social deprivation and the circumstances of some families were extremely complex and difficult. Many pupils were disconnected/detached from family, school and community social worlds and felt lonely and locked into a tangled web of constraints.

Secondly, African-Caribbean and Pakistani groups were strongly aware of negative and hostile stereotypes and attitudes about themselves. Pupils had very definite ideas in identifying stereotypes for Pakistanis and Caribbeans. This is a point which featured in equal measure across all three schools. Despite being aware of ethnic groupings within school, pupils displayed ambivalence and lack of understanding about why they occurred.

Thirdly, neighbourhood location was a significant marker of identity. Pupils saw their neighbourhoods as an important context and unpacking respondents' perceptions and experiences of where the boundaries around particular places lay emerged as an important identity activity. Neighbourhoods are made up of people and communities in places and there is great stability and cohesion in familiar settings.

Fourthly, neighbourhood location, postcode gangs and masculine 'gangsta' culture are imported into everyday school life fuelling violence/bullying which undermines attainment (reported by 43 per cent pupils in Jubilee School and 28 per cent Tannery Rise School). The physical divide between neighbourhoods was entrenched further through the existence of postcode gangs in the wider community. An important part of identity for both African-Caribbean and Pakistani pupils and particularly for boys was bound up with allegiance to specific areas. Overall much of this was bound up with ideas of 'hard' masculinity and involvement in gangs marked the transition to adulthood. It was a way to assert identity but the seriousness of the implications of this can however not be underestimated since there had been shootings in Brunsmere linked to gang wars. Pupil involvement in postcode gangs cut across disaffected and conformist identities in school. These connections between home environment, community and school are explored further in the next chapter which focuses on life inside school.

Chapter 6
Young People, Ethnicity
and Schooling in Northcity

Introduction

This chapter examines the significance of ethnicity in three multicultural schools in Northcity. It provides an introduction to the school contexts and examines the ways in which these schools have responded to issues of ethnic diversity. A critical analysis of the curriculum is given drawing on pupils' experiences. The social meaning of class, Whiteness and ethnicity and the ways in which they interact is then analysed and significant differentials in perceptions of schooling and relationships with teachers and peers are identified. Lastly pupils' educational and career aspirations are discussed. Northcity and the UK are rapidly changing and becoming more diverse which imposes greater challenges on already stretched schools which makes understanding the interaction between education and ethnicity all the more important.

In Northcity as a whole, there is evidence of racial and ethnic segregation at secondary school level which is significant in light of the fact that LEA (Local Education Authority)'s have had a statutory duty since 1976 to eliminated racial discrimination and promote good race relations and schools have had a specific duty to promote community cohesion since 2007. Pupils in Northcity are attaining at a lower rate than pupils nationally and schools in the city has made national headlines in recent years for behaviour problems. 21 per cent of the secondary school population in Northcity are from minority ethnic backgrounds (6,069 of a total of 30,801), compared with 11 per cent in 1998. Such rapid growth has brought about new challenges particularly to schools who have limited experience of managing and accommodating such change with some trends of city-wide reduced racial and ethnic segregation and suburbanisation of minority ethnic households.

However, the impact of an increased minority ethnic presence in schools can also be seen to have had powerful segregating effects over the last two decades as increasing concentration of these households in inner city areas also accompanies suburban movement, reflecting increasing internal socio-economic polarisation within minority ethnic populations, in other words increasing poverty for some families and increasing incomes for others (Law 2011). One school which is situated in the north-east of the city has a minority ethnic population of 91 per cent, predominantly Pakistani pupils. Rather than its composition being due to 'White flight', this is due mostly to parents actively making the choice to send their children to this school. On the other hand, the recent fate of another school situated across the city tells of a different story. Green Grove School is a former grammar school which had a historical reputation of academic excellence. By the 1980s, its catchment area was redefined to include areas of deprivation which meant increasing numbers of poor pupils began attending, a large proportion of whom were from minority ethnic groups. This rapidly resulted in 'White flight'. By the early 1990s the school's population had sunk from 2,200 to 500 pupils as middle class parents actively made the choice to send their children to an alternative school. In 2009 it was announced that the school would have to close. Only one other school had a significantly higher proportions of minority ethnic pupils (73.7 per cent) and seven schools remain predominantly White. In practice then the minority ethnic population is not spread equally among Northcity's secondary schools and racial and ethnic segregation is evident.

The school context

Although all the schools have large multiethnic catchments they differ in terms of achievement and attainment rankings. Of the three, Jubilee School has by far the largest Pakistani pupil population at 14 per cent but subsequently there are limited proportions of other ethnic groups. Although the lowest in pupil numbers, Tannery Rise School has proportionally the broadest ethnic social mix of the three schools with representation from a greater cross section of some minority ethnic communities including Somali (7.4 per cent) and Yemeni (3 per cent). According to the LEA's records, Tannery Rise School was also supposed to have a high proportion of Gypsy Roma pupils in comparison to other secondary schools in Northcity (1.8 per cent) but in practice, this was not the case.

Jubilee School (School 1) is the fifth biggest comprehensive in Northcity. It is a high performing school positioned joint fourth highest in Northcity's 2008 league tables and above the national average. It is the only school in the study to have a sixth form. The school is an impressive Grade II Listed Art Deco building which is currently undergoing a £27 million remodelling under the government 'Building Schools for the Future' initiative[1] (DCFS 2008a). In May 2009 it was the first comprehensive in Northcity to be accepted as an International Baccalaureate (IB) World School (http://www.ibo.org/) offering the Diploma programme as an alternative to 'A' Levels. Gaining IB World School status is prestigious since it is usually the preserve of public schools. There are only 195 IB World Schools currently in the UK and the qualification with its emphasis on critical thinking, is internationally recognised as an academically challenging pre university course. The school is situated in the affluent south west of the city. While its setting looks

---

1   A programme which aims at 'improving educational attainment and the life chances available to children, by providing educational, recreational and social environments that support modern teaching and learning methods'.

leafy and suburban (with low unemployment and a high rate of owner occupancy), the school's intake is mixed and from all over the city. 52 per cent of pupils do not live in the catchment.[2] 56 per cent of these pupils are shown to come from affluent families and 10 per cent are entitled to Free School Meals (FSM).[3] Minority ethnic pupils make up a third of the school population with the largest proportion being from of Pakistani origin. The school places great value on celebrating cultural difference. The school has a reputation for giving student voice a high priority. There is no school uniform and pupils dress independently, which is in opposition to most other secondary schools in the city. The school population is by far the most diverse of the three schools in terms of social class intake. When considering teenage tribal culture, it consists of 'rich kids', 'popular kids', emos, rockers, skaters, chavs and gangstas. Difference is marked through dress and physical appearance. Chavs wear Fred Perry and Lacoste whereas rich kids wear Ralph Lauren and D & G. Middle class White kids wear backcombed 'scruffy' hair whereas inner city girls wear their hair straightened and large hooped earrings.

Among staff, there is a strong professional culture and emphasis is currently on the transformation of learning. Innovation is evident in the recent review of the pastoral system which resulted in four vertical houses composed of mixed-age tutor groups. The aim was to create 'communities within a leaning community' by encouraging pupils to both socially mix and invest in the life of the school through involvement and loyalty. By grouping pupils in this way, there often runs an undercurrent of competition and rivalry in curricular as well as extra-curricular activities. For example, sports days may consist of inter-house tournaments. In this sense the house system may instrumentally have been enforced as a performance boosting measure as well as a cohesion strategy. Jubilee School opened in 1880 under a different name in the centre of Northcity and was renamed and relocated

---

2   The statutory school age admission system is based upon defined catchment areas and 'the principle of local schools for local children'. Northcity divides the city into catchment areas which were devised in the 1970s and are more or less stuck to today although there is some fluidity as new streets are added or exiting schools are closed down. Every address in the city is allocated one infant or primary school. When a child completes primary education he or she will transfer to the associated secondary school. In the event of oversubscription, places are offered in the following order of priority: Special Educational Needs and Looked After Children; Attendance at Linked Infant School; Catchment Area; Siblings; Contributory Feeder School; All other applicants; Tie-breakers.

3   Eligibility of Free School Meals (FSM) is the standard measure used to identify school pupils with high levels of social deprivation. FSM are available only to children whose parents/guardians are in receipt of one or more of the following benefits: Income Support; Income-Based Jobseeker's Allowance; Employment and Support Allowance (Income Related); Support under Part VI of the Immigration and Asylum Act 1999. Families in receipt of Child Tax Credit will also qualify provided that (a) they are not entitled to Working Tax Credit, and (b) their annual income, as assessed by Her Majesty's Revenue and Customs does not exceed £16,040 as at 6 April 2009 (subject to annual review); Guarantee element of State Pension Credit.

to its present site in 1933. Originally the building housed two separate single-sex grammar schools. They were merged into a single comprehensive school in 1969. An association which is run by the school's 'original' 'Old Boys' and 'Old Girls'[4] preserves nostalgic memories of the school from a bygone age. Schools 2 and 3 contrast strongly with this. Both are situated in areas of deprivation with a high proportion of council housing and housing association homes. Unlike Jubilee School, both have intakes which are restricted to working class pupils.

Proposal High (school 2) was originally built in the 1960s and is situated in the North East of Northcity. It draws its pupils from an area in Northcity that includes pockets of severe social deprivation. Unemployment is high and educational performance in the area has traditionally been low. In September 2002 the existing secondary school absorbed one of its feeder primary schools, which was in danger of becoming a failing school, and began accepting pupils from the ages of 3-16. This was the first school of its type in the country. The merger has had a positive impact. During December 2007 the primary phase was recognised as one of the most improved primary schools in the country. The school building is the antithesis of Jubilee School. It is in a secluded position, approached via a long driveway and adjacent to a large cemetery. The building is modern and orange and has a more corporate feel. The corporate ethos is reflected in a number of ways. A good working atmosphere seems to be of paramount concern. The reception, a vital part of the school, is a large glossy area with comfortable seating. Two pupils on daily reception duty get you to sign in on arrival and collect a visitor's badge. Rooms and subject areas are clearly signposted and classrooms and the corridors are always clean and fresh smelling. Pupils wear a school uniform consisting of a white or blue polo shirt, Black trousers and a royal blue sweatshirt bearing the school logo. Discrete jewellery is permitted.

The school applied the same level of control over religions dress, 'Muslim girls who wish to wear traditional clothing may wear Black Shalwar Kameez with a "Proposal High" sweatshirt and a Black headscarf' (school policy document). There is extensive cultural diversity within the school population. About 30 per cent of the pupils are from minority ethnic backgrounds, and PLASC data indicates that it has the third highest number of asylum seekers in the city. 20 per cent of the pupils have English as an additional language and, within this group, a wide range of first languages are spoken. Proposal High has the second highest population of Pakistani pupils in the city. 25 per cent pupils do not live in the catchment and of these, 54 per cent come from poor families. 23 per cent of pupils are entitled to free school meals.

Tannery Rise (school 3) is situated in the inner city North East area of Northcity in the Brunsmere ward. The school is situated on a residential street, just off a main artery road behind an old people's home and next to a dump site. 44 per cent of

---

4   This phrase originates from the notion of an 'Old Boy Network' which refers to exclusive social or business networks connections fostered between former schoolmates of male only public schools. It denotes preservation of a social elite.

pupils do not live in the catchment and of these 67 per cent are from poor families. 38 per cent are entitled to FSM. The school has a negative external image with a historically poor reputation for out of control pupil behaviour and low performance. In 2008 10 per cent of pupils who took GCSE exams achieved the standard of 5 A*–C grades, including Maths and English which is the minimum entry onto most Further Education (FE) courses. This is significantly lower than both the Local Authority average of 41 per cent and the national average of 48 per cent. In 2009, some improvement had been made with results rising to 22 per cent of all pupils achieving the 5 A*-C benchmark. The value added measure does change an initially negative picture though. A contextual value added score of 1004.1 per cent means that Tannery Rise School performed better than other schools with a similar mix of pupils and social factors. On this measure it outperformed Schools 1 and 2 and is ranked joint 8th out of Northcity's 27 secondary schools.

Tannery Rise School does have great challenges to overcome. Despite having the lowest size of student body, it appears to have much greater problems with discipline. A high proportion of pupils have been assessed as having behaviour difficulties. 19.3 per cent of the total pupil population was excluded[5] in 2008 which is very high not only in comparison to Schools 1 and 2, but is nearly double the national average of 10 per cent. Tannery Rise School also has the most exclusion drop outs. Discipline has been a historical problem at this school. The caretaker remembers pupils driving TWOCed[6] cars and joyriding them around the playground before a large fence was erected and the bus company threatened to stop running the service to Brunsmere because of poor pupil behaviour. It has undergone three name changes in the last 30 years and in 2008 the school pursued Academy status[7] under the sponsorship of an academic charitable trust. As a result of this, the school was replaced with an 11-16 Academy in 2009-2010, a year which is predicted to see the largest number of academies open so far. If the school follows the Academy programme's trend, its exam results will be expected to rise faster than the national average. The move to become an Academy has resulted in many changes. A new school uniform has been introduced from September consisting of a blazer with academy logo, white shirt, tie, v necked jumper with trim, Black or charcoal trousers, and plain Black shoes without motifs or logos. Academy blazers are a compulsory part of the uniform and must be worn on and around the academy site unless pupils are given permission by a member

---

5   Exclusions here refer to fixed term exclusions where a pupil is excluded for a specific time period. During this time the pupil is not allowed into school, onto school grounds or in a public space. Failure to comply could result in a fixed penalty fine. The school must ensure work is set and marked. Some City Councils have work packs which specifically relate to acts of unacceptable behaviour (Bristol City Council 2011).

6   Taken With Out Owner's Consent.

7   Academies are independent, all-ability state schools which are sponsored. The purpose of the Government's Academies programme is to replace underperforming schools (DfE 2011).

of staff to remove it. Shalwar and kameez are acceptable if they are grey and the academy blazer is worn over the top and headscarves are allowed if they are in school colours. Like Jubilee School, Tannery Rise School has also employed vertical tutoring and a House system with the aims of raising achievement levels and promoting a sense of unity and social cohesion. In addition every pupil is also assigned a mentor who they meet ten times during the academic year to discuss their individualised learning plan. The school itself is run down with old décor but it is due to move into new buildings in 2012.

Although improvement has been made over a number of years, the number of pupils achieving 5 GCSE A-C grades remains below the national average. Jubilee School by far outperformed schools 2 and 3. Likewise the survey results indicate that pupil performance in standardised SATs tests at Y9 did differ by school. Jubilee School outperformed Proposal High and Tannery Rise School in English and Maths. Noticeably a high proportion of pupils (11.6 per cent) achieved the maximum level 8 in Maths. No one achieved this in the other two schools. Proposal High had the largest spread in all subjects, with the bulk of pupils performing at level 5 in all subjects. As was expected gender was a significant factor for outcomes in all subjects. Girls outperformed boys in English, boys outperformed girls in Maths and Science. This persists in a uniform way along ethnic lines.

When taking into account socio-economic background as a factor, this level of performance needs to be considered in the context of the socio-economic profile of each school: the percentage of pupils entitled to free school meals (FSM), which is commonly used as a proxy indicator for disadvantage. Tannery Rise School which has the worst academic performance in the league tables and in this survey, also has the highest number of pupils eligible for Free School Meals. Although pupils with English as an additional language (EAL) require extra support, it is worth noting that they are not regarded as having SEN because it's not a learning difficulty. In 2008 21 per cent of all pupils taking their GCSEs at Tannery Rise School had statements or were supported at School Action Plus.[8] This compares to 9 per cent at Proposal High and 3 per cent at Jubilee School. If we look at pupils

---

8   School Action Plus: 'where the class or subject teacher and the Special Educational Needs Coordinator (SENCO) are providedd with advice or support from outside specialists, additional or different strategies to those provided for the pupil through School Action can be put in place. The SENCO usually takes the lead although day-to-day provision continues to be the responsibility of the class or subject teacher. A new Individual Education Plan (IEP) will usually be devised' (DfES, 2001: 213). Outside advice is usually offered from the LEA's support services, or from health or social work professionals (such as educational psychologists, speech and language therapists) to give recommendations as to how to work differently with the child in class. School Action Plus provision could include specialist equipment or information about the child's home circumstances that explains the changes in the child's behaviour and attitudes to learning which can then help the school to work with others to resolve the situation.

with SEN who are supported with School Action,[9] Proposal High marginally takes the highest position at 29 per cent, compared to Tannery Rise School at 28 per cent. At 2 per cent, Jubilee School has substantially fewer pupils in need of extra support.

Did sending disadvantaged students to the predominantly middle class affluent Jubilee School significantly affect their attainment levels? To examine this, the performance of pupils living in the inner city from Jubilee School was correlated with the performance of pupils living in the inner city at Proposal High and Tannery Rise School. Disadvantaged children attending Jubilee School did not achieve higher levels than peers at Proposal High and Tannery Rise School. Since these schools are situated in deprived areas with a mono class intake, results would indicate that social class remains a key explanatory factor in underachievement regardless of the context of the school.

Schools' treatment of diversity

At surface level diversity was appreciated and positively valued in all three schools. One of Tannery Rise School's aims was, 'To help students to understand the interdependence of individuals, groups, nations and the local environment, and to both comprehend and celebrate the multi-cultural nature of Northcity society'. This did not appear to be a superficial recognition of diversity, but one which played out on a daily basis. Over the years there had been enrichment activities aimed specifically at minority ethnic pupils, but a failure to focus explicitly on White pupils which can be read in two ways. First is the notion of a White 'cultureless' identity where White is not viewed as an ethnicity. Secondly an explicit focus on minority ethnic groups and an absence of focus on White pupils again serves to create a binary of 'insiders' and 'outsiders'. Extracts from staff news bulletins show an array of activities marking the significance of Black ethnic identities and cultures of pupils including Black History Month, African-Caribbean cookery, a Somali film project and Refugee Week. As well as activities within school, collaborative networks had been built which extended this beyond school provision. For instance pupils at all three schools had participated in Brunsmere Celebration of Success event, an event which exclusively catered for minority ethnic pupils living in Brunsmere.

---

9   School Action: 'where a class or subject teacher identify that a pupil has special educational needs they provide intervention that are additional to or different from those provided as part of the school's usual differentiated curriculum offer and strategies. An (IEP) will usually be devised' (DfES 2001: 213). In practice this could be further assessment, additional or different teaching materials, support from a teaching assistant (TA), training for staff or a different way of teaching. Teachers use IEPs to record the different or additional provision to be made for the child, teaching strategies, short-term targets for the pupil, success criteria, and what they have achieved.

African-Caribbean boys tended to show strong opposition to the creation of ethnic boundaries through schemes aimed specifically at them. African-Caribbean boys at Proposal High felt such interventions demonised them specifically,

> Well it's like they are targeted you because…
> You're Black.
> Yes you think you are going to achieve something but then they come along and say, "we think you need help" and it puts you down. Yes it puts you down and you are like, "so I am not doing that well", and you think you are doing really well and you know you are going to do well and then they just go and put you down. (African-Caribbean boys in focus group discussion).

One boy stated, 'I feel abused' by such projects. His emphasis was not on activities taking part within school but outside intervention projects brought into school. One mentoring scheme was referenced in particular. Its aim was to promote the inclusion of African and African-Caribbean young people who had already become disengaged, or those at risk of disaffection or disengagement,

> It is outside people, you know like (names project), it is a thing that helps you but we don't need no help, we are capable ourselves, but it puts us down anyway. It makes us think that we are dumb. (African-Caribbean Year 10 boy).

Intervention schemes which aimed to promote inclusion paradoxically were viewed by some as doing the exact opposite. They were stigmatising. When asked what should happen instead a African-Caribbean boy answered,

> Just like treat everyone equal. Don't just say "oh because you're Black or because you are different coloured we don't think you are doing as well"'. Just treat everyone like you would normally.

Opinion of the utility of such schemes was however mixed. While African-Caribbean boys did not like them, African-Caribbean girls did and felt they benefitted them on a personal level. This was the opinion of girls who were hard working, high attainers as well as those who did not. Perhaps it was because such a project was based around interpersonal skills (traditionally associated with 'feminine' qualities) which begs the question of what would work effectively for boys.

Teachers expressed different views on the value of activities being aimed at specific ethnic groups. In a conversation with one White female teacher she reflected that she felt minority ethnic pupils at the school had more advantages than their White counterparts. She connected this with recruitment practices employed by Northcity Council which as an equal opportunities employer promoted minority ethnic applicants above anyone else as they were under represented in certain areas of work.[10] 'If it said White people only there'd be uproar'. This teacher felt that the senior leadership team were often blind to the real problems. This may have stemmed from her own allegiances as she herself had grown up on the Tannery Rise estate and had attended the school in the 1980s when it was very much a White working class school. She therefore had a unique vantage point on watching its change to a minority ethnic school.

The absence of activities aimed specifically at White pupils can be viewed in two ways. On one hand it could be viewed as this teacher saw, as a mode of positive discrimination which privileged minority ethnic pupils over White pupils. On the other, it could paradoxically be seen as serving to reinforce White privilege. The 'multicultural' practices the school had employed to meet the needs of its diverse pupil population were the opposite of 'colour blindness' or 'bleaching' pupils' cultural heritage but paradoxically served the same end. While there was an abundance of activities aimed at specific ethnic groups, there was a limited amount done to promote social cohesion between different ethnic groups which was a pressing issue in Tannery Rise School and had been for a long time. Pupils continued to separate themselves into ethnic groups and the physical divide between White pupils living in Tannery Rise and minority ethnic pupils in Brunsmere played out on a daily basis within school as an ethnic divide although the divide was not as stark as it had been a few years ago. There had been some significant changes in social groupings with the entry of Eastern European children and evidence that they were becoming a target for pupil's hostility.

A White middle class curriculum taught by White middle class teachers

On the whole the majority of Pakistani and African-Caribbean pupils participating in the study did not feel school was responsive to the requirements of providing an education which catered to everyone. One African-Caribbean boy emphasised in his interview how he would like to know more about Rastafariansim, 'everyone thinks it's about smoking weed when it's about peace and love' (mixed minority ethnic focus group). Learning about other cultures, particularly about pupil's own cultural heritages was considered significant because it potentially could combat pre existing stereotypes. Although there were schemes in place which aimed to recognise and promote diversity and increase community cohesion between different ethnic groups, in practice they did not always work. Although there were posters around all three schools highlighting the fact it was Black History Month, discussions with pupils revealed that in practice it was not utilised effectively as a learning resources, 'We haven't done anything on Black history; I've done nothing on other people's history either' (African-Caribbean boy). Black History Month[11]

---

10   See section 38(1)(b) of the Race Relations Act 1976 and Section 49A(1C/E) of the Disability Discrimination Act 2005).

11   http://www.Black-history-month.co.uk/.

takes place every October in Britain to specifically highlight African-Caribbean and African achievements, icons and cultural history and experience. Although posters were put around school to promote Black History month, there were not any learning activities within lessons around it. This is perhaps unsurprising given the stringency in tackling the GCSE curriculum. But it does go some way to explain pupils' lack of engagement as its invisibility implies that Black history is not significant or does not really matter. Engaging pupils is key as much of what was covered in lessons was perceived as boring,

> When I used to go to RE and when I used to go to a History lesson in Year 9 because they were compulsory, I had them for an hour and I used to get so bored and I used to listen to music because I didn't find them interesting. (African-Caribbean Year 10 girl).

In places the academic curriculum excluded representation from minority ethnic groups. At Proposal High pupils complained that all they learned about in history was World War 2 and about Hitler which they felt was White people's history. Literature covered in English was Shakespeare and although efforts had been made to include more multicultural texts, they were still very much viewed as the traditional White literary canon, '...it's still from a White person point of view the choice of books'. In part this is due to structural constraints. Teachers are guided by the curriculum and the resources that the school has. In terms of resources, the English department at Jubilee School for instance is reliant on tatty sets of books which it has used for the past decade. Teachers too arrive into teaching from the experiences and understandings they have formed.

In other schools, a more proactive approach has been taken to working with pupils in a way not constrained by the curriculum. A head teacher who spoke at the Black community education workshops day stated,

> With our Y7s they do a project called British National Identity which looks at why the Pakistanis came over, African-Caribbean food. It was fantastic for me but some staff hated it. He (a teacher) decided to do it differently and he spent six weeks looking at slavery. "Imagine you're a slave in a slave ship. Write a diary entry for it". He brought the army in. He was looking at national identity in a totally different way. He thought that was what British identity was all about. (African-Caribbean Head Teacher).

Pupils considered the content of the curriculum a problem. Much of what was covered in school was boring. Citizenship lessons in Jubilee School and Prospect High were considered a waste of time. In part this was because it lacked the status of a 'proper' GCSE subject. But it was also because the content was mainly negative issues such as knife crime which for pupils felt too 'preachy' (pupil comment).

Another point which was brought out was the unequal coverage of different faiths and religions in Religious Education (RE),

> When we do RE and we have Islam time it's not so we only do Islam, we have
> Christianity for five minutes and then you learn about Islam ... but the teachers
> do not have enough resources to teach us about Islam. (...) They don't have
> enough knowledge about it, so I think they should bring different people in from
> different religions to explain it to us. (Pakistani Year 10 boy).

Although this was seen as stemming from teachers' lack of expertise in the
subject the implication could be that unequal worth is projected. A Pakistani boy
mentioned how he was seen as 'arrogant' when he corrected his teacher about an
incorrect fact about Islam that had been written in the textbook. This interrupted
the traditional asymmetric power dynamics of teacher and pupil. But some pupils
felt themselves more knowledgeable about those matters. Perhaps would be useful
to draw on their knowledge as a resource rather than a hindrance.

In the past research has shown teachers to view language use as a symptom
of inadequacy but there was clear evidence of individual teachers being inventive
in their teaching. For instance at Jubilee School one class of Year 10 students
were working on completing a draft of their assessed coursework on accent and
dialect. The function of the overall unit was to consider how language changes
over time. They were given two options and most had chosen to write a Catherine
Tate 'Lauren'[12] sketch. This provided an entertaining choice for pupils who were
thoroughly engaged with the material. Unlike previous research which revealed
how teachers held negative stereotypes about pupils' use of non-standard English,
it seems that today's teachers are utilising the skills and knowledge of pupils within
their classrooms. It was also very useful in understanding how pupils understood
different social groupings and the social relations within Jubilee School. For
instance one Black African-Caribbean boy had constructed a dialogue between
two characters.

> 1: Yo wassupman?
> 2: Yo what does 'wassup man' mean?
> 1: It means what is up blood
> 2: Oh ok so wassup, is that better?
> 1: Yeah way better dude.

Distinction here was made between a (White middle class) pupil living in the
south west of the city and a Black African-Caribbean pupil living in the inner
city. This example shows reflexive awareness of pupils' own status and roles
within the White middle class majority population at Jubilee School. Many
African-Caribbean pupils, born in England and never having been to Jamaica,
draw on a vernacular which drew on Los Angeles gangsta rap culture ('wassup',

---

12   Lauren is the well known character of comedy show The Catherine Tate Show.
She is an argumentative teenage girl often viewed as accurately portraying the current
generation of teenagers. She is associated with using the catchphrase, 'Am I bovvered?'

'blood',[13] 'dude'). This contrasted with the distinctly White middle class Northcity vernacular used by the second pupil. In this sense they are almost bilingual. This communication represents in part the complex mixed identities that these pupils displayed. It seems to evidence an identity they are perhaps often excluded from and have little in common with. Teachers' outlooks were often seen as homogenous and disconnected from pupils' experiences outside their lessons,

> …White people just think they know it all, I am not saying everyone does, but most of the teachers think they know what background you are from etc but they don't really. (African-Caribbean Year 10 boy).

Such examples within lessons are valuable as it provided a space for pupils to be the 'expert'. In this way pupils were enabled to subvert the dominant White middle class/subordinate minority ethnic working class group binary which was normalised in school. There still remained some uncomfortable boundaries between teachers and the African-Caribbean community mainly because of the gangsta image that was often embodied. For instance at the education workshops in Brunsmere an African-Caribbean head teacher reported how,

> A timid middle class teacher and a boy was causing havoc. I said go round to his home, she said "I can't do that"', so I said "I'll come with you" so we drive to the house and he's outside with his mates on one of those little bikes. He sees me and his teacher and he panics. From that her relationship with that boy changed. Because going round to the house and speaking to mum showed she cared. But it's really funny how some teachers are scared of Black boys. (African-Caribbean Head Teacher).

Social class distinctions, Whiteness and ethnicity in school

Social class distinctions were acutely felt but were rarely expressed in ethnic terms. Among the Pakistani community, pupils often initially reflected on social distinctions in terms of social class status. As conversation progressed it became clear that ethnicity was often entwined with wealth and status, 'White people are friends with posh people'. In an interview with troublesome twins they reflected on why their parents had made them move from Tannery Rise School to Prince Albert School, which is a high performing school much like Jubilee School in the south west of the city. White middle class status was intrinsically linked to intelligence and high achievement in school. The twins who were themselves disaffected from education believed that White middle classes were better at education because 'they are hardworking'. There was no sense of unfairness in the system. Pupils seemed to believe that schools were meritocratic and operated fairly so that they

---

13   The Bloods were a Californian street gang.

had equal chances to succeed. In underachieving fault lay with the individual. This was a point which arose in the focus group discussions throughout the schools.

In schools which had mixed social class intakes strong emphasis was given to neighbourhood and with that an implicit sense of social ranking. Pakistani pupils had very definite ideas about which areas were the best in Northcity. Areas in the south west were 'the best' in Northcity, and 'that is the area *they* (defined as the White middle classes) come from'. Brunsmere where these pupils lived was down market and living there equated to being inferior, 'how can you be posh if they live in Brunsmere?' Understanding residential segregation in this way shows keen awareness of social class and ethnicity. The salience of social class was viewed as material triumph but being posh (or White and middle class) did not translate into being flamboyant with money. In fact, in comparison to the Pakistani boys' everyday spending power, posh White pupils were limited,

> Yes posh people, they have lots of money. They have lots of money but their mums don't give them any. (…) Yes they save up and all that. Like say if they go to school they have no packed lunch, no nothing and they won't give them any money, only sometimes. … so they can think about how much it is going to cost. (Pakistani boys focus group).

The assumption was that White middle class families contributed less in financial terms in order for their children to learn and understand the value of money. These boys were each given £5 a day for their dinner money which they said was a lot more than posh people got. Money is not what separates pupils since there was no ways by which it provoked envy. However what is perhaps significant here is social class location and the different type of upbringing that White middle class pupils were seen as having. Money here can be used as a starting point for understanding a different relationship with the world. Social class is deeply etched into culture and into psyches and is implicated in the production of different types of social identities.

The White Head Teacher of Tannery Rise School drew on his experience of working at another school which had recently closed down to highlight the distinctions in the White middle class factions of the south west, 'The White students at Green Grove School were a remnant of the White middle class, so actually the White students were more like Jubilee School in nature'. By this he meant that the parents of the White children attending this school were like community activists. In his words, they were 'like urban guerrillas', actively having taken the choice to put their children in a multicultural school which had suffered White flight. Their actions in enrolling their children at a school which was viewed as rapidly deteriorating, had a moral purpose in challenging ethnic apartheid,

> …they had actively done that and wore it as a badge of honour and could be relied upon to be governors, to be in parents group, to chain themselves to

railings … and the only thing that I would say is that all the kids used to smoke dope all the time and that was the only thing I ever rang them up about and it was like, 'well what is the big deal?' Because I am sure it wasn't a big deal for them. So it was more like having a little bit of Jubilee School or… I don't know I think Jubilee School is a more liberal school than [this] School, which was associated with self-made-ness. (Head Teacher, Tannery Rise School).

Opinions of minority ethnic pupils at Tannery Rise School also expressed disdain for the local White working class community

..the kids in this area they live in the community and they still manage to come to School late. When people travel for miles, you know like in Africa when they go to Tannery Rise School miles away and that is actually walking, they don't have no buses, no form of transport and they still make it to School on time and here it's across the road and they are always late. (Somali Year 10 girl).

Among these minority ethnic pupils, Tannery Rise tended to represent a stagnant 'backwards' community and expressed a strong sense of educational urgency,

Do you know what I think this community hasn't seen change, like you see here the generation living here are all like … like kids that live in Tannery Rise they don't think "I want to achieve better and I want to go, I want to leave this area, I want to go abroad", they are just stuck here. There are people that left High School three or four years ago and they are still there, when I was in Year 7 they were leaving and they are still here. They don't want to do nothing; they just want to live there. (,..) It's like a cycle because that's what their parents did and their grandparents so they are just going to do it. (...) I want to break the cycle; I'm going to College and then University and want to get my degree and my Masters and that. I want to break the cycle. I want to be a Lawyer or a Teacher. (Somali Year 10 girl in focus group discussion).

Whiteness resonated very differently in the different schools due to the intersection with class distinctions. There was a general reluctance among pupils to view experiences through the lens of their ethnic identities. Rather they drew on other social identities, particularly White middle class pupils at Jubilee School. The word ethnicity provoked most opposition from White middle class pupils than any other group. Such opposition was surprising since race and ethnicity is an integral part of self-identity. Consideration thus must be drawn over the meaning, use, and influences of the term upon youth. In class discussions pupils were asked to explain what the word 'ethnicity' meant to them. At Jubilee School, comments from White pupils tended to invoke the idea of a cohesive shared 'whole' and the slogan 'We should treat people all as one race, "The Human Race"' was continually invoked in discussions among pupils. White middle class pupils tended to view race purely as a signifier of superiority versus inferiority. Their vocal opposition to the word 'ethnicity' seemed highly significant for this study. Although the reasoning cited was that of a common shared humanity where ethnicity is irrelevant, their resistance to differentiating groups by ethnicity seemed to mask a feeling of embarrassment which stemmed from their own ethnic and social class positioning. When asked whether defining pupils by ethnicity was any different from differentiating people by gender, pupils said yes, but were unable to articulate why this would be.

> I feel comfortable describing my ethnicity but I don't think there is any need for it. We should treat people all as one race, The Human Race. (African-Caribbean Year 10 girl).

> Ethnicity means nothing to me. It doesn't matter. Everyone is human. Why do we have to label ourselves. Does it really matter? (a different African-Caribbean Year 10 girl).

What this seemed to stem from was an unconscious awareness of the exclusivity of White privilege and a strong awareness of social inequality and difference which is apparent from this student's comment,

> If I have to I state my ethnicity but I don't go around feeling I'm better than other people because of my ethnicity. I don't think it matters what ethnicity you are. I don't like the idea of discrimination because of your ethnicity and how that affects your social category. (White Year 10 boy).

The majority of White pupils felt that their ethnicity did not play a role in their life. 15 per cent felt their ethnicity was advantageous and just 1 per cent said it was a disadvantage. Here the interplay between ethnicity and social background is crucial. 62 per cent of White (middle class) pupils living in the outskirts compared to just 39 per cent of White (working class) pupils living in the inner city felt their ethnicity did not play any role. Middle class White pupils experience 'culturelessness' in a way that White working class pupils do not. Perry's (2001) research in American schools goes some way to understanding White ethnic responses here. She illuminates the ways in which different institutional contexts influence different constructions of White identity as cultureless. Following a definition of cultureless whereby, '...White identity was understood to have no ties or allegiances to European ancestry and culture, no "traditions"', Perry (2001: 58) shows how culturelessness can serve, even if unintentionally, as a measure of White superiority. In her study, at the predominantly White high school White identities were constructed as cultureless because White cultural practices were taken for granted, naturalised and thus, not reflected on and defined. In contrast, at the multiethnic school, White culture was not taken for granted yet multiculturalism subversively helped constitute cultureless identities through what Perry (2001: 57) calls 'processes of rationalisation'. To the White youth, only ethnic minority people had ties to the past which put across the idea that White culture does not need special attention, the underlying message being 'White is the norm and standard'. At Jubilee School this also appeared to be the case.

However, a major problem with this kind of analysis is that it only focuses on the monocausal category of 'race' to explain inequality. Whilst many such studies have sought to expose the way White domination (through 'colourblind' practices or culturelessness) is sustained through 'invisibility', with the aim of disarming its 'cloaked perniciousness' (Perry 2001) interest should also turn to how this privilege is codified in White people at the margins of society. Although Perry (2001: 61) claims that 'cultural invisibility is a characteristic of all those who hold full citizenship and institutional power in the nation state', this surely serves to define the standard 'norm' of the White middle class. It is important to consider that working class pupils who are White may have cultural heritages which disadvantage them as well (Willis 1977). This is reflected through the fact that a high proportion of White working class pupils at Schools 2 and 3 felt that ethnicity did not play a role. How you identify yourself is to a large extent how society defines you so structurally they are only are not fully integrated into the cultureless norm by virtue of their social class or 'chav' status.

There was also hostility from some African-Caribbean girls to the recognition of ethnicity,

> I think the word ethnicity is a load of bullshit because it doesn't matter. (White Year 10 girl).

> Ethnic labels don't affect me. I don't care. It makes no difference. (African-Caribbean Year 10 girl).

Ethnic identity proved a very ambiguous subject for many young people. Locating and articulating what ethnic identity meant through discourse invoked subjectivities which were accomplished differently by individuals.

Despite these denials, when looking at the degree of ethnic solidarity, pupil responses indicate varying patterns. The majority of White pupils did not remember ever feeling they shared solidarity with those that share the same ethnicity. This does not follow the same pattern for minority ethnic pupils. 65 per cent of Pakistani and 64 per cent of African-Caribbean pupils said they felt solidarity with those sharing the same ethnicity. Minority ethnic pupil perceptions were also strongly reflected in classroom organisation where all pupils tended to self group with pupils of the same ethnicity. Yet, over half of African-Caribbean pupils and White pupils reported that 'same ethnicity is definitely not important' in friendship choices whereas over half of Pakistani pupils did see 'same ethnicity is important'. This is a significant finding and may suggest that Pakistani pupils find greater bonds of solidarity with other Pakistani pupils.

Pupils' attitudes towards their own ethnicity tended to bring mixed feelings and ethnicity was shown to be a particularly slippery and elusive concept for

White and Pakistani pupils. The majority of both groups had 'positive self esteem with uncertainties'. On the other hand the majority of African-Caribbean pupils expressed 'strong positive self esteem' about their ethnicity, but only a third of White and 27 per cent of Pakistanis shared the same feeling. African-Caribbean pupils seem able to run a strong positive sense of ethnic identity in parallel with feeling more socially integrated within school. This is an important distinction from Pakistani pupils who do not negotiate their ethnic identities alongside the same perceived level of social integration. However, despite feeling more socially integrated the majority of African-Caribbean pupils felt that they had experienced racism compared to just under a third of Pakistani pupils and only 11 per cent of White pupils. For this group racism is perceived as more a part of everyday life. On the surface pupil responses would indicate that schools are relatively ethnically integrated but this did not appear to be the case in practice.

Ethnic differentials in perceptions of schooling

Predominantly pupils viewed school with 'mixed feelings'. In Jubilee School and Proposal High, almost half of pupils had strong positive feelings about school, being slightly lower at Tannery Rise School. Positive feelings about school do appear to be connected in part to ethnicity. 48 per cent of White pupils, 44 per cent of African-Caribbean pupils and just 34 per cent of Pakistani pupils had strong positive feelings about school. Pupils' perceptions of school work also show disparities. 18 per cent of White pupils compared with 9 per cent of Pakistani and 7 per cent of African-Caribbean felt 'good' about school work. The degree to which ethnicity accounts for social alienation, acceptance and differences in feelings about school seems of crucial importance when data on school exclusions indicate that pupils from African-Caribbean and White and African-Caribbean groups are among the most likely to be permanently excluded from schools. Moreover most boys continue to dominate the numbers of permanent exclusions nationally which warrants study of how gender intersects with this.

While there was a tendency for White pupils to be more positive about school, there was a contradiction in pupils' perceptions of unjust treatment. The majority of all pupils thought they experienced unjust treatment from 'time to time'.

Exploration into what unjust treatment encompasses shows variation in perceptions across ethnic groups. Setting by ability has been viewed negatively by much research (Ball 1981, Keddie 1970) but despite this the present emphasis continues to be on instrumental outcomes and league tables which means schools are under pressure to 'perform'. Setting pupils by ability is widely used as a sorting mechanism to enable pupils to reach targets. Despite the potential for negativity, not much of this has seemingly seeped down to minority ethnic pupils only a small proportion of Pakistani and African-Caribbean pupils indicated unjust treatment with selection into classes. However, 23 per cent of White pupils felt unhappy with selection into classes. The negative impact of setting on educational motivation and aspirations remains a problem across all ethnic groups.

Social class could also be a key explanatory factor since there was some disparity between schools. At Jubilee School, 20 per cent of all pupils felt they had been unfairly grouped which compares to 17 per cent at Proposal High and just 12 per cent at Tannery Rise School. This could perhaps be significant given that Jubilee School has a mixed social class intake. Existing studies of schools with mixed class intakes have indicated that setting was not just by ability, but clearly by social class (Ball 1981, Lacey 1973). Setting was thus viewed as a sorting mechanism which created and maintained inequalities as working class pupils tended to be placed in the lower sets. This study has been unable to demonstrate that social class is a factor here since at Jubilee School the same proportion of working class pupils felt they had unfair treatment as middle class pupils. Moreover this school had actively organised classes so that each had an equal balance of pupils according to gender, socioeconomic and ethnic backgrounds. It is difficult to explain why White pupils felt unhappy about selection into classes, but it might be related to the competitive culture of achievement which emphasises differences in ability, or perhaps they were unhappy with the way existing classes were mixed.

Overall pupils felt positively about school work. This was the case for the vast majority of Pakistani and White pupils. African-Caribbean pupils felt less positive (74 per cent). More pupils felt they had unjust treatment with the judgement of individual academic performance. This was the case for 31 per cent of Pakistani, 28 per cent of White but just 20 per cent of African-Caribbean pupils. Behaviour was cited as a reason for unjust treatment but this did differ according to ethnicity. White and Pakistani pupils had the same perceptions on this measure at 55 per cent. Despite this, punishment, or the way sanctions were distributed among pupils was not seen as a significant reason for unjust treatment. Only a small proportion of Pakistani pupils and White pupils identified this as an issue.

However, the majority of African-Caribbean pupils (73 per cent) felt that they had experienced unfair treatment because of behaviour. This factor would therefore seem to strongly shape African-Caribbean pupils' feelings about the school and is significant in light of the fact African-Caribbean pupils are most likely to be excluded from school at national level. African-Caribbean pupils were twice as likely to feel the way sanctions were distributed among pupils was an issue compared to White and Pakistani pupils. This factor would seem to strongly shape African-Caribbean pupils' feelings about the school and impacts on academic achievement. Combined with contextual factors such as the fact this group is more likely to suffer a dramatic event (which may cause conflict at home), this has adverse social implications. School should be a safe non-confrontational space for pupils which is achieved through school climate and ethos.

Ethnic differentials in teacher and peer relationships

With ethnic diversity apparent in all the schools and classrooms, as well as different personalities and learning needs, assessment of the classroom environment is an important facet of the study. Atmosphere in the classroom provoked different responses along ethnic lines. 45 per cent of White respondents viewed the atmosphere in their classrooms as 'friendly and cohesive' compared with 35 per cent of African-Caribbean and just 26 per cent Pakistani pupils. This is a significant finding and may reflect the fact that Pakistani pupils are more likely to feel less social support in school from both teachers and peers which is significant when these social relations are often seen as an important protective factor. There was some difference between schools as well. Pupils at Tannery Rise School were more likely to feel that their class was 'friendly and cohesive' than at Jubilee School, whereas less than half felt this way at Proposal High. In general, therefore, it seems that Tannery Rise School has created a more relaxed and more enjoyable classroom environment.

Overall most pupils indicated that several teachers liked them which shows that despite the different power positions of teachers and pupils, there are good interpersonal relationships. In the eyes of students, teachers are likely to be supportive and are likely to motivate and enhance self-esteem. This was the case across all schools. While there was not much difference in response according to school context, there was some difference in response according to ethnicity. Over half of Pakistani pupils felt that several teachers liked them but a significant minority did not know. This is in contrast to both African-Caribbean and White pupils who displayed more confidence. 60 per cent of African-Caribbean pupils and 65 per cent of White pupils felt their teachers liked them. Although much research has focused on teacher-pupil relationships, what has emerged here is the need to consider pupil-pupil dynamics. The vast majority of pupils identified themselves as having several friends in school. This was the case across all three schools and all ethnic and social class groupings. However, while the relationships pupils have with teachers seem to be ubiquitously positive, social relations between pupils seemed to be more fraught. The majority of pupils had a 'not unanimously positive experience' with peers in school. This was the case for all pupils across the social class and the ethnic divide. There was a slight difference with African-Caribbean pupils. Those (working class) pupils living in the inner city were more likely to report a negative social experience than those (middle class) pupils living on the outskirts. The combined influence of social class and ethnicity therefore does appear to be more pronounced for African-Caribbean pupils.

Hostile groups were identified in classrooms among about a quarter of White, Pakistani and African-Caribbean pupils. In addition to this, bullying occurred 'occasionally' in all three schools. Over a third of pupils at Tannery Rise School reported that bullying 'frequently' occurred. This was predominantly the case for all ethnic groups. However, bullying occurred in different places at different times according to the school context. At Schools 1 and 3, bullying occurred in the classroom, around school and outside school. At Proposal High, bullying mainly occurred outside the classroom, around school. This perhaps gives an indication of the different educational ethos and routine of each school. Bullying was seen to occur because of a number of different factors. Pupils perceived bullying to occur between pupils living in different neighbourhoods. This was the case for half of African-Caribbean pupils, and about a third of Pakistani and White pupils. On this measure, there was variation between schools. Pupils attending Proposal High were least likely to report any bullying between pupils living in different neighbourhoods. Bullying between pupils of different social backgrounds was most apparent at Jubilee School. Pupils also felt that bullying occurred between pupils of different ethnicities. Perceptions of this varied according to ethnicity. White and Pakistani pupils shared more or less the similar perceptions but far more African-Caribbeans (64 per cent) felt that bullying occurred between pupils of different ethnicities.

Although pupils felt that setting was fair, the competitive, achievement oriented-environment of school does seem to have had an impact on some pupils more than others. Pakistani pupils were much more likely to perceive their class as highly individualised which has implications for participation, compared with White and African-Caribbean pupils. A range of reasons for this could be suggested. The institutional organisation of classes where pupils are seated individually at desks in rows with the expectation to sit quietly and often work independently discourages social interaction. Coupled with the fact that Pakistani pupils were more likely to perceive hostile groups in their classroom, the mediating effect is one of diminished confidence and insularity.

A worrying finding was the number of pupils who found no comfort anywhere with significant ethnic differences, varying from about a quarter of White pupils to over a third of Pakistani and half of African-Caribbean pupils. It is very difficult to *define* exactly what is meant by this because you need to take into account a range of personal as well as social factors, but this does suggest a significant cohort of young people who are unhappy and insecure.

In summary, classroom interaction between peers of different social categories does involve subtle pressures and tensions. When studying classroom interaction Delamont (1976) states we need a less static concept than the notion of the clique to understand how pupils sometimes act together and sometimes isolate individuals. Observation of classroom dynamics in all three schools indicated that pupils tended to choose to sit with friends of the same ethnicity most of the time.

Altogether findings demonstrate that pupil-pupil relations within school are troubled. Placing emphasis on how the learner *perceives* the educational environment and social relations of their school, alongside external structural barriers such as gender, ethnicity and social class has allowed a clearer picture of ethnic differences in school to emerge. In sum, school experience varies according to ethnicity. Whereas White pupils feel secure in school possibly as a result of being the majority population, Pakistani pupils are more likely to feel unhappy and insecure. African-Caribbean pupils feel much more socially integrated with the student body than Pakistani pupils and feel the classroom is a friendly and sociable place, but perceive unfair treatment on the grounds of behaviour. Ethnicity matters in everyday school life.

Pupils self-segregated themselves according to ethnicity to varying degrees in all three schools. At Jubilee School there was also the added dimension of a predominantly White middle class catchment. Like so many other studies of teenagers in school, social groupings and peer networks were easily identified and made visible through discussion of cliques. Particular groups hung around in particular areas of the school. This was summed up by one African-Caribbean girl, 'Everyone is trying to fit in to different groups so they are not left out. (…) It is all to do with looks and stuff like'. These cliques were widely referred to by the names used among teenagers at national level, 'We have goths and stuff and then you have got chavs and then you have got people that think they are hard and people that we actually know are hard really…'. Another African-Caribbean girl said much of the same, 'we all just hang about with each other. Everyone goes in to different groups to be honest though'. Pupils openly discussed social groupings in each school. Dress styles and music tastes were sites of 'coolness' which characterised pupils' discussions of social groupings. Pupils reported socialising with pupils from a range of different ethnic backgrounds and for many the role of ethnicity was not recognised or acknowledged but in practice it operated to differentiate pupils' everyday social experience.

Emos and chavs were universally disliked. Discussion of these groups featured across all three schools and often provoked strong reaction, 'We have like Goths, Emos and Chavs and stuff like that. (…) I am just going to be truthful, I hate them.' (African-Caribbean boy). This was a pattern which emerged through all schools but to varying effect. Emos and Goths invoked a particular type of White ethnicity which sat uncomfortably with all Pakistani and African-Caribbean pupils interviewed. The terms emo and goth were used interchangeably to distinguish a group which were situated on the periphery of the everyday world of school, 'Goths stick together, they just get to the point where they just don't…they just do their own thing'. In understanding why emos were a peripheral group four main dimensions of this identity emerged. First was the salience of ethnicity, 'it's mostly White people'. Identities were marked by particular clothing choices, 'They just wear dark clothes, grow their hair right long and everything they wear is Black'. Some pupils displayed blurred identities, 'there are some people where they are kind of goths because they like listening to the rock music and that, but they don't dress themselves like goths, I don't know they just like listening to rock music and all that'. The boundaries which demarcated social identity could be fluid and could be experimented with. However the pupils which fell fully into emo identity provoked most negative discussion. Emo tastes were marked differently with preference to listening to heavy rock metal rather than the mainstream's preference for R 'n' B music. It was the specific ideology underlying emo/goth identity which caused offence,

> There is this guy, I am not too sure what his name is but he always talks about how his life is crap and that he wants to die. It is really depressing being around him. You say "shut up there is nothing wrong with your life, you should be happy". (Pakistani 10 girl).

Emos were the polar opposite of chavs, which was another branch of 'White' identity embodied by pupils at Schools 2 and 3 in particular. Chavs were constructed as a version of working class White identity. Pupils' descriptions fit Tyler's (2008: 17) interpretation of 'disgust reactions' received by 'the grotesque and comic figure of the chav'. 'Hardness' was a term widely used to delineate prestige to physical strength, 'he's reet hard' and on corridors at Schools 2 and 3, chavs would talk of 'banging people out'. However, African-Caribbean pupils in particular associated White Chav identity with physical weakness and empty threats. In lessons chavs were viewed as being the group most likely in school to get into trouble. White identities were also seen as under attack, apart from perceptions of emos and chavs, White boys in Tannery Rise School complained of being called 'White bastards'. White middle class boys at Jubilee School felt they had tried to forge friendships with African-Caribbean boys but these were often rebuffed.

The main area of inter-ethnic antagonism was not between White and Black pupils, but between African-Caribbeans and Pakistanis, this has not been identified adequately in existing research. This finding was based on analysis of a range of evidence and observations of a number of interactions within the schools. Sometimes these divisions came out seemingly playfully but they were always instigated by African-Caribbeans against Pakistanis. In a focus group discussion about connections to other countries, one African-Caribbean boy commented, 'Yes Pakistan. They used to run round playing football in bare feet' [laughs] to which the Pakistani boy responded with, 'Ha ha no they didn't' Later on when asking a Pakistani boy why having more Pakistani teachers would be a good thing, the same African-Caribbean boy responded with, 'They have more fear of terrorists. [Laughs]' to which the Pakistani boy responded with, 'I'll slap you you Black shit' [laughs] (Year 10 Focus group). Although both boys were laughing which suggests harmless fun, there was a deeper layer of significance behind these exchanges. These were not examples of injecting humour into social interaction. Neither did it seem to be a marker social intimacy. Rather these were micro insults given by the African-Caribbean boy to the Pakistani boy and the laughter from both boys served to reduce the potential tension. When the meaning of these remarks was challenged the African-Caribbean boy stated, 'No it is just a joke; we are only messing about with each other'. However, this was a feeling in all three schools which suggests a wider social division between the two groups than school based issues. What was significant was that Pakistanis tended to 'accept' these exchanges. Although there was evidence of active challenging this was not a case of resistance within accommodation but seemed to signal subservience.

Aspirations

Young people's aspirations are a large part of their decisions to participate in further education (FE). When comparing the employment aspirations of these young people with the outcomes of their parents results show that they have higher aspirations. The fact that pupils from Pakistani backgrounds were more likely to think they will live better indicates aspirations but exploration into how pupils expect upward mobility to be achieved shows that it is not by entry into professional occupations. 67 per cent of African-Caribbean and 65 per cent of White pupils aspired towards white collar work, but a lower proportion of Pakistani pupils (58 per cent) had these aspirations. Although Pakistani pupils have aspirations to provide a better standard of living, it does not seem to be through the endorsed professional occupational route which may reflect disillusionment about prospects. Aspirations of disadvantaged pupils were no different to aspirations of advantaged pupils. However, perhaps in reality it poses more risk for working class pupils since the financial burden to support further education rests with parents. They do not have the safety net of financial resources so have to make decisions which safeguard their security perhaps. In looking at worries and concerns the majority of White and African-Caribbean pupils cited 'country, nation and society'. Pakistani pupils worried more about personal and family life and the impact of wider social issues on these spheres.

The rhetoric espoused about the value and need to engage in further and higher education (with the emphasis being upon employment as the main route out of poverty) does seem to have had an impact on individual students which cuts across ethnicity lines. 70 per cent of White pupils, 72 per cent of Pakistani pupils and 74 per cent of African-Caribbean pupils intend to continue studying after GCSEs which is a fairly optimistic indicator that pupils are motivated, have raised aspirations and subscribe to the endorsed view that education brings better prospects.

To some extent findings would indicate that some pupils feel they have no control over their destiny. Of the pupils who did not expect to continue studying the main reason cited was 'I have to earn money'. 17 per cent of African-Caribbean students and 7 per cent of Pakistani students cited this as a reason. There was also a distinction made between schools. Schools 1 and 3 with 9 per cent and 10 per cent of all pupils compared to 5 per cent in Proposal High. This difference between school contexts may be explained by social class or pupils' families' existing social status. Perhaps this indicates that pupils with limited financial resources are less prone to worry simply because you can't lose what you never had. Having financial worries and being focused on alleviating financial constraints in the present is significant since it can be viewed as detrimental to the longer term goal of securing employability through education. Given the impact that post-compulsory qualifications have on future earnings (and with it, future life chances) this is a point of significance for educational policy. How to get rid of the 'dual economy' in higher education and more effectively widen participation? How can you achieve equity without perhaps creating a 'cloyingly supportive environment that patronises or mollycoddles them (working class students) and undermines their self-esteem' (Derham 2003). This is concerning as recent research on the impact of the recession predicts that one in five young people who collected their GCSE results this year could be on unemployment benefits/Jobseekers Allowance by the time they are 21 (Prince's Trust 2009).

Conclusion

This chapter confirms general trends in the literature on education and ethnicity (reviewed in Chapters 2 and 3) and contributes new evidence on the importance of ethnic differentials in school experiences, patterns of informal ethnic segregation and the significance of inter-ethnic and peer hostilities in school life. This research also challenges any connection between ethnicity and low educational aspirations, apart from the case of Gypsies, Roma and Travellers where high dropout and high levels of disaffection with school are particularly marked. The UK experience shows that despite significant achievements in developing integrated, non-discriminatory educational systems persistent patterns of hostility, segregation and inequality remain. The next chapter considers the significance of these findings in the context of other selected European countries, particularly as in Central and Eastern Europe where the progress towards integrated, non-discriminatory educational systems has been much more limited.

There are a number of clear messages arising from this research. Racial and ethnic polarisation is evident across secondary schools in this city context. Negative perceptions and experiences for Pakistani and African-Caribbean pupils confirms ethnic differentials in life at school. Everyday informal ethnic segregation was common in school and inter-ethnic hostility was particularly focused on Pakistanis. Minority ethnic pupils did not appear to benefit in terms of attainment from attending a 'better, more middle class' school. Institutional processes of streaming fuelled dynamics of inclusion/exclusion but there is evidence that some pupils could negotiate differing roles, e.g. across 'boffin' (achievement orientated) and 'gangsta' (street orientated) positions which challenges the binary of academic achiever/disaffected. Over 70 per cent of pupils from all ethnic majority and minority groups (apart from Gypsy and Traveller pupils who were not represented amongst this group of pupils) strongly recognised that education was a key means of improving life-chances and despite widely varying home backgrounds and school experiences aspirations were high with no significant ethnic differentials. However, over a quarter of pupils did not take this view and this educational disaffection across all groups needs addressing. Highly complex and differentiated positions, strategies and perceptions were articulated by young people in relation to their experiences of school and community life. Young people's yearning to escape being 'othered' was strongly voiced with some able to articulate narratives of emancipation and liberation from differential and discriminatory treatment.

But many felt locked into and unable to escape a tangled web of constraining circumstances and social worlds with serious consequences in terms of declining educational aspirations and dropout from the educational system altogether.

To conclude the policy implications of the findings presented both in this chapter and in Chapter 5 are now considered. There is an urgent need to prioritise the objectives of racial and ethnic equality and multiculturalism in educational experiences, institutional arrangements and achievement and actively develop and support programmes, initiatives and interventions to achieve these objectives in mainstream schooling. There are many ways in which individual schools and local education authorities and agencies can and have been responding to these challenges. Diversity was emphasised in the schools examined here through focusing on the surface manifestations of ethnicity, which served to socially articulate and maintain differences through 'boundary maintenance' rather than offering cohesive provision. Firstly, it is necessary for schools and local educational authorities and agencies, and central government to acknowledge and recognise the nature and extent of these processes identified here and to re-affirm and prioritise racial and ethnic equality and multiculturalism in educational contexts. The likelihood that these concerns and objectives will be downgraded in the current economic context is of serious concern given the real prospects of increasing racial and ethnic inequalities amongst children, for example in poverty and material conditions. Secondly, it is necessary to actively develop and support programmes, initiatives and interventions to achieve these objectives in mainstream schooling. There is still a great need for stronger leadership, creative innovation and transformative change on these matters. At national level the strengthening of multiculturalism (Modood 2010) and a renewed commitment to racism reduction and anti-discrimination (Law 2010) are urgently needed.

Increasing the participation of Gypsy, Roma and Traveller (GRT) children in secondary education is urgently required. The continued failure to arrest declining educational attainment requires a new creative national campaign to address literacy and generate aspirational capital amongst these communities, led by these communities with government, LEA and school support. Some local initiatives have shown that entrenched patterns of school non-attendance can be substantially transformed with effective outreach programmes but they remain marginal and insecure and it is vital to build on the success of targeted initiatives like the Achievement Service programmes and Early Years Outreach teams and also that schools show positive leadership and do not turn away these children due to concerns over absence figures. Empowerment of GRT community organisations, mobilising adult mentors and securing involvement of families and parents is also vital in achieving this objective.

There must be intensive efforts to reduce ethnic differentials in school experiences, particularly for Pakistani pupils in their perceptions of the unfair treatment of their school work, in the classroom and in their general perceptions of schooling, and particularly for African-Caribbeans in their perceptions of unfair treatment of their behavior. Ofsted have a key role to play here in adequately addressing this issue in inspection regimes. Head teachers and governors have a statutory duty here to eliminate racial and ethnic equality and racial discrimination, and promote good relations and cohesion between all groups.

Reducing informal ethnic segregation and peer to peer hostilities in all areas of schooling, and particularly inter-ethnic hostility between African-Caribbean and Pakistani pupils, and also reducing societal racial stereotyping of Gypsies, Roma and Travellers, African-Caribbeans and Pakistanis is needed and also support for pupils in consciousness raising, understanding and dealing with these issues. The Education and Inspections Act 2006 inserted a new section 21(5) in to the Education Act 2002 introducing a duty on the governing bodies of maintained schools to promote community cohesion which came into effect on 1 September 2007. The wealth of UK good practice in 'racism reduction' (Law 2010) outside school contexts, and in school (for example Knowles and Ridley 2006, Runnymede Trust 2007) provide a valuable evidence base of successful interventions. It would also be valuable to allow pupils the space to understand about the African-Caribbean, Pakistani and Gypsy Roma presence in Britain, specifically in relation to the local context. Although all the schools examined here promoted Black History Month, there were not any learning activities developed around this. White ethnic identities are currently often left out of these sorts of 'ethnic' provisions and should be included.

There must be an on-going commitment to the professional development and training of both teaching and non-teaching staff working in multicultural schools. Too little assistance is provided to teachers to help them observe and construct the meanings and knowledge that guide their actions in the classroom. Teachers appear scared about the issues of race and ethnicity which seems to stem from hyper-awareness and insecurity. Measures to address this could include training days and workshops with parents and community members where they break from the everyday insular routine and are able to learn about the ethnically diverse groups they teach in a very practical way. Greater attention needs to be paid to how teachers working in inner city schools are trained, hired, and manage with the distinct challenges of inner city teaching in ethnically diverse classrooms. There are two achievable options here. Option A is a PGCE (postgraduate certificate in education) specifically aimed at teachers wanting to teach in inner city settings. This differs from the 'mainstream' PGCE as greater emphasis is placed on understanding pupil behaviour and the specific challenge of classroom management. Option B is to ensure that a statutory requirement of gaining Qualified Teacher Status is that all trainee teachers must successfully undertake a placement in an inner city school. Following this there must be an on-going commitment to the professional development and training of both teaching and non-teaching staff working in inner city schools. Too little assistance is provided to teachers to help them observe and construct the meanings and knowledge that guide their actions in the classroom. Measures to address this could include offering a mentoring scheme or offering opportunities for team teaching where they break from insularity and can learn from others' professional practice through action and reflection in a very practical way. It would also be of benefit for all teachers to be offered the opportunity to 'see outside the box' and observe practice in a range of other types of schools. For instance, teachers working in inner city schools may observe teaching practice in the differing contexts of independent schools, pupil referral units, academies, faith schools and special schools to gain a broader level of social insight in order to be equipped to trial new methods and make change in their own milieu. Such experience would equip teachers with an understanding of how different groups of pupils of the same age perform in different settings with different organisational and social contexts. This could generate higher expectations of the pupils in their classes and could generate ideas for innovating lessons. To ensure a better understanding of teaching ethnically diverse groups of pupils the content of the PGCE should also develop skills, knowledge and understanding in managing ethnically diverse groups and in addressing racial hostility and ethnic and religious identities in school.

Reducing the influence of postcode gangs and masculine 'gangsta' culture on young people and everyday school life is an increasing priority. Schools in this study were generally sensitive to the issues surrounding postcode gangs and some had taken a clear stance of zero tolerance, but much more work needs to be done to develop effective interventions to achieve this goal. The Department for Children, Schools and Families has issued guidance and a toolkit for action for schools in dealing with gangs and group offending (DCSF 2008b), and there are useful lessons set out in the experiences of the Tackling Gangs Action Programme which was carried out in 2007/8 (Home Office 2007/8). There are also a variety of other toolkits and guides for example *Gangs at the Grassroots* (Brand and Ollerearnshaw 2008). Work must continue around boys' damaging and limited models of being masculine in the context of postcode gangs and also in addressing attitudes and patterns of behaviour that demean girls and women. Schools are well placed to address gender issues through specific units of work which explicitly discuss conceptions of gendered identity. Programs may be either gender-specific or gender-relevant but should address social justice issues which allow pupils to build and explore individual identities and also girls' assertiveness and issues of sexual exploitation.

Institutional processes of streaming and setting fuel pupil and teacher dynamics of inclusion and exclusion, they have little impact on increasing attainment and they can reduce educational aspirations and attainment and they can also be detrimental to children (Blatchford 2005). A key challenge for policy makers at national level is to find ways to promote the motivational disposition which encourage aspirations through education and learning. While interventions in disaffection usually focus on 'fixing' the pupil, focus must also be drawn to the role of the curriculum and pedagogy, which currently remains standardised and uniform. This exists as a consequence of school evaluation and pupil assessment which emphasises a narrowed range of outcomes. It is logical that a flexible, permeable and responsive continuum of support and provision is needed to target the most challenging young people based on their particular continuum of need. What is needed is a flexible and creative response which offers an alternative to traditional education to meet the demands of challenging pupils. This requires more innovative measures than just tweaking the timetable. There is a need for a pedagogy that captures and sustains pupils' interest in learning. The goal of educational work with disaffected pupils should be one of social justice and schools should provide the space and resources for pupils to broaden their horizons and improve relationships. Schools are unable to affect the social circumstances in which pupils are living; but policy could do more to offer a curriculum which permits young people to make choices, to build self-confidence, and to see the connections between learning and a better life.

Chapter 7

Ethnicity and Education in Europe, Comparisons and Case Studies

Introduction

This chapter will place both England and the Northcity case study in a comparative context drawing on similar studies in the nine EU countries that have participated in the EDUMIGROM project, England, Germany, Denmark and Sweden in Western Europe and Romania, the Czech Republic, Slovakia and Hungary in post-socialist Central and Eastern Europe. The nature and complexity of relations between the movement of people (migration), the formation of boundaries between groups of people who have shared cultural meanings, memories and descent (ethnicity) and the formation and negative treatment of racial groups (racism) and the interactions between these three processes and schooling is a key focus for this chapter. This chapter will firstly present key comparative findings based on an analysis of the cross-national survey data and then some of the key findings from the country case studies are presented, drawing on selected extracts from these studies. An extremely rich data set has been produced from each country team and it is not possible to do justice to the depth of this data here, all the country team reports are available on the EDUMIGROM website (www.edumigrom.eu). These case studies form the basis for the meta-analysis in the next section of this chapter which focuses on identifying key themes and issues from the qualitative studies of schools and community contexts carried out in the different national contexts. A summary European Policy Brief identifying key messages and policy recommendations can be found at http://www.edumigrom.eu/news/2011-04-04/ new-publication-european-policy-brief.

Lastly, consideration is given to theorising the intensification of anti-Roma racism in Central and Eastern and the implications of contemporary debates in the UK over multiculturalism, segregation and education.

Cross-national themes and issues arising from survey evidence

The EDUMIGROM project team carried out a survey of 14-17 years old students attending schools in multi-ethnic working class communities in eight EU countries in 2008 (not including Sweden). 105 schools with 287 classes completed the survey, yielding data on 5,086 students. Individual country reports detailed students' experiences with schooling, significant relationships offered by adolescent life, and the ways schools opened up, or for that matter, limited the choices and aspirations of teenagers in multi-ethnic communities. In interpreting the findings the overall survey report (Szalai, Messing and Nemenyi 2010) defined three country clusters rather than drawing comparison between individual countries. This enabled comparison to be drawn to the inter-ethnic attitudes in the present day being importantly shaped by differences in historical development leading to century-old and traditions of inter-ethnic relations and ethnic hierarchies. The country clusters were: post-colonial countries (France and the United Kingdom); countries of economic migration (Denmark, Germany) and post-socialist countries (Czech Republic, Hungary; Romania and Slovakia). The data confirmed significant differences in the life, schooling, and opportunities of young people from 'visible' minority ethnic groups in these three contexts particularly between those in the 'West' and in the 'East'. There are very limited rights, provisions and political institutions that protect Roma in the post-socialist context, with Roma youth frequently facing harsh exclusion and racialised 'ghettoisation' in schooling and beyond, that has been accompanied in recent years by increasing questioning of their citizens' rights by vocal and influential majority groups which has a harmful impact on identity development and aspirations. Young people belonging to 'visible' minorities in the post-colonial contexts tend to consider themselves parts of the country where they were born in a more routine manner than the respective groups in the countries of economic migration. Children of 'visible' migrant families in the post-colonial countries seem to face somewhat smaller risks of becoming severely marginalised than those in countries of economic migration.

In using this data to examine the interactions between the ethnic composition of school and students' performance, self esteem and aspirations Messing (2010) identified a number of key findings:

- the impact of ethnic segregation/separation of students in school is far from evident. Various patterns of separation affect students' performance, self-esteem and aspirations towards further schooling and labour market participation quite differently, and, naturally, the wider social and structural circumstances seem to have a determining influence as well.
- divergence between new and old member states of the European Union in how ethnic background and school environment affect students' performance, self-esteem, and aspirations. In new EU member states, there are significant differences between minority ethnic and majority students studying in the same environment. In particular, ethnic background as well as the ethnic composition of a school influence students' performance, self-esteem, and aspirations. While old EU member states are by no means homogeneous, these relationships are generally not so pronounced.
- The most clear-cut relationship between a school's ethnic composition and respondents' performance, self-esteem, and aspirations is that the correlation between performance in school and self-esteem is not inherently

positive. Minority ethnic students studying in schools that are dominated by the country's ethnic majority perform well and have high aspirations regarding further schooling and employment, but tend to have a more negative self-image and, in general, and feel less comfortable at school. By contrast, minority ethnic students have higher self-esteem and feel more comfortable in schools in which they form a majority, but perform poorly and have limited aspirations regarding their education or labour market participation. Both relationships are especially pronounced in countries in Central and Eastern Europe.

- The least favourable environment both for majority and minority ethnic students in terms of performance, self-esteem, and aspirations comprises schools where segregation is practised within the walls of the institution.
- Taking into account all aspects investigated here, under certain conditions, an ethnically mixed school and class environment seems to best meet the needs of both majority and minority ethnic students. Mixed schools appear to provide students who perform well with opportunities to continue suitable education, and they also assist with the healthy development of students' self-esteem and interpersonal relationship (Messing 2010: 1).

In England the long-established legal context of challenging segregating and racially discriminatory practices and the development of mixed comprehensive schooling without early tracking, does support this general vision. Of all countries researched here, England has on the surface one of the most fair education systems with a high proportion of minority ethnic minority students having access to popular high achieving schools. Despite this relatively high degree of ethnic mixing, in practice this alone does not work to ameliorate social divisions. Students self segregate on the grounds of ethnicity and social class and to varying degrees live separated to ethnic 'Others', particularly White pupils. So, informal segregation, inter-ethnic hostilities and severely inadequate inclusion of Gypsy and Traveller children and young people remain a tolerated and to some extent accepted part of the educational system. This finding has implications for other European countries in that these issues need addressing at the same time as more formal de-segregation measures, which are also failing in most of the Central and Eastern European contexts considered below (Szalai, Messing and Nemenyi 2010).

Despite major differences in educational policies and the structure and organisation of schooling, educational systems throughout Europe have proved rather inefficient in ameliorating the effects of family background. The quantitative survey found that students from highly educated families are nearly five times more likely to attain 'excellent' qualifications than their peers from poorly educated parental backgrounds. Living conditions were also a crucial factor directly affecting the ways children perform in school. Students from relatively well-off families enjoy the facilities of well-equipped homes, opportunities for quiet studying and being saved from taking part in income-raising duties, and those that did not living in poor and destitute conditions have less than half the chance of concluding their studies with outstanding results. Gender did have an impact on achievement levels but it was significantly less than those of one's socio-economic or ethnic background. Girls better adjust to the official requirements of schooling than boys and have an 8 per cent higher chance of receiving 'excellent' grades than boys. Ethnicity is deeply entwined with socioeconomic status, and nearly one-third of students of a White 'ethnic majority' background attained 'excellent' qualifications compared to only one-tenth of their peers from minority ethnic groups (Szalai, Messing and Nemenyi 2010).

There were significant differences in patterns of openness and acceptance of 'Others' between students residing in Western, as opposed to Central European communities. Students in Denmark, Germany, France and the United Kingdom seemed to attribute far smaller significance to the family background or ethnic identity of their (potential) partners: the proportion of those mentioning socio-economic or ethnic background as an important factor in choosing a partner is almost twice as high among respondents in the 'new' than in the 'old' member-states (about 56 per cent, in contrast to about 25 per cent, for both these factors). The history and traditions of inter-ethnic relations play a key role in distancing social and ethnic groups from each other. Students seem to refuse the 'Other' (both, in ethnic and social terms) least in those countries that are characterised primarily by migration from the one-time colonies (France, UK). In these countries, only 15 per cent of the respondents mentioned that ethnicity or social background (would) make a role in forming partnerships. This proportion is more than the double (30 per cent) in countries where migration is a more recent process and where it has been kept in motion primarily by economic needs of the 'host' country (Germany, Denmark). The ratio of those who identify different ethnic or social background of their (potential) partner as a significant factor in their choice is much higher in post-socialist contexts (56 per cent). This reflects different patterns of inter-ethnic relations and indicates the significance of ethnicity in shaping young people's private lives (Szalai, Messing and Nemenyi 2010).

In school contexts wide variations in peer relations were reported. Very few students in the Czech Republic reported bullying, whereas over 90 per cent of students in France, UK and Hungary did. Ethnic composition of the school is important here. Bullying between pupils takes place less frequently in schools where the student body is ethnically homogeneous. In schools with a White majority student population, bullying is less typical (67 per cent) than in schools where ethnic separation exists (80 per cent). Patterns differ in schools where there is a dominance of ethnic minorities within the school population. In Central European countries, bullying in ethnically homogeneous environments is considerably lower when compared to other schools (50 per cent and 75 per cent), while a similar environment in the West produced higher levels of such conflict (84 per cent and 68 per cent). Inter-ethnic hostility and associated bullying occurs with remarkable frequency as well as almost one-third of students reported such experiences (Szalai, Messing and Nemenyi 2010).

A key message from this research, borne out by the quantitative survey data, is that there is a major benefit from creating ethnically and socially mixed schools both in the achievement of disadvantaged and/or minority ethnic students and all (majority *and* minority) students with regard to their attained social and cultural skills. This should be a primary goal for local educational authorities (Szalai, Messing and Nemenyi 2010: 117). Patterns of inter-ethnic conflict, and bullying are also likely to be lower where there is no ethnic separation or segregation *within* the school in terms of classes or streams, i.e. no racial and ethnic direct or indirect discrimination. These patterns and problems may still be higher in mixed school contexts than where ethnic groups are segregated in different schools and where there is less opportunity for conflict, and this requires recognition and intervention to address these difficulties in mixed contexts, as in the UK (Szalai, Messing and Nemenyi 2010). The next section provides some illustrative evidence from case study material in individual countries

Germany case study: conflict over Islam in Berlin schools

This section draws on and summarises the final report by the German EDUMIGROM team (Mannitz et al. 2011). Research for this case study was carried out in two schools in two typical immigrant districts of Berlin. Turkish and Lebanese young people were selected for study here as their performances are significantly lower than average and as they appear to be the main target group of public discourse on failed integration, increasingly codified as 'Muslims'. The chosen schools were an integrated comprehensive school (*Gesamtschule*), and one grammar school (*Gymnasium*) which facilitated insight into the situation of more successful students with the same family background. The difference between these two schools in terms of teachers and parents attitudes was significant. In the *Gesamtschule* very few students gave an example of supportive, motivated and friendly teachers, unlike the *Gymnasium* where they stated that most teachers there were good and the general atmosphere was open, respectful and friendly. Teachers were motivating the students with positive responses to their ideas and suggestions. In contrast, in the *Gesamtschule* some teachers tried to 'tame' the class to ensure an atmosphere where learning was possible, while others simply did not really interact with the students or constantly blamed them. Although the teachers of the *Gesamtschule* were well aware of the underprivileged situations their pupils lived in, they mostly saw it as a burden which made their job too exhausting, and respond to it by reducing their teaching standards. Language problems and other difficulties of their students were blamed on the pupils and their families and many felt that their home and ethnic origins were not appreciated at all. The importance of active and conscious parents and committed teachers made a huge difference in the *Gymnasium*, in comparison to the pessimistic and disrespectful atmosphere in the *Gesamtschule* (Mannitz et al. 2011).

Intensifying conflict over Islam was a major theme in the German study. A key finding was that students and parents on the one hand, and with teachers and other school staff on the other is that Islam is not really accepted (students and parents) or does not really fit (teachers) into German society. Pupils identified teachers and other adults working in the school environment as key in the process of 'othering', particularly as school was the site where students interact with members of the majority population most regularly. Several Muslim girls felt discrimination because of their headscarf. Some explained that they felt bothered by discussions in school lessons about arranged or forced marriages and family life in Islam as well. This feeling seems to be due to the fact that teachers present these issues in such a way that the Muslim students feel put under pressure; the teachers' intention in most cases seems to be to make the pupils adopt German majority views and not to resolve negative stereotypes about Islam. Students of Muslim background who subscribe to norms of premarital sexual abstinence are perceived by the majority as representing outdated attitudes, or as being the objects of family oppression, and do not want to justify themselves all the time. They prefer to spend time with peers who share similar thoughts and accept them the way they are. Some students even argued that it is better to be in a school where minority ethnic pupils are in a majority because it offers a kind of protection against discrimination. For young people outside school, residential segregation and differences in teenage lifestyles serve to embed ethnic segregation and separation between Muslim minorities and the German majority, which increase in importance and significance with the beginning of adolescence. Whenever pupils from Turkish, Arab and Muslim backgrounds said that it would be better if there were more Germans at school, this was not motivated by an interest in closer interactions but by the desire to become fluent in German language, or that it would improve the image of the school. Past experiences of being 'othered' discouraged these from approaching Germans unless necessary and this experience seems to be an important part of everyday life for Muslim minorities in Germany.

Family solidarity was seen by many as being of these pupils as an asset in which Germans were lacking. The need for minority ethnic pupils to close ranks with their parents by stressing how much they agree with them, and that their own obedience of certain norms is completely deliberate has to be interpreted as a reaction to the mainstream discourse about Islam as a repressive force. The interviewees were well aware that most Germans regard norms like chastity, covering of the hair, or marriage at an early age as signs of parental oppression. In their schools students are often faced with discussions about these issues, and they experience that they are not able to change their teachers' or German peers' negative perceptions of their families and religion. Closing ranks with all Muslims in Germany and sometimes even to non-Muslim minorities who were described as sharing similar cultural norms of respect, chastity and honesty was also expressed by some pupils, particularly amongst the Arab group. There was a complete absence of identification as Germans despite almost all being German citizens. Some students also argued that the Germans would not accept them as being alike. To fully assimilate and finally become a 'real German' is evidently not within the range of options that students of Turkish, Arab or Muslim background regard as realistic (Mannitz et al. 2011). These findings confirm a track record of research evidence on minority ethnic identities in Germany and the significance of the 'losing battle' between teachers and pupils over Islamophobia and the role of Muslim communities in this national context (Schiffauer et al. 2004). The German and the British state's parallel political construction of the failure of multiculturalism seeks to put the blame for inter-ethnic conflict and segregation on multicultural policy rather than on the racialisation of political discourse, the construction of citizenship, the rhetoric of integration rather than inclusion and the failure to construct shared political space. Contradicting mainstream political rhetoric, greater multiculturalism and antiracism, in terms of attention to the human needs arising from ethnic, cultural and religious diversity in education rather than less is required here.

Denmark case study: new stereotypes of Muslim pupils and schools as a 'zone of exception' in Copenhagen

This section draws on and summarises the final report by the Danish EDUMIGROM team (Moldenhawer and Padovan-Özdemir 2011). Seven schools in two different areas of Copenhagen were chosen for study. Both areas have been targeted for special educational intervention due to the high concentrations of minority ethnic groups in order to promote equality in education outcomes, social cohesion and inter-ethnic stability, but are perceived differently. Belleview seems to receive very limited public and political attention, whereas Fraser is often characterised as a ghetto and as an area dominated by lack of integration into the Danish society (Moldenhawer et al. 2010: 11). 50 per cent of Belleview School's student body is of minority ethnic background, whereas 90 per cent of Fraser School's student body is of minority ethnic background. Minority ethnic families primarily being of lower socioeconomic status, it is evident that minority ethnic students score lower in school than do their ethnic majority peers. Ethnic majority girls receive the highest grades, whereas minority ethnic boys receive the lowest. This confirms earlier and present research often explaining this pattern as a result of female gendered socialisation processes being more adaptive to the education system (Jakobsen and Liversage 2010: 49-51). This explanation may additionally be qualified by the qualitative teacher interviews, where they often explain the ethnic category in gendered terms differentiating between 'the quiet hard-working minority ethnic girl' and 'the misbehaving Muslim boy' (Moldenhawer et al. 2010: 33; Gilliam 2010). Nevertheless, this data show that minority boys from lower-status families report that they get higher grades than majority boys form the same social position (Moldenhawer and Padovan-Özdemir 2011). The construction of new stereotypes of Muslim pupils has also been identified in the British context (Shain 2011).

Minority ethnic pupil's aspirations were strong and they were more likely to aim for a white collar job than majority students despite their parents' lower average education level. Teachers, on the other hand, speak of too high ambitions among minority ethnic students and their parents. Even the most school-reluctant minority students express an understanding of the importance of schooling, being in the most extreme case a route the passage out of crime (Moldenhawer et al. 2010: 56). Dominant discursive linkages between minority ethnic groups and crime, violence and unemployment were frequently identified by pupils. Pupils' strategies of commitment to educational goals, particularly amongst girls, and an instrumental approach to these goals were clearly identified, whereas strategies of opposition were not. In terms of ethnicity pupils advocated a variety of positions ranging from 'ethnic pride' to downplaying ethnicity and promoting mixed ethnic/ immigrant identities that are converted into sub-cultural and locally anchored identities (i.e. 'hip hop'/'gangsta' – attitudes) particularly amongst boys.

The school stands out as a 'zone of exception', the ethnically diverse school may be understood as a sanctuary from the negative representations of ethnic minorities in public and political discourses, especially when it comes to social interaction and the social well-being of the students (Moldenhawer et al. 2010: 57). There is also evidence of a high level of inter-ethnic interaction among the students. Girls interact more than boys and social upper-status boys interact the least and there is a high level of inter-ethnic interaction amongst minority ethnic students exclusively. Outside school inter-ethnic interaction appeared very limited except in sports contexts. The notion of school as a zone of exception is particularly relevant where it is situated in a so-called 'ghetto-area' like the Fraser school, and where local residential areas become a key feature of belonging as they do for many pupils. The research sample consists of both Muslim independent schools and public schools with different concentration levels of minority ethnic students and there appears to be a general feeling of safety and recognition among the students in schools with high proportions of minority ethnic students (Moldenhawer and Padovan-Özdemir 2011). The significance of local/ neighbourhood identities and related gang/gangsta cultures was also identified in the English case study, together with greater levels of inter-ethnic interaction amongst minority ethnic students rather than those of the majority indicating the forging of new identities and living multiculturalism and the need for schools to recognise these trends, counteract negative trends and nurture and support positive processes of interaction.

Sweden case study: the negative impact of segregation and selection on ethnic minority groups in Stockholm

This section draws on and summarises the final report by the Swedish EDUMIGROM team (Carson et al. 2011). The principal explanation of the frequent occurrence of 'othering' identified by the respondents from this fieldwork is the segregation in housing and schools in Stockholm. As a result of spatial separation, groups with different social and ethnic background have fewer opportunities to interact in the kinds of social settings that contribute to developing personal relationships, which gives rise to prejudice and stereotypical thinking. However, seeking to create a multicultural environment does not provide a simple remedy, as tensions can arise between groups of Swedes and immigrants, and between different immigrant groups. Such tensions are obviously not limited to ethnic or cultural differences, as evidenced by the tensions and occasional violence between rival soccer gangs. School personnel and the parents have developed somewhat different strategies to counteract 'othering' and discrimination including working with and supporting young people to improve level of motivation and access to upper secondary schools and work. In some cases parents seem more resigned to this condition, and want to protect their children from 'othering' by keeping them close to people with the same background. This is mostly the case among parents with low levels of education. More highly educated parents tend to be more oriented toward the surrounding society. Three distinct patterns or strategies of identity formation among the students regarding their ethnic belonging and relationship to the native Swedish population were identified including firstly students with a strong ethnic identification combined with weak integrationist aspirations and strong desire for building bonding social capital within their ethnic group, secondly students with a more open and distanced attitude towards their ethnic origin and thirdly students with a self-conscious acceptance and pride of the ethnic belonging accompanied by strong integrationist aspirations. Teachers often interpret equality as similarity, which means providing children with a similar education (Burns et al. 2005). Teachers' interpretation of equality as meaning similarity, or treating students similarly, has discriminatory effects on students with a foreign background (Carson et al. 2011). The reticence to address ethnicity directly by teachers is a theme across a number of these case studies.

In the process of a decade-long experiment with independent schools where public financing follows the student there are indications that this will lead to increasing problems for young people from migrant groups particularly where the best students gravitate to the same schools and poorly performing students would be left concentrated in struggling public schools which may then on the verge of closing due to falling enrolment and financial difficulties. It remains unclear to what extent this development will ultimately have a disproportionate impact on students with an immigration background. However, the evidence suggests that selection pressures are making it increasingly difficult for schools located in areas considered less desirable. Students who suffer from the disruption of closing schools appear at this point more likely to be members of groups that have immigrated to Sweden (Carson et al. 2011). The negative effects on some minority ethnic groups of current changes in the structure of educational systems is also a recurring theme across a number of these case study contexts.

France case study: major divide between teachers and pupils in the recognition of ethnicity and racism in Paris and Bordeaux

This section draws on and summarises the final report by the French EDUMIGROM team (Schiff 2011). The French study was carried out in six different high-schools, located in a disadvantaged Parisian suburb of the Seine-Saint-Denis district and in the agglomeration of Bordeaux. In the schools under investigation the proportion of students belonging to the 'selected' minority groups (Maghrebian-Turkish, African-Caribbean) ranged from approximately 40 per cent in Bordeaux to over 90 per cent in Paris and the student population was overwhelmingly of lower class status. These groups were located at the bottom of the local hierarchy of schools in Bordeaux, but represented the local norm in the Seine-Saint-Denis given the lower class status of the area's residents as a whole. The French study is therefore about lower class youth enrolled in low prestige schools, more than it is about a particular ethnic group or a particular local community. Compared to countries such as Germany, Austria, Belgium or the Netherlands, the French school system produces greater polarisation of educational outcomes for second generation youth (Schiff 2011).

The failure of teachers, heads and other key educational informants to recognise key problems of ethnic differentials and acknowledge their significance was striking, such as the unequal distribution of ethnic groups across streams or the over-representation of minority students among school leavers and among the lowest performing students of certain classes. But, there was no evidence of racial or ethnic discrimination against minority ethnic students in terms of grading, of tracking, or in terms of the treatment of students in class. Although some teachers might hold racist sentiments or hold negative stereotypes of minority students, they clearly appear as exceptions to the rule. Teachers' ignorance of these issues and the almost total absence of any mention or discussion of students' ethnicity in normal everyday school interactions and official discourse was striking. The contrast between a student body for whom ethnic, racial and religious distinctions are an integral part of social interactions and a vehicle for expressing a range of feelings and opinions about oneself and others, and the Republican school culture for whom such references remain largely taboo, creates a real cultural divide between students and teachers in the most disadvantaged urban schools (Schiff 2011).

Students did voice their feelings of injustice or their difficult relationship to authority in terms or racial or ethnic discrimination. Ethnic identification of self and others, inter-ethnic tensions and demands for recognition of cultural or religious differences, were very much a function of the manner in which students related to their schooling and how they felt about themselves as students. Students from the least desirable classes and those who felt most constrained in their educational prospects tended, much more than students in the more prestigious programs, to refer openly to their ethnic, national or religious origins as a source of pride and to denigrate their peers using racial terminology. This did not mean that the higher performing students had a weaker ethnic or religious identity than those who had been negatively selected, but simply that they did not feel the need to assert such an identity as a way of compensating for their inferiority within the educational hierarchy and that this remained relatively independent of their educational experience and of their view of themselves as students (Schiff 2011).

Minority ethnic students paradoxically had both higher rates of entry into the non-vocational streams which prepare for entry into higher education as compared to their majority origin peers of similar socio-economic status, and to be over-represented among those who drop-out of high-school (as well as university) without having obtained proper certification and in remedial type classes or in classes which were in relatively low-demand and were equally numerous among those receiving poor grades or who were considered by school personnel to be 'troublemakers'. This finding, as well as those of other studies on the school trajectories of minority ethnic students (Brinbaum and Kieffer 2009, Beaud 2003, Felouzis 2005) confirm that other more structural mechanisms are at work here which explain why students of immigrant origin often face deep discrepancies between the aspirations which they develop during their primary and middle-school years, which are largely encouraged by their parents, and the possibilities which are available to them once they enter into upper-secondary school where tracking takes place and where academic requirements are more demanding than in disadvantaged urban middle-schools. Local contextual factors and differences born of the structural inequalities between schools, classes and educational tracks all played a central role in shaping students' perceptions of themselves and of their educational and professional opportunities (Schiff 2011).

Minority ethnic pupils tended to reside in low-income public housing areas and to have been educated in the local schools which are quite segregated both socially and ethnically, while majority origin students, even those of lower-class status, often lived outside of such areas and had therefore attended more mixed middle-class schools (Felouzis 2005). For this reason they are much more likely to have been average students in very disadvantaged schools, while the majority origin students are likely to have been disadvantaged and poor performing students in average more mixed schools. Upon entering into vocational or technical high-school the children of immigrants thus experience a disheartening drop in their relative academic status, while members of the majority group experience, on the contrary, the relief of finding themselves in an institution which better conforms to their working-class status and to their potential and aspirations. The phenomenon of relative frustration and disillusionment, which is much more prevalent for minority pupils, explains the propensity for many of them to rebel against the system or to become disengaged from their studies. Students in France frequently experience transition into a vocational stream as a form of 'punishment' inflicted upon those whose academic performance and behaviour do not fit the norm. This sentiment is particularly pronounced among the descendants of migrants from the African continent whose parents have suffered disproportionately from de-industrialisation and the economic crisis and who view schooling as the only means for their children to escape from their inferior condition. These parents tend to view vocational schooling as a negative last resort, since they want their children to avoid the types of low-status jobs which they were obliged to occupy after migrating. Their disappointment and feeling of failure are proportional to the hopes and aspirations placed on the school system. The burden felt by students who carry the guilt of having failed to live up to both their parents and the school systems' expectations seems particularly heavy to carry for second generation boys, who are expected to redeem the family's honour and status which has often been tarnished by the immigration process (Schiff 2011).

There was no evidence of clear-cut ethnic hostility between different groups. In the least desirable classes and in schools in which teacher-student relations were the most tense, the tendency was for minority students, especially boys of Maghrebian origin, to have the upper hand in displays of youthful social competition and power relations. The French survey study revealed that 'White' students rather than other ethnic groups experienced more isolation in their everyday peer relations.

The survey study also showed that ethnic identity represents more of a social resource than a stigma for minority origin students. It is a source of pride and solidarity for most of them, though this in no way prevents them from also having friends and intimate relations that are, more often than not, mixed. Within this world of interethnic sociability, the students in the majority group seemed however less cohesive than those in the two minority groups. They were less proud of their origins and displayed less solidarity with their schoolmates. Indeed, for the minority groups, the conversion of stigma into pride and solidarity plays a role in the construction of their social identity. The lesser degree of ethnic solidarity displayed by 'White' students also reveals the relative fragility of these individuals who benefit less from collective resources in their everyday school lives, while suffering equally from the negative reputation and low status of their schools (Schiff et al. 2010).

Despite denials that no racism existed amongst peers, racial characterisations and ethnic tensions (as well as inter-ethnic friendships) were part and parcel of students' everyday social relations. While most students admitted that racial slurs, put downs and teasing about each other's ethnic origins were a common feature of their daily exchanges, this was never interpreted as being a form of racism, but rather was deemed to be simply the expression of friendly joking and ordinary banter. Even isolated incidents of bullying and confrontation which appeared to teachers and researchers alike to be racially motivated, were never openly regarded as such by students whose natural tendency was to downplay (or to deny) any form of ethnic hostility among peers. The ethnic school mix and the position and status of the schools and neighbourhoods relative to other schools and neighbourhoods in the area all have a considerable influence on the way inter-ethnic relations and identities are formed and evolve. Young people suffer at least as much from the negative image associated with their schools and neighbourhoods, as well as from the social pressures exerted by peers who most conform to the roles and reputations associated with such neighbourhoods, than they do from the objective disadvantages of their residential situation, such as limited access to cultural resources, urban insecurity or poor living conditions. While the minority students encountered in Bordeaux appeared much less exposed than their Parisian counterparts to the ills of urban life, such as gang violence, police brutality, limited geographic mobility and overcrowded living conditions, they were clearly more deeply affected by the stigma associated with their inferior position relative to that of young people living in more middle class areas attending more prestigious secondary schools. Such schools can serve as a safe-haven for those who are most exposed to the harsh realities and strict social controls of the 'ghetto'. Yet they can also exacerbate students' feelings of exclusion and lead to forms of bullying among students that constitute a way of inversing the dominant hierarchies and norms of success through a process which transforms the victim into the victimiser (Schiff et al. 2010), as in the English study where inter-ethnic hostility between African-Caribbeans and Pakistanis was identified.

Romania case study: raft of desegregation measures fails to improve educational opportunities for the Roma

This section draws on and summarises the final report by the Romanian EDUMIGROM team (Vincze 2011). This study was carried out focusing on 13-14 years old pupils in nine secondary schools in two regions of Romania in Multiculti town and the neighbouring Sunny village in Transilvan town and the neighbouring Mountain village. Both cities are multicultural but the proportion of Hungarians is much bigger in Transilvan than in Multiculti, so the Roma people in the former setting might have had experiences of 'minoritisation' and strong hostility from both the Romanian majority, and the local Hungarian minority. In Romania, by and large, 'multicultural education' is based on the idea that ethnic minorities should learn (in) their mother tongues and should have their own educational units. For the Hungarian minority this is an achievement for the politics of cultural autonomy and is a way of cultivating ethnic distinctiveness with pride. But for the Roma minority, as it struggles with marginality, exclusion and discrimination, separation means segregation involves stigmatisation and lower quality of education (Vincze 2011).

Interviews with Roma parents and students show that in terms of separation/ isolation from the outer world an inter-generational change is going on. Younger people had a more powerful desire to comply with the requirements of majority society. They did not internalise mechanisms of exclusion as profoundly as their parents did. For older members of the Gipsy-Gabor community staying apart from the majority is the accepted norm. For their children, especially for sons who attend school and stay close to the educational system for a longer period integration serves as a key aspiration. But, many Roma children who are performing badly and being devalued at school show strong resistance to the school regime. Educational inequalities are also exacerbated by the unequal (re)distribution of income and wealth which result in disadvantages for Roma children in accessing to and advancing in school education. Many Roma families are living on the margins of towns with frequent changes of home, experiencing periods of unemployment and day labouring in the informal economy, low levels of school education and with difficult access to quality school education. But there was also evidence of high educational aspirations of/for their children and a desire for integration into the majority society despite minoritisation through shared experiences of segregation, unequal treatment and exclusion in a variety of different domains of life and persistent poverty and immiseration (Vincze 2011).

Despite denials that there was no conscious principle of differentiating among the parallel classes, or between Roma and non-Roma, or between boys and girls, teachers constructed hierarchies under the pressure of current institutional arrangements, for example grouping students in foreign language classes, which resulted in the formation of 'good' and 'weak' classes. Students of the latter were mostly active in the sense of resisting the teacher, while the ones of the former were had a collaborative strategy of participation. By the middle of the 1990s, one school initiated the formation of separate classes for Roma which was more or less hidden as classes for children with special educational needs. Over the last decade desegregation led to these classes being closed and the majority of students were directed towards the separate special school. In some cases parents were not informed in time about these changes, and in many cases they accepted this 'proposal' due to the free transport and free meal that this school offered to their enrolled students. Here, material constraints structured parental choices and prevented these children from having a decent education. Progressive interventions including the institution of Roma school mediators, the assurance of separate places for Roma at high schools and university, the Second Chance Programme, the programme for Children with Special Educational Needs, the Summer Kindergarten programme, the right to learn Romani language or Romani history in schools, and defining school segregation as a form of discrimination could not structurally improve the access of disadvantaged Roma children to quality school education due particularly to a failure to address wider socio-economic inequalities. These deficiencies are also reflected in the new Romanian law on education which totally neglects the issue of school segregation (Vincze 2011). Despite these failures this raft of interventions aimed at the Roma is far above the range and level of UK interventions aimed at inclusion of Gypsy, Roma and Travellers and there is much that may be useful here in developing new strategies.

Czech Republic case study: complex mechanisms of educational segregation for Roma including concentration in Basic Practical Schools

This section draws on and summarises the final report by the Czech EDUMIGROM team (Marada 2011). Since the 1990s, the segregation of Roma pupils in the Czech educational system has been symbolised by their concentration in Basic Practical Schools. Entry here is based on an examination carried out by an expert in a specialised pedagogical-psychological centre. Where the child is found to not have the appropriate predisposition towards attending common basic school, he or she can be placed into a specialised institution with trained pedagogical staff. These schools, however, provide less demanding, substandard education, which limits the possibility of future educational success. During the Communist regime, the proportion of Roma pupils in these types of schools was high and after 1989, the number of non-Roma pupils in these schools declined significantly. Research commissioned by the Ministry of Education found out that approximately 30 per cent of Roma pupils attend Basic Practical Schools, whereas for children from non-Roma families, this proportion is far lower (approximately 2 per cent). With the introduction of a requirement of parents' explicit consensus when placing their child into a Basic Practical School, the rules that allow for the systematic and involuntary segregation of Roma pupils into Basic Practical Schools – which was the main reason the Czech Republic was designated as a country where the right to an equal education is infringed – have been gradually transformed and a policy of inclusive education has been established alongside traditional approaches which favour specialised institutions and staff (Marada 2011).[1]

Many heads of schools and teachers remain highly skeptical about the integration of Roma pupils into mainstream schools. In schools where Roma pupils are in the majority, but which are not Basic Practical Schools, similar problems are evident (see Marada et al. 2010), in three aspects: providing substandard education (although Basic Practical Schools offer lower quality education), Roma pupils do not carry on with further education, and the segregation of Roma pupils takes place at both school types on the basis of very similar mechanisms. Segregation mechanisms in the Czech educational system result from a complex of factors including the attitude of the majority towards Roma populations, the strategies of particular schools, the educational strategies of Roma and non-Roma parents, the setting of the educational system (marketisation and introduction of market principles in the 1990s), and urban structure (Marada 2011).

Slovakia case study: intensifying everyday anti-Roma hostility and racial abuse and discrimination by teachers

This section draws on selected key findings from the quantitative and qualitative reports produced by the Slovakian EDUMIGROM team (Kusa et al. 2010,

---

1   Despite this fact, there are still potential ways to evade this measure, and even a paradoxical situation occurs when pupils and parents themselves struggle for unjustified placement into a Basic Practical School. This happens in those cases when pupils, due to disciplinary problems, expect to be excluded from common basic schools and to be put into a preventive-corrective institution. In such cases, a pupil can try to pretend to be suffering from a learning disorder and/or a minor mental handicap and start attending Basic Practical School, thus staying with his or her family.

Kusa et al. 2011). This research studied pupils, parents and teachers and representatives of organisations that are associated with ten schools in two districts Hrdé and Krásne in Slovakia (names are fictitious). Although Hrdé has a stronger local economy, there are some common trends. Neo-Nazi and skinhead groups are active both in the towns and in poor Roma neighbourhoods. Non-Roma parents tend to be generally hostile and discourage play, social interaction and friendships with Roma children. They carefully examine the ethnic composition of schools in order to avoid those with 'too high' numbers of Roma pupils. Destitute living conditions were common with 60 per cent of Roma pupils living in families without regular monthly income. Parents' expectations that children would provide for household livelihood as soon as possible was a key reason for Roma pupils leaving school too early (about one third of surveyed Roma pupils intended to quit school early). Roma pupils do not express a higher level of dissatisfaction toward school in comparison to Slovak or Hungarian pupils. Both the Roma parents and the teachers advocate the benefits of ethnically mixed classes. They consider the presence of 'White children' to be important for providing a norm to follow and a stimulus for educational aspirations (Kusa et al. 2011).

Despite the bulk of pedagogues which support integrated education of non-Roma and Roma, almost all elementary schools implement streamlining and divide pupils according to their school marks and special talents for maths and languages. In big schools with several parallel classes, the top performing classes generally contain no Roma pupils, with these groups concentrated in the least demanding classes which are dominated by norms of relaxation and fun as the principle and reason for school attendance. The sneering hostility of 'elite' children towards others and the Roma in lower classes is a key source of conflict. As a result of lower teachers' and pupils' expectations towards school performance, the majority of Roma pupils choose vocational schools where they move to at age 11 and where there is a high level of inter-ethnic tension and fights. No attention is given to the problematic nature of relations in ethnically mixed classes. Roma students described that there are teachers who make allusions to their colour and there are even those who address pupils directly with derogatory references to Gypsy lifestyles. In Hrdé such hostility is particularly common in everyday situations. In schools Roma girls from Hrdé were particularly critical of racial discrimination by teachers, due partly to their greater self-consciousness and confidence, and the ways in which they had lower expectations of Roma students and under-estimated their academic potential.

The Slovakian team observed that teachers very often make divisions between good and bad Roma pupils and their 'civilising habits' or lack of them. Roma themselves accept this categorisation and use it. Though Roma accept this division, they distinguished themselves from strong stereotypical categorisations of the Roma as having deficient hygiene, not enough clean clothing and being noisy and rude. Stereotypes that divide the Roma and non-Roma community particularly affect Roma with darker skin. Interviews suggest that the colour of one's skin matters more than one's socio-economic status. Roma with a pale skin have an advantage in that they can communicate with non-Roma young people directly and develop relationships. Verbal abuse of Roma pupils was common with standard insults such as 'dirty Gypsy' being widely used, and teachers' insults tended to arise in conflict situations as a way of disciplining pupils (Kusa et al. 2011).

Hungary case study: failure of integration policies and increasing ethnic divisions

This section draws on and summarises the final report by the Hungarian EDUMIGROM team (Messing, Neményi and Zolnay 2011). This report presents evidence drawn from research in two urban areas where the estimated rate of Roma students was higher than the average in Hungary. This study confirmed that the extreme inequalities of Hungarian public education originate from the multiplicity of selective processes driven by diverse social, political, and economic interests that produce ethnic segmentation of the school system.

Three intersecting factors led to diverging quality of schools. Firstly, the impact of residential inequalities has increased, producing both high status areas and impoverished minority ethnic slums and Roma ghetto-villages on the other. Secondly, the right of free choice for schooling produced a massive flight of the middle classes from poor and ethnically mixed areas and intensified socio-geographic differentials. Thirdly, divergent policies of the schools, responding to parental pressures led to the implementation of 'streaming' children into homogenous class-communities and reinforced divisions and segregation between Roma and non-Roma children and young people. Ethnicity was found to be of more important significance than gender or class in determining educational achievement. The devaluing of school results achieved in weaker institutions where Roma pupils are concentrated leads to their concentration in low-prestige institutions known for hardly useable poor-quality training, disinterest in students' occupational advancement, low career aspirations and high rates of dropout (Messing, Neményi and Zolnay 2011).

Setting in schools and the separation of Roma and non-Roma students into parallel classes produces the most damaging environment for both ethnic majority and minority students. The everyday experience of separation and discrimination is damaging in terms of relationships as well as performance and aspirations. In such school setting bullying, mocking and rivalry dominates the general atmosphere of the school. Segregation between schools provides an inferior environment for school advancement and future aspirations, but inter-group relations and identity formation seem to be less damaged than among circumstances where separation and discrimination occurs inside schools as an everyday experience of adolescents. Integrated schooling and class environments provide the best circumstances for the healthy development of adolescents' personalities, and it does not necessarily hinder the academic advancement of majority students and it may improve school achievement of minority ethnic students (Messing, Neményi and Zolnay 2011).

Despite Hungarian educational policy advocating integration in education and the implementation of positive incentives including finance, teacher training and review of special needs education, educational segregation has increased in the last decade (Kertesi and Kézdi 2010). Current policy fails due to its inability to engage and address the concentration of Roma in marginalised, ghetto settlements, White flight and widespread hostility from local government and majority parents. Amongst young Roma, frustrations about institutionalised discrimination and manifest exclusion turn most frequently into interethnic conflict, quarrels and gang fights. School and teacher responses to integration policy range from superficial acceptance through passive resistance to active rejection. Three discursive strategies were identified, firstly, 'fatalist discourse' which sees the fate of children from under-educated Gypsy families as pre-determined leading to a cycle of low teacher/pupil aspirations was common. Secondly, a 'social/class' discourse which sees Roma pupils lower performance and aspirations as being due to social and economic disadvantage and thirdly, racist discourse where 'Gypsy' means genetic and racial inferiority. The weak school performance and limited future aspirations of most Roma students are closely connected with a sense of racial and ethnic discrimination, which was mentioned in nearly every interview, and strongly felt both inside and outside school, in their relations with their teachers and with fellow students. Prevailing negative perceptions of Roma identity led many children to express a desire to melt into the social majority, give up family traditions and adopting majority norms. Policies of educational integration have failed, ethnic divisions are increasing and 'Roma' is still synonymous with being socially useless, deviant and a danger to public safety in Hungarian society (Messing, Neményi and Zolnay 2011).

Conclusion and summary of cross-national themes

This section presents and summaries some of the key comparative findings examined in the nine Community Study reports, produced by the EDUMIGROM country teams in 2010 (Szalai 2010) and identifies some key themes and issues arising from this cross-national analysis. For a summary of key European policy messages see http://www.edumigrom.eu/news/2011-04-04/new-publication-european-policy-brief. The persistence, durability and, in some cases, increasing strength of ethnic identities, divisions and conflicts across these national contexts is evident (Law et al. 2009). There are significant variations and differences in migration processes, economic development, welfare provision and forms of citizenship across these countries and there are differences in ethnic composition, ethnic mobilisation and patterns of racialisation which makes a direct comparison of the countries a complex task. But, this research has identified a cross-cutting set of key themes and issues in the perceptions and experiences of 'othering'.

In terms of teachers and the (re)production of the differentiated school performances of minority ethnic/majority youths there is a convergence of discourse around five key themes. Firstly, processes of ethnic separation and segregation, including streaming, characterise Central and Eastern European countries and this was seen as normal by many teachers. Secondly, the emergence of schools with a considerable, and in some cases increasing, share of minority ethnic students ('minority ethnic schools') through 'White flight' and 'socio-economic flight'. Thirdly, lower learning standards and reduced curriculum in 'minority ethnic schools' has been accompanied by the development of an 'Island Culture' where minority ethnic students feel relatively safe and comfortable and where teachers have reduced learning expectations. Fourthly, teachers tended to perceive many parents of minority ethnic children as problematic through a process of 'othering'. Parents were seen as uninvolved in their children's education careers with low attainment resulting from poor family backgrounds, and sometimes this involved negative moral judgements of these families, with an accompanying decline in teachers' responsibilities. Evidence of racialised teachers' perceptions was documented as well as evidence of exceptional teachers who faced up to these varied challenges. Fifthly, national policy approaches to ethnicity and education, whether colour blind (France), colour conscious (UK) or segregationist (Central and Eastern Europe) were not always evident in school based approaches and in teachers' perceptions with differing and in some cases oppositional narratives in the foreground (Law et al. 2010).

In examining community representatives' views it was clear that processes of structural discrimination in social and economic contexts, together with the power of White middle class norms and values were seen as central to understanding ethnic differentiation. Paralleling teachers' views home circumstances were also seen as key to educational achievement, but they were much more ready to acknowledge racial and ethnic inequalities and discrimination. Community representatives were also critical of both the need to engage with and change aspects of community values and norms, as well as informal and formal practices which maintained ethnic boundaries within schools. Parents' narratives confirmed the sense of cultural divide and conflict which existed between home and school and they pursued a number of varied strategies to both protect their children from discrimination and hostility and provide a range of forms of caring and support to facilitate their progression through life. This evidence contradicted teachers' perceptions. Parents identified patterns of residential segregation as a key constraining factor on young peoples' life chances, as did the young people themselves.

In these varying situations of school-based and community-based 'othering' young people from minority ethnic groups adopted a range of responses. Three types of peer relations were identified; 'mono-ethnic', 'pluri-ethic' and 'ghetto-youth' amongst young people with some having very little contact outside their own ethnic group, some having weak social and friendship networks, others where strong bonds were formed. Young people did perceive teachers as generally fair but language barriers and extracurricular activities provided key sites of conflict.

Outside school young people provided highly diverging accounts of racism and discrimination ranging from little experience (France) to being a central topic of conversation (Hungary), with linkages between 'othering', racialisation and criminalisation being a key site for conflict and criticism. This research has identified the main types of reported experiences of racial and ethnic 'othering', which include teasing and joking, verbal hostility and abuse, forms of racial and ethnic discrimination, patterns of segregation and other types of differential treatment. It has examined how inter-ethnic mixing and patterns of informal ethnic segregation characterise everyday life, and how practices of 'othering' are enacted in the domains of school and peer relations and also in wider neighbourhood and family contexts, for example through downplaying hostility to oppositional showing off. It also shows where and under what circumstances children have experiences of discrimination and the factors that might lead to students perceiving ethnic bias (Law et al. 2010).

Social processes such as residential segregation, avoidance strategies of middle-class majority origin families, tracking systems which result in the high concentration of minority ethnic students in certain types of schools and classes, explain that individual schools do not always have the power to implement the integration measures which are required from them. Schools do carry out practices which range from the negative segregation of minority ethnic pupils into relegated and devalued dead-end classes reserved for handicapped, troubled or very low performing students which do not address their particular needs (mostly Roma in the Central European countries), and as a result seek to protect the majority from contact with them. Whereas some schools have recruited qualified personnel of minority ethnic origin and have developed specific pedagogical measures to respond to the needs of these groups, such as bilingual students in Denmark and Sweden. In other national contexts, such as in Britain and France, the treatment of minority ethnic students does not appear to have such clear negative or positive consequences on their educational trajectories and academic performances.

Pupils' strategies in relation to schooling whether being commitment, instrumentation or opposition depend both on factors, such as parents' cultural capital, and intrinsic factors, such as the existence of a clear hierarchy between classes. Schools may represent both the means for individual success and emancipation and a possible investment in order to increase one's chances of overcoming the lower status associated with one's ethnic group, or the active agent of exclusion to be resisted. It appeared that the more underprivileged and potentially oppositional students were most sensitive to their particular school's policies and practices regarding differential treatment, while the highest performing, most committed students asserted an unflinching belief in the meritocratic principle regardless of the reality of segregation or of their actual chances of success.

The manner in which teachers relate to minority students is the result of a combination of national traditions and ideologies regarding the role which should be played by ethnicity and the recognition which it is due, of the individual school's organisation and coherence (notably the authority of the school head and the manner in which reform has been implemented), and of the training received by teachers in matters such an inter-cultural communication, bilingualism and the implementation of differential pedagogical styles. The analysis of some of the major means by which students identify themselves and assert similarities and differences with their peers revealed the fact that, compared to the often simplistic ethnic and cultural distinction which adults tend to resort to, for minority youth there exist complex intersections between ethnicity, local neighbourhood identities, cultural style, leisure activities and personal tastes. Youthful humour, inter-ethnic bantering and the use of derogatory ethnic epithets can serve either as a way of making light of latent racial tensions, or as a means for deepening inter-ethnic animosities and reinforcing strong socio-ethnic hierarchies. Young people are particularly sensitive to dominant social hierarchies and racial stereotypes, but are also as representatives of a globalised culture capable of transcending and subverting national traditions of differentiation and ethnic categorisation (Schiff et al. 2010).

The colour-blind French ethos prevailing at schools as well, prioritising citizenship rights over everything else, clearly impacts on all visible minority adolescents, including those following Muslim religious traditions. Schools in Central European states, where ideas of equality and inclusion are reluctantly acknowledged but not yet embedded in institutional practices, produce Roma youth who regard themselves as second-rate citizens. In countries of migration where schools reinforce separation some, for example Muslim youth may benefit from such policies in terms of self respect. So, educational policies may sometimes reinforce and at other times mitigate, displace or override the aspirations of minority ethnic groups, and hence may either undermine or, intensify (and often distort) the significance of ethnic or religious differences and divisions and 'minoritisation'.

The decline of multiculturalism as policy, the growth of hostility focused on minority ethnic groups, and the increasing anxieties over differences between Muslims and Christians, and Roma and non-Roma provide a context where schools have been transformed into sites of ethnic and religious conflict and/or suppression of identities. The sharpening of differences as a result of the contemporary political climate and associated institutional mechanisms, has mobilised a sense of oppositional solidarity amongst some minority ethnic groups with attempts to separate from, or occasionally even aggressively confront representatives of, majority societies. The rise of such self/group-consciousness has lead to the articulation of claims for recognition and action. But, the reinvigoration of nationalisms and the reinforcement of anti-minority voices and political forces mark a conservative turn both in the East and the West. Yet, this research, shows that in schools ethnically mixed, integrated education, as long as it is coupled with multiculturalist principles, diversity-conscious sensibilities and readiness to reflect upon (the consequences of) differences, results in better school achievement, improving perspectives of further education, and generating more positive future aspirations (Szalai, Messing, and Neményi 2010).

But, there is a significant threat to this objective and other, more majoritarian and anti-minority solutions may become dominant (Kallstenius et al. 2010). Finally, the intensification of anti-Roma racism and the mainstream political rhetoric about multiculturalism in the UK, Germany and other EU countries and the calls for muscular, aggressive majoritarianism are now briefly addressed.

A note on the intensification of anti-Roma racism

Today the Roma are subject to an intensification of hostility, discrimination, violence and political racism, why has this happened? Also, why did the collapse of the Soviet Union, the sweeping away of the Communist logics of racial proletarianisation, and the introduction of liberal democracy produce such an outcome? The highly durable power of anti-Roma racism across centuries and nations in this region cannot be explained by regime change, neither can this enduring, ancient hatred explain adequately why there are differing patterns of violence and discrimination across both localities and nations, and across Communist and post-Communist regimes. It plays a contextual, shaping role but not a determinate one. Macro theories, such as those which emphasise competition and the structural context of economic conditions, institutional arrangements such as the policies of nationality and nationhood in the Soviet Union or globalisation and the formation of radical ethno-nationalisms as a reaction to global elites, are inadequate too. These types of explanation also fail as they necessarily involve theorisation of simple determinate linkages between economic, institutional and global processes and anti-Roma racism. There is no necessary correspondence between racist logics and these social forces. Racial violence and neo-Nazi activity can erupt in situations where there is an absence of competition for jobs and housing for example in areas where there are few, isolated, vulnerable Roma families, and globalisation has also invigorated anti-racist, indigenous and Roma struggles for recognition and rights. Anti-Roma racism amongst children can better be explained by processes of socialisation and the operation of norms and values within families, peer groups and schools, rather than by processes of economic competition

   The historical cultural reservoir of nationally shaped racism is highly significant in providing a persisting repertoire of hostile images, perceptions of superiority and legitimation for brutality and violence against many different groups. The narratives of neglect and decline elaborated in local communities, and the output of the extreme right may all adopt a 'backward-looking' frame of reference to this and related sets of key memories. The significance of national political debate and government policies may be paramount in focusing and amplifying local tensions, and there is evidence of a direct connection here. The targeting of racialised groups in political discourse has in many national contexts led to significant increases in racist violence, for example Germany, Sweden and the UK, and evidence from the CEE countries confirms this process happens here too. The extent to which racist hostility is permitted in both public debate and through the failure of government responses to racist violence, may parallel the sanctioning and failure to condemn amongst local communities. Factors which strengthen the bonds between families, including changing economic opportunities and isolation from social networks outside the local area, can strengthen mobilisation to respond to external threats and dangers.

Strong communities may often be highly exclusionary. A key to understanding how this process works is to examine local norms, values and sanctions to conform operating across a range of networks including families, friends/peer groups and other informal forms of association. Within these social contexts individuals act in different ways and micro forms of explanation focusing on individuals will also be necessary to explain patterns of racial hatred and violence (Law 2010). The success of both racist and radical ethno-nationalist discourse depends on its ability to re-code and make sense of everyday life. Emotional, ideological, bigoted, criminal and territorial motives for racist hostility and violence need to form part of a multi-layered account which also integrates both meso-, or contextual, and macro-forms of sociological analysis. In a context of high levels of uncertainty, frustration and fear of the loss of fragile advantages anti-Roma racism brings an unearned easy feeling of superiority. Pleasure, joy and triumphant emotions may for some drive the process of race hate rage, particularly when preceded by a sense of personal humiliation or emotional anxiety. The shame, envy and disgust experienced by living in vulnerable, insecure economic and social settings, together with both a sense of personal failure and a sense that others are receiving more favourable opportunities are all relevant here. Anti-Roma racism can provide a temporary release from such anxieties and Roma households provide an uncomfortable reminder of the inability of the majority to secure decent lives for themselves and their families. No wonder then that racial distancing and constructing the 'Roma-line' characterise these societies in an effort to keep the contamination of Roma poverty, disease, stink and dirt from seeping into the foundations of mainstream and majority social worlds (Law 2012).

A concluding note on ethnic segregation in education in the UK

Segregation and integration are 'chaotic concepts' and their misrecognition and mis-interpretation provides fertile ground for 'myths to grow' (Finney and Simpson 2009). There are many myths associated with schooling in the UK, including a current government view that multiculturalism has facilitated segregation and that minority ethnic groups prefer segregated schools. Multiculturalism, in terms of the recognition of the human needs that arise from ethnic diversity in social policy, and anti-racism, in terms of the recognition of the need to challenge the fundamental basis of racial hostility and associated violence, have not led to increasing spatial, structural or cultural segregation, and these objectives remain legitimate policy goals. Despite the political rhetoric, ethnic managerialism, recognising the need to respond to ethnic diversity in the provision of public services and applying 'new public managerial' strategies to this issue is prevalent across all sectors, for example the sanctioning of faith schools and adapting institutions, law and professional practice (Law 1997, Modood 2011). Also, the failure of institutions to adequately identify and respond to differing needs does lead to poor quality service provision and reproduces patterns of exclusion, as in the case of the failure of secondary education in relation to Gypsy and Traveller children (also recently confirmed in evidence on Scotland, Netto et al. 2011) and the very limited attention to issues of racism and ethnic diversity in the national curriculum (Ball 2009). Race relations law in the UK defines segregationary practices as direct discrimination, treating someone less favourably because they are a member of a specific group, and cases of for example segregation of minority ethnic children in special remedial English classes which deprive them of learning from the national curriculum have been found to be unlawful.

In relation to schooling, ethnic composition is not growing over time and there is a strong desire for ethnically mixed schools among both White and minority ethnic families (Weekes-Bernard 2007), although a minority of both White and minority ethnic parents do prefer schools where their child is a part of the ethnic majority in the school. Ethnic composition of schools and resulting segregation arises largely from differentials in income and wealth and decisions in the housing market and the resulting mismatch between choice of schools and outcomes (Finney and Simpson 2009). Here, the statutory legal duty placed on schools to promote both 'good race relations' and 'community cohesion', for example in contexts where there are, concentrations of either White or minority pupils, and also where there is evidence of inter-ethnic conflict, is of particular importance. Further, all minorities, including Muslims, want to live in mixed neighbourhoods and increasing residential concentrations in certain areas is caused by those who move out. Paradoxically, both increasing suburbanisation and increasing inner-city concentrations characterise the housing outcomes for all minority ethnic groups result from both increasing socio-economic polarisation within minority ethnic groups and 'White flight'. White middle-class children often had little interaction with children from other backgrounds. These children rarely had working class friends and their few minority ethnic friends were predominantly from middle-class backgrounds. It was clear that there was little evidence of social mixing despite the ethnic mix of the school as a whole, confirming the persistence of embedded ethnic and racial divisions.

So, in response to the segregating tendencies in education it is paramount to both address the attitudes of White children and young people as well as ethnic differentials in child and adult poverty through the tax and benefit system, the minimum wage and implementation of the race relations legislation. Persistent disadvantage and complex barriers to both work and benefits are experienced by minority groups. The creation of destitution amongst some asylum-seekers, rising unemployment differentials and failure by the Department for Work and Pensions to implement statutory race equality strategies (Law 2011) are all further signs that indicate poor prospects for the future and the likelihood of increasing ethnic differentials in both poverty and in income and wealth, and hence the reproduction of current patterns of ethnic polarisation in schools. The relative vulnerability of minority ethnic groups in a variety of market contexts means that the current economic recession and associated cuts in welfare are having and will have a greater negative impact on these groups and also on school outcomes.

In addition to the policy recommendations set out at the end of the last chapter, fully implementing the eradication of direct and indirect racial and ethnic discrimination in school could go a long way to dismantling segregationist practices, for example in differential examination entry and setting, across schools. Race relations legislation has placed a statutory responsibility on schools in this regard since 1976. There have been successful formal investigations and court cases but currently the lack of leadership, data collection, accurate analysis and action within schools on issues of racial and ethnic equality indicate that this is a low priority, and this reflects the prevailing reticence to grasp these issues effectively at national (and international) level. Racial and ethnic inequalities, racial and ethnic hostilities and patterns of racial and ethnic segregation in education are known, broadly understood and largely they are ineffectively dealt with in political, policy and professional contexts. Yet a post-ethnic, post-racial society is being built as declining racist attitudes, increasing mixed-ethnicity friendship groups amongst young people, increasing ethnic mixing in residential neighbourhoods, and the demand for ethnically mixed schools are evident as positive social trends in the UK. These trends are constrained, counteracted and frustrated by the powerful effects of hostile political rhetoric and divisive structural forces, such as the marketisation of education and increasing child poverty. We need to change the terms of the political debate about ethnicity and education and build educational policies and practices which nurture and facilitate these positive multicultural social trends. Despite the constraints of politics, policy and markets everyday multiculturalism is a living, powerful social process which will not be denied.

References

Abbas, T. 2007. British South Asians and pathways into selective schooling: social class, culture and ethnicity. *British Educational Research Journal*, 33(1), 75-90.

Ahmad, F., Modood, T., and Lissenburgh, S. 2003. *South Asian Women and Employment in Britain: The Interaction of Gender and Ethnicity*. London: Policy Studies Institute.

Ahmed, P., Feliciano, C. and Emigh, J.R. 2001. *Ethnic Classification in Eastern Europe*. Paper presented at the American Sociological Association Annual Meeting, Anaheim, CA.

Ajegbo, K. 2007. *Diversity and Citizenship: The Impact in Schools*. London: DfES.

Allen, R. and Vignoles, A. 2007. What should an index of school segregation measure?. *Oxford Review of Education*, 33(5), 669-677.

Nayak, A. 2006. Displaced Masculinities: Chavs, youth and class in the post-industrial City. *Sociology*, 40(5), 813-831.

Aps, W. and Blair, A. 2005. What not to wear and other Stories: Addressing religious diversity in schools. *Education and the* Law, 17(1-2), 1-22.

Arai, L. 2005. *Migrants and Public Services in the UK: A Review of the Recent Literature*. Oxford: ESRC Centre on Migration, Policy and Society (COMPAS), http://www.compas.ox.ac.uk/publications/Resources_Lit_Review_1205.shtml.

Arora, R. 2005. *Race and Ethnicity in Education*. Aldershot: Ashgate Publishing.

Ball, S.J. 1981. *Beachside Comprehensive: A Case-study of Secondary Schooling*. Cambridge: Cambridge University Press.

Ball, S.J. 2009. *The Education Debate*. Bristol: Policy Press.

Donnor, J.K. and Brown, A.L. 2011. The education of Black males in a post-racial world. *Race, Ethnicity and Education*, 14(1), 1-5.

Beaud, S. 2003. *80% au bac... et après? Les enfants de la democratisation scolaire*. Paris: La Découverte.

Beck, U. 2006. *The Cosmopolitan Vision*. Cambridge: Polity.

Berthoud, R. 1999. *Young Caribbean Men and the Labour Market*. York: Joseph Rowntree Foundation.

Berthoud, R. 2005. Family formation in multicultural Britain, in *Ethnicity, Social Mobility and Public Policy*, edited by G. Loury, T. Modood and S.M. Teles. Cambridge: Cambridge University Press, 222-253.

Bhopal, K. 2004. Gypsy travellers and education: Changing needs and changing perceptions. *British Educational Research Journal*, 52(1), 47-64.

Blair, T. 2006. *Public Lecture*. London: Runnymede Trust.

Blakey, H., Pearce, J. and Chesters, G. 2006. *Minorities Within Minorities: Beneath the Surface of South Asian Participation*. Joseph Rowntree Foundation, accessed online: http://www.jrf.org.uk/bookshop/eBooks/1972-involving-south-asian-communities.pdf, accessed 14 June 2010.

Blatchford, P. 2005. *Improving pupil group work in classrooms*, http://www.tlrp.org/pub/documents/BlatchfordRBFinal_001.pdf, accessed 7 January 2011.

Bradford, B. 2006. *Who Are the Mixed Ethnic Group?* London: Office for National Statistics.

Brand, A. and Ollerearnshaw, R. 2008. *Gangs at the Grassroots, Community Solutions to Street Violence*. London: New Local Government Network.

Brinbaum, Y. and Kieffer, A. 2009. Trajectories of immigrants' children in secondary education in France: Differentiation and polarization. *Population-E, INED*, 64(3), 507-554.

Bristol City Council. 2011. *Work Packs for Pupils on Fixed Term Exclusion*. Bristol: BCC. http://www.bristol-cyps.org.uk/teaching/behaviour/work_packs.html.

Buck, N. and Gordon, I. 2004. Does spatial concentration of disadvantage contribute to social exclusion?, in *City Matters: Competitiveness, Cohesion and Urban Governance*, edited by M. Boddy and M. Parkinson. Bristol: The Policy Press, 237-254.

Burgess, S. and Wilson, D. 2004. *Ethnic Segregation in England's Schools*. London: CASE, LSE.

Burgess, S., Gardiner, K. and Propper, C. 2001. *Growing Up: School, Family and Area Influence on Adolescents' Later Life Chances*. London: CASE Paper No. 49, London School of Economics.

Burns, T.R., Carson, M., Lilja, M., Lipponen, S., and Kamali, M. 2005. WP-9 Report, Analysis and Policy Recommendations for Project: the European Dilemma: Institutional Patterns of Racial and Ethnic Discrimination. Unpublished.

Byfield, C. 2008. *Black Boys Can Make It: How They Overcome the Obstacles to University in the UK and the USA*. Stoke-on-Trent: Trentham Press.

Cabinet Office. 2010. *State of the Nation, Poverty, Worklessness and Welfare Dependency in the UK*. London: Cabinet Office.

Carson, M., Kallstenius, J., Sonmark, K. and Hobson, B. 2011. *Sweden Country Findings and Policy Recommendations*. Unpublished.

Cemlyn, S. and Clark, C. 2005. The social exclusion of Gypsy and Traveller children, in *At Greatest Risk: The Children Most Likely to be Poor*, edited by Gabrielle Preston. London: CPAG, 146-162.

Cemlyn, S., Greenfields, M., Burnett, S., Matthews, Z. and Whitwell, C. 2009. *Inequalities Experienced by Gypsy and Traveller Communities: A Review*, Research Report: no. 12, Manchester: Equality and Human Rights Commission.

Children's Society. 2007. *This Is Who We Are*. London: Children's Society.

Clark, C. and Greenfields, M. 2006. *Here to Stay: the Gypsies and Travellers of Britain*. Hatfield: University of Hertfordshire Press.

Clark, K. and Drinkwater, S. 2007. *Ethnic Minorities in the Labour Market: Dynamics and Diversity*. York: Joseph Rowntree Foundation.

Clarke, L. 2003. Supporting asylum seekers in schools. *Support for Learning*, 18(4), 177-183.

Commission for Racial Equality. 2007. *A Lot Done, A Lot To Do*. London: CRE.

Commission For Racial Equality. 2006. *Common Ground: Equality, Good Race Relations and Sites for Gypsies and Irish Travellers*. London: CRE.

Connolly, P. 1995. Racism, masculine peer-group relations the schooling of African-Caribbean infant boys. *British Journal of Sociology of Education*, 16(1), 75-92.

Craig, G., with Adamson, A., Ali, N., Ali, S., Atkins, L., Dadze-Arthur, A., Elliott, C., McNamee, S. and Murtuja, B. 2007. *Sure Start and Black and Minority Ethnic Populations*. London: HMSO.

Craske, O. 2000. Breathing uneasy sighs of relief. *Central European Review*. 2. 27. July, http://www.pecina.cz/files/www.ce-review.org/00/27/craske27.html, accessed 6 August 2008.

Crick, B. 1998. *Education for Citizenship and the Teaching of Democracy in Schools*: *Report of an Advisory Group on Citizenship*. London: DfES.

Crozier, G. and Davis, J. 2006. Family matters: a discussion of the Bangladeshi and Pakistani extended family and community in supporting the children's education. *Sociological Review*, 54(4), 678-695.

Crozier, G. and Davis, J. 2007. Hard to reach parents or hard to reach schools? A discussion of home-school relations, with particular reference to Bangladeshi and Pakistani parents. *British Educational Research Journal*, 33(3), 295-313.

Crozier, G., Reay D., James D., Jamieson, F., Beedell P., Hollingworth, S., and Williams, K. 2008. Middle-class parents, identities, educational choice and the urban comprehensive school: dilemmas, ambivalence and moral ambiguity. *British Journal of Sociology of Education*, 29(3), 261-272.

Culic, I., Horvath, I.-L. and Marius-Magyari, N.L. 1998. *Romani si maghiari in tranzitia postcomunista*, [Romanians and Hungarians in post-communist transition]. CCRIT, Cluj.

Dale, A. 2002. Social exclusion of Pakistani and Bangladeshi women. *Sociological Research Online*, 7(3). http://www.socresonline.org.uk/7/3/contents.html.

Dale, A. et al. 2002. Routes into education and employment for young Pakistani and Bangladeshi women in the UK. *Ethnic and Racial Studies*, 25(6), 942-968.

DCLG (Department for Communities and Local Government) 2006. *Improving Opportunity, Strengthening Society*. London: DCLG.

DCLG (Department for Communities and Local Government). 2007. *Improving Opportunities, Two Years On*. London: DCLG.

DCSF (Department for Children, Schools and Families). 2007. *The Inclusion of Gypsy, Roma and Traveller Children and Young People*. London: DSCF.

DCSF (Department for Children, Schools and Families). 2008a. *Building Schools for the Future*. London: DCSF.

DCSF (Department for Children, Schools and Families). 2008b. *Gangs and Group Offending, Guidance for Schools.* London: DCSF.

Delamont, S. 1976. *Interaction in the Classroom.* London: Methuen.

Demie, F. 2005. Achievement of Black Caribbean pupils: good practice in Lambeth schools. *British Educational Research Journal*, 31(4), 481-508.

Derham, M. 2003. A call for real class. *Times Higher Educational Supplement*, 17 January http://www.timeshighereducation.co.uk/story.asp?storyCode=174170 &sectioncode=26.

DfE (Department of Education). 2011. *Academies.* http://www.education.gov.uk/ schools/leadership/typesofschools/academies.

DfE (Department of Education). 2010. *Schools, Pupils and their Characteristics.* London: DfE.

DfES (Department for Education and Skills). 2001. *School Action Plus.* London: DfES.

DfES (Department for Education and Skills). 2003. *Aiming High: Raising the Achievement of Minority Ethnic Pupils.* London: DfES.

DfES (Department for Education and Skills). 2005. *Ethnicity and Education: The Evidence on Minority Ethnic Pupils.* London: DfES.

DfES (Department for Education and Skills). 2006. *Ethnicity and Education: The Evidence on Minority Ethnic Pupils Aged 5-16.* London: DfES.

DfES (Department for Education and Skills). 2007. *Pupil Absence in Secondary Schools in England.* London: DfES Discussion Paper.

Donnor, J.K. and Brown, A.L. 2011. The education of Black males in a 'post-racial' world. *Race, Ethnicity and Education*, 14(1), 1-5.

EHRC (Equality and Human Rights Commission). 2010. *How fair is Britain? The First Triennial Review.* London: EHRC.

Esman, M.J. 2004. *An Introduction to Ethnic Conflict.* Cambridge: Polity.

Felouzis, G. 2005. Ethnic Segregation and its effects in Middle School in France. *Revue Française de Sociologie*, 46(5).

Finney, N. and Simpson, L. 2009. *'Sleepwalking to Segregation'? Challenging Myths about Race and Migration.* Bristol: Policy Press.

Finney, S. 2011. *Black Aspirations: An Empirical Study of Young Black Males.* Unpublished MA thesis, University of Leeds.

Foucault, M. 1995. *Discipline and Punish, The Birth of the Prison.* New York: Random House.

FRA (Fundamental Rights Agency). 2005. *Majorities attitudes towards migrants and minorities: key findings from the Eurobarometer and European Social Survey.* Vienna: FRA.

FRA (Fundamental Rights Agency). 2006a. *Migrants' Experiences of Racism and Xenophobia in 12 EU member states.* Vienna: FRA.

FRA (Fundamental Rights Agency). 2006b. *Roma and Travellers in Public Education.* Vienna: FRA.

Fraser, D. 1980. *A History of Modern Leeds.* Manchester: Manchester University Press.

Gallagher, T. 2004. *Education in Divided Societies*. Basingstoke: Routledge.

Gilbert, D. 2004. Racial and religious discrimination: The inexorable relationship between schools and the individual. *Intercultural Education*, 15(3), 253-266.

Gillborn, D. and Mirza, H. 2000. *Educational Inequality: Mapping Race, Class and Gender.* London: Ofsted.

Gillborn, D. 2006. *Citizenship Education as Placebo*. London: Sage Publications.

Gillborn, D. 2008. *Racism and Education, Confidence or Conspiracy.* London: Routledge.

Gokulsing, M. 2006. Without prejudice: an exploration of religious diversity, secularism and citizenship in England (with particular reference to the state funding of Muslim faith schools and multiculturalism). *Journal of Education Policy*, 21(4), 459-470.

Goldstein, H. and Noden, P. 2003. Modelling social segregation. *Oxford Review of Education*, 29(2), 225-237.

Goodhart, D. 2004. Discomfort of strangers. *Guardian*, 24 February.

Gundara, J. 2000. *Interculturalism, Education and Inclusion*. London: Paul Chapman Publishing.

Gwent T.E.C. 1997. *Mapping Disaffection in the Gwent TEC Area*. Gwent: Gwent TEC.

Hancock, I. 1997. *Gypsy Politics and Traveller Identity.* Hatfield: University of Hertfordshire Press.

Hanley, L. 2007. *Estates: An Intimate History*. London: Granta Books.

Hansen, R. and Weil, P. (eds.). 2001. *Towards a European Nationality*. London: Palgrave.

Harff, B. 2003. Assessing the risks of genocide and political mass murder since 1955. *American Political Science Review*, 97(1), 57-73.

Haynes, J., Tikly, L. and Caballero, C. 2006. The barriers to achievement for White/Black Caribbean pupils in English schools. *British Journal of Sociology of Education*, 27(5), 569-583.

Hemmerman, L., Law, I., Simms, J. and Sirriyeh, A. 2007. *Situating Racist Hostility and Understanding the Impact of Racist Victimisation in Leeds.* Leeds: CERS.

Hetto, G., Sosenko, F. and Bramley, G. 2011. *Poverty and Ethnicity in Scotland: Review of the Literature and Datasets.* York: Joseph Rowntree Foundation.

Hill, A. 2010. Gypsies prepare to fight government housing policy, *Guardian* 8 June. http://www.guardian.co.uk/society/2010/jun/08/gypsy-traveller-housing-government-backlash.

Holmes, C. 1988. *John Bull's Island: Immigration and British Society, 1871-1971.* London: Palgrave Macmillan.

Holmes, C. 1991. *Tolerant Country: Immigrants, Refugees and Minorities.* London: Faber and Faber.

Home Affairs Committee. 1986. *Bangladeshis in Britain*. London: HMSO.

Home Office. 2007/8. *Tackling Gangs Action Programme.* London: Home Office. http://www.compas.ox.ac.uk/publications/Resources_Lit_Review_1205.shtml.

Huggan, G. and Law, I. (eds). 2009. *Racism, Postcolonialism, Europe.* Liverpool: Liverpool University Press.

IPPR (Institute for Public Policy Research). 2010. *Recession Leaves Half Young Black People Unemployed.* London: IPPR.

Jenkins, R. 1997. *Rethinking Ethnicity.* London: Sage.

Jenkins, S.P., Micklewright, J. and Schnepf, S.V. 2006. *Social Segregation in Secondary Schools: How does England Compare with other Countries?.* IZA Discussion Paper No. 1959. http://ssrn.com/abstract=881567.

John, G. 2008. Quoted in 'The Silent Majority', *Media Guardian*, 25 August 2008.

Johnston, L. 2003. From 'pluralisation' to 'the police extended family': discourses on the governance of community policing in Britain. *International Journal of the Sociology of Law*, 31(3), 185-204.

Kallstenius, J. and Sonmark, K. 2010. Denmark: Community Study. *EDUMIGROM Community Studies*. Budapest: CEU, Center for Policy Studies.

Keddie, N. 1971. Classroom knowledge, in *Knowledge and Control*, edited by M. Young. London: Collier-Macmillan.

Kendall, S. and Derrington, C. 2003. *Gypsy Travellers in English Secondary Schools; a Longitudinal Study*. Stoke on Trent: Trentham Books.

Kertesi, G., Kézdi, G. 2010. Segregation in primary schools in Hungary, a descriptive study using data from the National Assessment of Basic Competencies, in *The Hungarian Labour Market 2010*, edited by K. Fazekas, A. Lovász and A. Telegdy. Budapest: Institute of Economics and National Employment Foundation, 99-119.

Khan, O. 2008. *Financial Inclusion and Ethnicity.* London: Runnymede Trust.

Knowles, E. and Ridley, W. 2006. *Another Spanner in the Works: Challenging Prejudice and Racism in Mainly White Schools*. Stoke-on-Trent: Trentham Press.

Kocsis, K. and Kovács, Z. 1999. A cigány népesség társadalomföldrajza [Sociogeography of the Gypsy Population], in *A cigányok Magyarországon [The Gypsies in Hungary]* edited by F. Glatz, compiled by I. Kemény. Budapest: HAS.

Kymlicka, W. 2007. *Multicultural Odysseys, Navigating the New International Politics of Diversity*. Oxford: Oxford University Press.

Lacey, C. 1973. *Hightown Grammar*. Manchester: Manchester University Press.

Lattimer, M. 2008. Peoples under threat, in *State of the World's Minorities*, edited by the Minorities Rights Group. London: MRG.

Law, I. with Henfrey, J. 1981. *History of Race and Racism in Liverpool, 1660-1950*. Liverpool: Merseyside Community Relations Council.

Law, I. 1997. Modernity, anti-racism and ethnic managerialism, *Policy Studies*, 18(3/4), 189-206.

Law, I. 2002. *Race in the News*. Basingstoke: Palgrave.

Law, I. 2008. *Defining the Sources of Intercultural Conflict and their Effects*. Strasbourg: Council of Europe.

Law, I. 2010. *Racism and Ethnicity, Global Debates, Dilemmas, Directions.* London: Pearson Education.

Law, I. 2011. Poverty and income maintenance, in *Understanding Race and Ethnicity*, edited by Gary Craig, Understanding Social Welfare Series. Bristol: Policy Press.

Law, I. 2012. *Red Racisms, Racism and Ethnicity in Communist and post-Communist Contexts.* London: Palgrave. (forthcoming).

Law, I., Nekorjak, M., Daniel, O. and Vajda, R. 2009. Comparative Analysis of Ethnic Relations. *EDUMIGROM Comparative Papers.* Budapest: CEU, Centre for Policy Studies.

Law, I., Feischmidt, M., Mannitz, S., Strassburger, G. and Swann, S. 2010. *The Experiences and Consequences of Othering.* Working Paper 8. Budapest: CEU, Centre for Policy Studies.

Lawler, S. 2005. Disgusted subjects: the making of middle-class identities. *The Sociological Review*, 53(3), 429-446.

Leech, D. and Campos, E. 2003. Is comprehensive education really free?: a case-study of the effects of secondary school admissions policies on house prices in one local area. *Journal of the Royal Statistical Society: Series A (Statistics in Society)*, 166(1), 135-154.

Leeming, C. 2010. 'We are not ashamed, we are proud of being Roma'. *Big Issue in the North.* 842, 20-26 September, 16-17

Lemos, G. 2005. *The Search for Tolerance: Challenging and Changing Racist Attitudes and Behaviour in Young People.* York: Joseph Rowntree Foundation.

Levinson, M.P. and Sparkes, A.C. 2003. Gypsy masculinites and the home-school interface: exploring contradictions and tensions. *British Journal of Sociology of Education*, 24(5), 587-603.

Lewis, B. 2004. *Keep Calm and Carry on and Other Second World War Posters.* Unpublished PhD thesis, University of Winchester

Liederman, L. 2000. Pluralism in Education: The Display of Islamic Affiliation in French and British Schools. *Islam and Christian-Muslim Relations*, 11(1), 105-118.

Longhi, S. and Platt, L. 2008. *Pay Gaps Across Equalities Areas.* London: Equality and Human Rights Commission.

Loury, G.C., Modood, Tariq, and Teles, Steven M. (eds.). 2005. *Ethnicity, Social Mobility and Public Policy.* Cambridge: Cambridge University Press.

Lupton, R. 2004. *Schools in Disadvantaged Areas: Recognising Context and Raising Quality.* Case Paper 76: Centre for Analysis of Social Exclusion. Accessed online: http://sticerd.lse.ac.uk/dps/case/cp/CASEpaper76.pdf.

Macinnes, T., Kenway, P. and Parekh, A. 2009. *Monitoring Poverty and Social Exclusion.* York: Joseph Rowntree Foundation.

Macneil, M., Stradling, R. and Clark, A. 2005. *Promoting the Health and Wellbeing of Gypsy/Travellers in Highland.* Scotland: Highland Council.

MacPherson, Sir W. 1999. *The Stephen Lawrence Inquiry.* Cmnd 4262. London: The Stationery Office.

Mannitz, S. in collaboration with Frauke Miera, Rainer Ohliger, Gaby Strassburger, and Meryem Ucan. 2011. *Ethnic Diversity in Public Discourses and School in Germany*. Unpublished.

Marada, R., Nekorjak, M., Souralova, A. and Vomastkova, K. 2010. Czech Republic: Community Study. *EDUMIGROM Community Studies*. Budapest: CEU, Center for Policy Studies.

Marada, R. 2011. Policy recommendations in domestic contexts: the Czech case. Unpublished.

Mawhinney, P. 2010. *Seeking Sound Advice, Financial Inclusion and Ethnicity.* London: Runnymede Trust.

McLeod, J. and Yates, L. 2000. Young people and the politics of racial discourse, in *AARE 2000 Conference Papers*: 1-4, edited by P. Jeffrey. London: Routledge, AARE, Sydney.

Messing, V. 2010. Interactions between the ethnic composition in school and students' performance, self-esteem and future aspirations. *EDUMIGROM Policy Brief No. 3*. Budapest: CEU, Centre for Policy Studies.

Messing, V., Neményi, M., Zolnay, J. 2011. *Policy Recommendations in the Domestic Context of Hungary*. Budapest: CEU, Centre for Policy Studies.

Mir, G. 2007. *Effective Communication with Service Users*. London: Race Equality Foundation.

Modood, T. 2003. Ethnic differentials in educational performance, in *Explaining Ethnic Differences,* edited by David Mason. Bristol: The Policy Press.

Modood, T. 2005. *Multicultural Politics, Racism, Ethnicity and Muslims in Britain*. Edinburgh: Edinburgh University Press.

Modood, T. 2010. *Still Not Easy Being British, Struggles for a Multicultural Citizenship*. Stoke-on-Trent: Trentham Press.

Modood, T. 2011. This is not a minority problem. Guardian. 8 February.

moosa, Zohra and Woodroffe, Jessica. 2010. *Poverty Pathways: Ethnic Minority Women's Livelihoods*. London: Fawcett.

Moldenhawer, B., Kallehave, T. and Hansen, S.J. 2010. Ethnic Differences in Education in Denmark: Community Study. *EDUMIGROM Community Studies*. Budapest: CEU, Center for Policy Studies.

Moldenhawer, B. and Padovan-Özdemir, M. 2011. *Policy Brief Policy Recommendations in the Domestic Context of Denmark*. Unpublished.

Morris, L. 2002. *Managed Migration: Civic Stratification and Rights*. London: Routledge.

Morris, L. 2004. *The Control of Rights: The rights of workers and asylum seekers under managed migration*. London: Joint Council for the Welfare of Immigrants.

Morris, M. and Rutt, S. 2004. *Analysis of Pupil Attendance Data in Excellence in Cities Areas*. London: NFER/HMSO.

Morris, R. and Clements, L. 2001. *Disability, Social Care, Health and Travelling People*. Cardiff: Traveller Law Research Unit.

Morris, R., and Clements L. (eds.) 1999. *Gaining Ground: Law Reform for Gypsies and Travellers.* Hertford: University of Hertfordshire Press.

Morris, R. 2003. *Factsheet; Travelling People in the UK.* http://www.cf.ac.uk/claws/tlru/Factsheet.pdf (accessed August 2008).

Myers, M., McGhee, D. and Bhopal, K. 2010. At the crossroads: Gypsy and Traveller parents' perceptions of education, protection and social change. *Race, Ethnicity and Education*, 13(4), 533-548.

NEP (National Equality Panel). 2010a. *Summary, An anatomy of economic inequality in the UK.* London: Government Equalities Office/LSE.

NEP (National Equality Panel). 2010b. *An Anatomy of Economic Inequality in the UK.* London: Government Equalities Office/LSE.

NUT/NALDIC. 2010. *National Ethnic Minority Achievement Grant Survey.* London: NUT/NALDIC.

Office for National Statistics (ONS). 2008. *Information paper, recommended questions for the 2009 Census Rehearsal and the 2011 Census: ethnic group.* London: ONS.

Office for National Statistics (ONS). 2006. *Focus on Ethnicity and Religion.* London: HMSO.

Ofsted. 2003. *The Education of Asylum-seeker Pupils.* London: Ofsted.

Okely, J. 1983. *The Traveller Gypsies.* Cambridge: Cambridge University Press.

Okley, J. 1997. Some political consequences of theories of Gypsy ethnicity. The place of the intellectuals, in *After Writing Culture. Epistemology and Praxis in Contemporary Anthropology*, edited by A. James. London: Routledge.

OSI (Open Society Institute). 2007. *Equal Access to Quality Education for Roma.* Budapest: OSI.

Palmer, G. and Kenway, P. 2007. *Poverty Among Ethnic Groups: How and Why Does it Differ.* York: JRF.

Panayi, P. (ed.). 1996. *Racial Violence in Britain in the Nineteenth and Twentieth Centuries.* Leicester: Leicester University Press.

Parekh, B. 2000. *The Future of Multi-Ethnic Britain.* London: Profile Books.

Peach, C. (ed.). 1996. *Ethnicity in the 1991 Census, Vol. II: The Ethnic Minority Populations of Great Britain.* London: HMSO.

Peach, C. 2005. Social integration and social mobility: spatial segregation and intermarriage of the Caribbean population in Britain, in *Ethnicity, Social Mobility and Public Policy*, edited by G. Loury, T. Modood and S.M. Teles. Cambridge: Cambridge University Press, 178-203.

Pearce, S. 2005. *You Wouldn't Understand: White Teachers in Multi-Ethnic Classrooms.* Stoke-on-Trent: Trentham Books.

Perry, P. 2000. White means never having to say you're ethnic: White youth and the construction of 'culturelessness' identities. *Journal of Contemporary Ethnography*, 30(1), 56-91.

Pilkington, A. 1999. Racism in schools and ethnic differentials in educational achievement: a brief comment on a recent debate. *British Journal of Sociology of Education*, 20(3), 411-417.

Pons, E. 1999. *Ţiganii din România – o minoritate în tranziţie.* Bucureşti: Compania.

Princes Trust. 2009. *Deprived youth hit hardest by recession.* http://www.princes-trust.org.uk/about_the_trust/what_we_do/research/rethinking_recession.aspx.

Robinson, V., and Valeny, R. 2005. Ethnic minorities, employment, self-employment and social mobility in postwar Britain, in *Ethnicity, Social Mobility and Public Policy*, edited by Glenn Loury, Tariq Modood and Steven M. Teles. Cambridge: Cambridge University Press, 414-448.

Rollock, N. and Gillborn, D. 2010. *Enough talk, not enough action*, Runnymede Trust e-conference, Are we getting it right yet?, http://www.runnymedetrust.org/events-conferences/econferences/econference/enough-talking-not-enough-action.html (accessed 7 January 2011).

Runnymede Trust. 2007. *Promoting Community Cohesion through Schools.* http://www.runnymedetrust.org/uploads/projects/education/EducationConference-Nov07.pdf (accessed 7 January 2011).

Saggar, S. 1992. *Race and Public Policy.* Aldershot: Avebury.

Salman, S. 2006. Victory over Violence. *Guardian*, 4 October.

Sandu, D. 2005. *O hartã socialã a comunitãtilor de romi* [A social map of Roma communities]. Bucharest: The World Bank.

Save The Children. 2001. *Denied a Future.* London: Save The Children.

Schiff, C. with Evelyne Barthou, Joelle Perroton and Jessica Pouyau. 2010. 'Ethnic' differences in education in France: Community Study. *EDUMIGROM Community Studies*. Budapest: CEU, Center for Policy Studies.

Schiff, C. 2011. *France Country Findings and Policy Recommendations.* University Victor Segalen, Bordeaux. Unpublished.

Schiffauer, W., Baumann, G., Kastoryano, R. and Vertovec, S. (eds). 2004. *Civil Enculturation: Nation-State, School and Ethnic Difference in the Netherlands, Britain, Germany and France.* New York: Berghahn.

Shain, F. 2000. Culture, Survival and Resistance. *Discourse: Studies in the Cultural Politics of Education*, 21(2), 279-288.

Shain, F. 2011. *The New Folk Devils, Muslim Boys and Education in England.* Stoke-on-Trent: Trentham Press.

Shyllon, F. 1977. *Black People in Britain 1555-1833.* Oxford: Oxford University Press.

Singh, B. 2001. Citizenship education and the challenge of racism, discrimination and disadvantage. *Contemporary Politics*, 7(4), 176-190.

Singh, E. 1987. A question of interest: tackling racism in the curriculum, in *Producing and Reducing Disaffection*, edited by T. Booth and D. Coulby. Buckingham: Open University Press.

Skelton, C., Francis, B. and Valkanova, Y. 2007. *Breaking Down the Stereotypes: Gender and Achievement in Schools.* Manchester: EOC.

Somerville, W. 2007. *Immigration under New Labour.* Bristol: Policy Press.

Stone, J. 2003. Max Weber on race, ethnicity and nationalism, in *Race and Ethnicity, Comparative and Theoretical Approaches*, edited by J. Stone and R. Dennis. Oxford: Blackwell.

Swann, S. and Law, I. 2009. *Survey Report-UK, Working Paper 5*. Budapest: EDUMIGROM.

Swann, S. and Law, I. 2010. *Community Study-UK, Working Paper 7*. Budapest: EDUMIGROM.

Sveinsson, K. 2008. *A Tale of Two Englands, Race and Violent Crime in the Media*. London: Runnymede Trust.

Szalai, J. (ed.). 2010. *Being 'Visibly' Different: Experiences of Second-Generation Migrant and Roma Youths at School*. Budapest: CEU, Centre for Policy Studies.

Szalai, J., Messing, V. and Neményi, M. 2010. Ethnic and social differences in education in a comparative perspective. *EDUMIGROM Comparative Papers*. Budapest: CEU, Centre for Policy Studies.

Thomas, B., Pritchard, J., Ballas, D., Vickers, D. and Dorling, D. 2009. *A Tale of Two Cities*. The Sheffield Project. Social and Spatial Inequalities Research Group. Accessed online: http://sasi.group.shef.ac.uk/research/sheffield/a_tale_of_2_cities_sheffield_project_final_report.pdf (12 November 2010).

Tomlinson, S. 2005. Race, Ethnicity and Education Under New Labour. *Oxford Review of Education*, 31(1), 153-171.

Tomlinson, S. 2008. *Race and Education: Policy and Politics in Britain*. Maidenhead: Open University Press.

Travellers Law Reform Project. 2007. *Response to Discrimination Law Review: A Framework for Fairness: Proposals for a Single Equality Bill for Great Britain: a Consultation Paper*. http://www.travellerslaw.org.uk/pdfs/single_equality_response.pdf.

Travellers Law Reform Project. 2008. *The Education and Skills Bill and Related Matters*. http://www.travellerslaw.org.uk/pdfs/education_and_skills_bill.pdf.

Tyler, I. 2008. 'Chav Mum Chav Scum': Class disgust in contemporary Britain. *Feminist Media Studies*, 8(1), 17-34.

Van Cleemput, P., Parry, G., Peters, J., Moore, J., Walters, S., Thomas, K. and Cooper, C. 2004. *The Health Status of Gypsies and Travellers in England*. Sheffield: University of Sheffield.

Vertovec, S. 2006. *The Emergence of Super-Diversity in Britain*. Centre for Migration, Policy and Society, Working Paper No. 25, Oxford: University of Oxford.

Vincze, E. 2011. Policy recommendations in domestic contexts: the Romanian case. Unpublished.

Vogue. 2010. *Homing Instinct*. London: Vogue.

Walby, S., Armstrong, J. and Humphreys, L. 2008. *Review of Equality Statistics*. Research report 1, Manchester: Equality and Human Rights Commission.

Walvin, J. 1973. *Black and White: The Negro in English Society, 1555-1945*. London: Allen Lane.

Ward, I. 2006. Shabina Begum and the headscarf girls. *Journal of Gender Studies*, 15(2), 119-131.

Warren, S. 2005. Resilience and refusal: African-Caribbean young men's agency, school exclusions, and school-based monitoring programmes. *Race, Ethnicity and Education*, 8(3), 243-259.

Weekes-Bernard, D. 2007. *School Choice and Ethnic Segregation: Educational Decision-making Among Black and Minority Ethnic Parents*. London: The Runnymede Trust.

Weller, S. 2008. You need to have a mixed school... Exploring the complexity of diversity in young people's social networks, in *Social Capital, Professionalism and Diversity: New Relations in Urban Schools*, edited by J. Allan, J. Ozga and G. Smyth. Rotterdam: Sense.

Whiteman, R. 2005. Welcoming the stranger: A qualitative analysis of teacher's views regarding the integration of refugee pupils into schools in Newcastle upon Tyne. *Educational Studies*, 31(4), 375-391.

Whitty, G. 2000. *Privatisation and marketisation in education policy*, London http://k1.ioe.ac.uk/directorate/NUTPres%20web%20version%20(2%2001). doc.

Wilkins, C. 2001. Student teachers and attitudes towards race: Westminster. *Studies in Education*, 24(1), 7-21.

Willis, P. 1977. *Learning to Labour*. Farnborough: Saxon House.

Wood, M., Hales, J., Purdon, S., Sejersen, T. and Hayllar, O. 2009. *A Test for Racial Discrimination in Recruitment Practices in British Cities*. DWP Research Report No 607, London: DWP.

Youdell, D. 2003. Identity traps, or how the black students fail. *British Journal of Sociology*, 24(1), 3-20.

Yosso, T.J. 2005. Whose culture has capital? A critical race theory discussion of community cultural wealth. *Race Ethnicity and Education*, 8(1), 69-91.

Index

GRT=Gypsies, Roma and Travellers. Page numbers in *italics* refer to figures and tables.